ISABELLA AND SAM

The Story of Mrs Beeton

ISABELLA AND SAM

THE STORY OF MRS BEETON

by

SARAH FREEMAN

———————— ◇ ————————

LONDON
VICTOR GOLLANCZ LTD
1977

© Sarah Freeman 1977

ISBN 0 575 01835 6

920 BEE

EQUAL OPPORTUNITIES
COMMISSION
INFORMATION
CENTRE
1953

Printed in Great Britain by
Ebenezer Baylis and Son Limited
The Trinity Press, Worcester, and London

To Jean

ACKNOWLEDGEMENTS

A great many people have helped in one way or another in the writing of this book, and I am extremely grateful to them all. I particularly want to thank the following for supplying me with material about the Beeton and Dorling families: Rodney Levick, Mrs Audrey Levick, Mrs Marjorie Killby, Lady Fisher, Mrs H. D. Fellowes, Mrs Georgina Ballance, Miss Caroline Newman, Sister Mary Gabriel, Christopher Mayson, Anthony Dorling, Dr and Mrs Leslie Holliday, and Mr and Mrs Philip Smiles.

Others to whom I am especially grateful are Harford Montgomery Hyde, for his generous help, encouragement, and suggestions; Mrs Adriana Davies, for research assistance; Miss Janet Clarke, antiquarian cookery bookseller, who lent me many early editions for a long period; Peter Day, for invaluable editorial advice; Mrs Rita Hughes and Miss Clare Sheppard, for secretarial help; Miss Leslie, of Senate House Library, University of London; Miss Ratcliffe of Birmingham Central Library; Mr Large of the National Magazine Co.; and above all to my husband and children for their endless patience and good humour.

CONTENTS

1*

Part four
'...A LIFE OF TORTURE...'

Photographs of Elizabeth Dorling, Sam and Isabella, and Mount Pleasant, by kind permission of Rodney Levick Esq.; portrait of Myra and Meredith Browne, of Mrs Marjorie Killby; drawing of the Dorling family, of Lady Fisher.

FOREWORD

You will search the pages of the *Dictionary of National Biography* in vain for the names of Isabella Mary Beeton and her publisher-husband Samuel Orchart Beeton who brought out the earlier editions of her classic books on household management and cookery under his imprint. Such omissions from the standard reference work of British biography are all the more surprising in view of the remarkable literary partnership which existed between husband and wife in the editorial and publishing field of magazines and books, particularly for women and young people in the Fifties and Sixties of the last century. Indeed, for long after the Beetons were dead, few middle-class English families at home and overseas were without 'Mrs Beeton', an invaluable standby for successive generations of British housewives. But it was not until Mrs Beeton's youngest son Sir Mayson Beeton presented a portrait of his mother to the National Portrait Gallery in 1932 that the general public learned for the first time the essential details of his parents' lives and work. The picture was reproduced by the gallery on a postcard for sale, the card being accompanied by a few explanatory words written by Mrs Margaret Mackail, which emphasized how husband and wife were 'mutually helpful in their literary work' and how to his inspiration her own principal book 'distinguished by its intellectual and interesting qualities', owed its origin.

The portrait, a coloured daguerreotype photograph, reproduced in Sarah Freeman's book, was taken when Isabella was twenty-one, in the year after her marriage; it shows a strikingly intelligent looking and beautiful young woman. As she died in 1865 when she was only twenty-eight, having given birth to four children and written two literary classics as well as having turned out a continuous stream of journalism during the nine years of her married life, it will be realized that she was very far removed from the stout middle-aged kitchen figure of popular imagination.

Here I must declare an interest. My paternal grandmother's

sister Julia Johnstone married Sam Beeton's cousin Edmund Beeton, and as a boy I came to know most members of the Beeton family then alive, including Sir Mayson. (Incidentally Julia Beeton and her sister, my grandmother Emma Hyde, were daughters of the newspaper proprietor James Johnstone, whose principal paper *The Standard* warmly praised the Beeton publications for 'doing great work in our national education'.) Following the interest aroused in the press as a result of the exhibition of Isabella's picture in the National Portrait Gallery and the sale of the postcards, Sir Mayson Beeton suggested that I should write his parents' biography and I agreed to do so. However, delays occasioned by other professional commitments at that time, followed by five years' war service in the army and various post-war distractions, delayed the publication of my biography until 1951.

One advantage which I enjoyed in writing it was that I made the acquaintance of Isabella's half-sister Lucy, who had been a bridesmaid at Isabella's wedding to Sam Beeton in 1856, and she gave me a vivid description of the reception which took place at the Grand Stand on Epsom Racecourse, where her father Henry Dorling, whom Isabella's mother had married after her first husband's death, was Clerk of the Course. It is worth noting that Lucy Dorling later married William Smiles, son of Samuel Smiles, whose *Self-Help* was another Victorian classic, and she went to live in Belfast where William managed the large ropeworks there. I remember meeting Mrs Lucy Smiles at her home in Belfast in 1939 when she was in her ninetieth year, and a very sprightly and vivacious old lady she was, with a remarkable memory. I am glad that Sarah Freeman has used some of Lucy's first-hand information in this book. Lucy and William Smiles had eleven children, including the late Sir Walter Smiles, MP, father of Lady (Nigel) Fisher. Another of the Smiles children was Norah who married George Spain; their daughter the late Nancy Spain also wrote a biography of Isabella and Sam, first published in 1948. In fact it was to avoid conflicting with Miss Spain's book that I further postponed the publication of my own.

Through her researches Mrs Freeman has been able to deal in greater and more interesting detail than either Nancy Spain or I were able to do in our relatively short biographies, with the details of the Beetons' amazing literary collaboration. Sam Beeton was an editor and publisher of exceptional ability who made a fortune (which he subsequently lost) through the first publication in this country of the American Harriet Beecher Stowe's anti-slavery epic *Uncle Tom's Cabin*. He had many other publishing successes, some with his wife such as *The Queen* and *The English-woman's Domestic Magazine*, as well as his wife's great classic, which he largely inspired. He never really recovered from the blow of Isabella's death. In the following years financial troubles due to a bank failure obliged him to assign the copyrights in all the Beeton publications to another publishing house. However, he struggled bravely on, dogged by increasing ill-health; he suffered from chronic tuberculosis and in the event he survived his wife by barely a dozen years.

Now that more than a quarter of a century has passed since the publication of my book and Nancy Spain's, I feel that the time has come for a new assessment of the lives of one of the most remarkable couples of Victorian times, who were devoted to each other in the home and in the office. I am glad that Sarah Freeman has undertaken this work which I am convinced will be recognized as the definitive biography. She has written an exciting and poignant story, packed with fascinating information of the times in which Sam and Bella Beeton lived and worked in their unique but tragically short partnership.

H. Montgomery Hyde

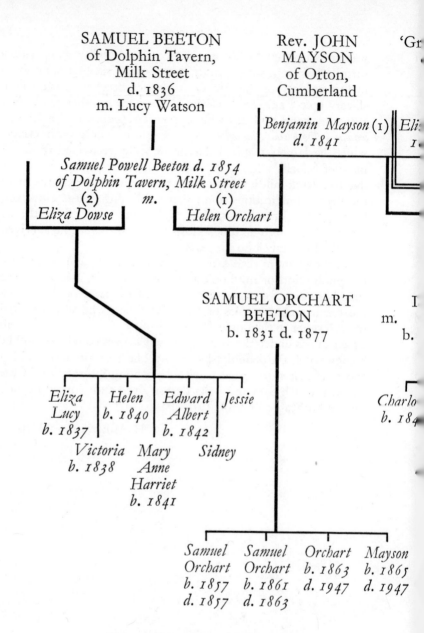

The Family Tree of the
BEETONS-MAYSON & DORLINGS

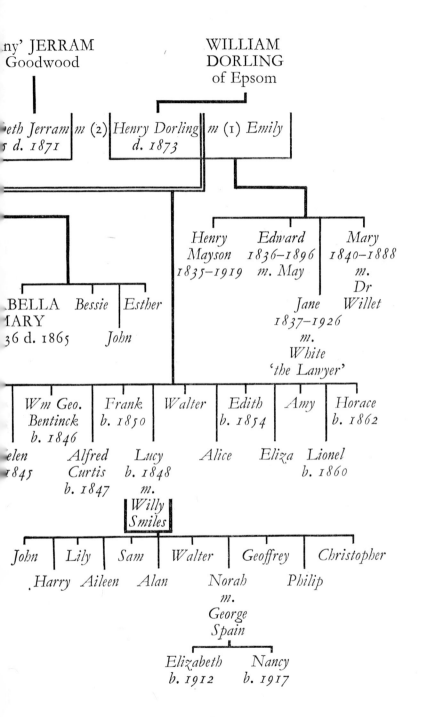

ny' JERRAM
Goodwood

WILLIAM
DORLING
of Epsom

...eth Jerram m (2) Henry Dorling m (1) Emily
...y d. 1871   d. 1873

Henry   Edward   Mary
Mayson   1836–1896   1840–1888
1835–1919   m. May   m.
                                         Dr
...BELLA   Bessie   Esther   Jane   Willet
...MARY   1837–1926
...36 d. 1865   John   m.
                                          White
                                      'the Lawyer'

Wm Geo.   Frank   Walter   Edith   Amy   Horace
Bentinck   b. 1850   b. 1854   b. 1862
b. 1846

...elen   Alfred   Lucy   Alice   Eliza   Lionel
...845   Curtis   b. 1848   b. 1860
               b. 1847   m.
                           Willy
                           Smiles

John   Lily   Sam   Walter   Geoffrey   Christopher
.Harry Aileen Alan   Norah   Philip
                            m.
                          George
                           Spain

Elizabeth   Nancy
b. 1912   b. 1917

PART ONE

Miss Mayson

DICKENS'S EPSOM

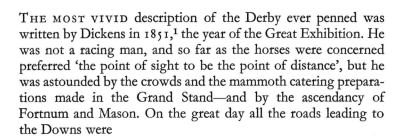

THE MOST VIVID description of the Derby ever penned was
written by Dickens in 1851,[1] the year of the Great Exhibition. He
was not a racing man, and so far as the horses were concerned
preferred 'the point of sight to be the point of distance', but he
was astounded by the crowds and the mammoth catering preparations made in the Grand Stand—and by the ascendancy of
Fortnum and Mason. On the great day all the roads leading to
the Downs were

> so thronged and blocked by every description of carriage that
> it is marvellous to consider how, when, and where they were
> all made—out of what possible wealth they are all maintained—
> and by what laws the supply of horses is kept equal to the
> demand . . . barouches, phaetons, broughams, gigs, four-
> wheeled chaises, four-in-hands, Hansom cabs, cabs of lesser
> note, chaise-carts, donkey-carts, tilted vans made arborescent
> with green boughs and carrying no end of people, and a cask
> of beer,—equestrians, pedestrians, horse-dealers, gentlemen,
> notabilities, and swindlers, by tens of thousands. . . . Never, to
> be sure, were there so many carriages, so many fours, so many
> twos, so many ones, so many horsemen, so many people who
> have come down by 'rail', so many fine ladies in so many
> broughams, so many of Fortnum and Mason's hampers, so
> much ice and champagne! If I were on the turf, and had a
> horse to enter for the Derby, I would call that horse Fortnum
> and Mason, convinced that with that name he would beat the
> field. Public opinion would bring him in somehow. Look
> where I will—in some connexion with the carriages—made
> fast upon the top, or occupying the box, or tied up behind, or
> dangling below, or peeping out of a window—I see Fortnum

and Mason. And now, Heavens! all the hampers fly wide open, and the green Downs burst into a blossom of lobster-salad!

On the Monday before the race he made a tour of the Grand Stand, and was lured into the basement by the smell of cooking:

wine-cellars, beer-cellars, larders, sculleries, and kitchens, all as gigantically appointed, and as copiously furnished as if they formed part of an Ogre's castle. To furnish the refreshment saloon, the Grand Stand has in store two thousand four hundred tumblers, one thousand two hundred wine-glasses, three thousand plates and dishes . . . a whole flock of sixty-five lambs have to be roasted, and dished, and garnished, by the Derby Day. Twenty rounds of beef, four hundred lobsters, one hundred and fifty tongues, twenty fillets of veal, one hundred sirloins of beef, five hundred spring chickens, three hundred and fifty pigeon pies; a countless number of quartern loaves, and an incredible quantity of ham have to be cut up into sandwiches; eight hundred eggs have got to be boiled for the pigeon pies and salads. The forests of lettuces, the acres of cress, and beds of radishes, which will have to be chopped up; the gallons of 'dressing' that will have to be poured out and converted into salads for the insatiable Derby Day, will be best understood by a memorandum from the chief of that department to the *chef-de-cuisine*, which happened, accidentally, to fall under our notice: 'Pray don't forget a large tub and a birch-broom for mixing the salad!'

But all this happened only once a year. All the rest of the time Epsom was, as Dickens put it, 'as unlike the Desert of Sahara and the interior of the Palace of Glass at Hyde Park' (the Crystal Palace, which housed the Great Exhibition). It was small, quiet, dull, and parochial, enlivened only by wonderfully spicy tales of the annual influx of gamblers and vagabonds and the usual little rivalries and jealousies that sustained the inhabitants of every country town. It had a clock tower, a large, muddy pond, and elms and poplars growing down the High Street, its only distinction being a disproportionately large number of inns. The spectacle of a grand carriage rumbling past the bland houses was sufficiently unusual to cause the populace to cluster at their windows and stare inquisitively—for there were not many people of consequence in the neighbourhood: the local gentry consisted of the Baron and Baroness de Tessier, the Briscoes, who owned some of the land over which the race course lay, and Sir Gilbert Heathcote and his son Arthur; nor were there many more middle-class families of any pretensions. Among the latter, by far the most conspicuous were the rich, numerous, talented, *nouveaux-riches* Dorlings. It was as a member of this family, remarkable yet unexceptionable, against the extraordinary contrasts of Epsom, that Isabella Mayson, the future Mrs Beeton, spent the formative years of her childhood.

Henry Dorling, her stepfather, was clerk of the race course, a post he had held for nearly ten years, during which time he had, by luck, hard work, and his own and his wife's perspicacity, become virtually dictator of the races; and if he has not come down to posterity as one of the great men of the century, he is still remembered with veneration by all those connected with the turf. As the official in charge, he conducted the none-too-gracious Dickens round the course; it seems that Dickens found him somewhat condescending, for he referred to him disparagingly as the 'Great Man', and did not fail to report that he overheard him whispering to one of his trainers, Mr Filbert, that he (Dickens) was quite harmless—' "green" was the exact expression'—and much too ignorant to be able to pass on confidential details about the horses.

Henry had not been born to the turf, like so many who devoted their lives to it, but had come to it via the activities of his father William, a printer. It seems that the Dorlings originally came from a remote village in Suffolk called Dalling Hoo, from which their name is thought to have been derived; William, however, was first heard of in Bexhill, on the south coast, where a rhyme about him and his printing (which he had probably written himself) appeared in the local directory. He was a rather fearsome-looking character, with thick black hair, inherited by Henry, and a hooked nose, which still occasionally crops up in the family. Being energetic and ambitious, he had soon exhausted the limited resources of Bexhill, which was then no more than a village, and began to look around for somewhere which might offer an

up-and-coming printer more scope. According to his great-
grandson Edward, who made him out to be simply a cheerful,
light-hearted adventurer, he rode off on his pony one fine spring
morning and stopped at Epsom because he was entranced by its
prettiness;[2] more likely, he selected it because he had heard of
the racing, and reckoned that it would offer just the kind of
opportunity he wanted. At any rate, he moved there about 1820,
and established his printing press and family of five, of whom
Henry was the eldest, in a large house at the end of the High
Street, opposite the track which led to the race course and just in
front of the site of the station, though that was not built for
nearly another twenty years.

By 1830 he was not only printing almanacks, hymn books,
and other useful items, but selling almost every miscellaneous
article racegoers could possibly want, including writing paper,
shaving cakes, lavender water, and even pianos; but already his
principal business was printing and selling race cards. The first
'Dorling's Genuine Card List' went on sale for the 1827 Derby,
and listed as far as possible the runners, owners, jockeys, colours,
and horses' pedigrees. He collected the information by going up
on the Downs before race meetings and battering everyone in
sight with questions, from stable-boys to bookmakers. The cards
were not designated as 'official' until Henry became clerk of the
course, but they were a much-needed innovation, and within a
few years William had made enough money to buy a substantial
number of shares in the Epsom Grand Stand Association.[3] This
was a strategic move, for although he himself used them merely
as an investment, they were worth far more than that to his son,
to whom they gave automatic status in the racing world, enabling
him to grow up as familiar with the shareholders and their ilk
as with grooms and trainers.

The Grand Stand Association was formed in 1829 to finance a
proper building for spectators in place of the miscellaneous
assortment of makeshift stands and sheds which until then had
been all that was provided. It was born of greed and local jealousy,
for it was set up in the first instance to oust a speculator from
Doncaster called Charles Bluck, who had been inspired by the
new Grand Stand at Doncaster to come south and copy the idea
at Epsom. The locals were furious at the idea of having such a
plum snatched from under their noses, and determined to get

rid of him, a procedure which turned out to be both difficult and expensive; but they succeeded in the end, and carried out his plans for the Stand by issuing a thousand £20 shares.[4] The building was completed with quite remarkable speed and was ready for use in time for the Derby of 1830.

By this time William had sent Henry to London as a printer's apprentice—probably in 1827, the same year as his first race card appeared, since the seven-year apprenticeship ended around 1834. In London, Henry lodged with Mrs Jerram, a kindly, middle-aged widow, whose father, Standish, may have been known to William since he had been a groom and was said to have had some connection with the race course at Goodwood. She had married another groom, William Jerram, who set himself up as the keeper of a stables on the Portsmouth Road, and died soon after the couple had produced a daughter. Mrs Jerram then moved to London to make her living by taking in lodgers.

One of Henry's companions in her house was a linen wholesaler called Benjamin Mayson, some ten or eleven years older than himself, who became his greatest friend, and also his rival in love—for Mrs Jerram's daughter Elizabeth grew up into a girl of exceptional beauty, and both young men fell in love with her. From photographs taken when she was quite old, one can imagine that Mrs Jerram too had been very good-looking when young, though not in such a delicate way as her daughter: a portrait painted of Elizabeth at the age of eighteen shows an almost too perfect face, fine-boned and aristocratic, but with a cool, determined, calculating expression which suggests that she was not quite of that warm, dependent nature which was commonly regarded as the feminine ideal. Although Henry, who was depicted some years later as tall and dashing, was a handsome youth with considerable charm and an excellent manner, she preferred Benjamin: he was a man of education who passed as a gentleman, and had his own very respectable business—(wholesaling was definitely a cut above retailing, and if he had kept a shop, like Henry's father, she might have considered him less eligible). Henry, always a realist, may have recognized from the outset that his suit was hopeless; at any rate, as soon as his term of apprenticeship was over, he married another girl, Emily Clarke, who was said to be rather domineering and in some respects not unlike Elizabeth herself.[5]

Henry and Emily Dorling returned to Epsom and settled in the house in the High Street; they had four children, the eldest of whom was given the second name of Mayson, after his father's friend. Henry Dorling went into his father's business—probably as a partner though his exact status is not clear—and at the same time set about ingratiating himself with the racing authorities, having evidently already decided that it was with the turf that his main interest lay. He took the first important step in his career between 1840 and 1843, when he was appointed to replace a Mr Farrall as clerk of the course.[6]

His second break followed soon after, as a result of a notorious but amusing scandal. The Derby of 1844 was won by a horse called Maccabeus, who was officially ineligible because he was over the regulation age of three, and had been entered disguised by black hair dye as another horse, Running Rein. The deception was uncovered by the most distinguished member of the Jockey Club, Lord George Bentinck, who had evidently been tipped as to what had happened and interviewed all the hairdressers in Regent Street until he discovered the assistant who had sold the dye. This incident encouraged him to put into practice various reforms he had been contemplating for some time, which brought him automatically into contact with Henry.

Lord George, second son of the Duke of Portland and owner of one of the most famous studs in the country, was by repute almost a caricature of the popular idea of the hot-tempered, overbearing aristocrat, but he was also very hard-working, and a loyal ally—as a supporter and close friend of Disraeli, his sense of duty eventually forced him to abandon racing and go into politics, for which his abilities were by no means so well adapted —and once Henry had managed to convince him of his genuine dedication to the interests of racing, he gave him all the support that his own authority and the backing of the Jockey Club could lend. The excellent relationship with Lord George was an outstanding proof of the tact and charm which, when all was said and done, were the chief ingredients in Henry's success. Without them he could never have reconciled the numerous conflicting interests upon which his position depended: he was almost as skilful at dealing with Bentinck's eccentric successor at the Jockey Club, Admiral John Rous (who apparently disapproved of betting) as with Bentinck himself; and only almost superhuman patience and diplomacy could have kept him simultaneously on peaceable terms with the landowner Briscoe and his wife, who took a tiresome interest in the racing, the racing stewards, and the diverse members of the Grand Stand Association. It was not surprising that as the years went by the strain of maintaining his public image began to tell, to the disadvantage of those who had to deal with him in private.

The respect he managed to inspire in Bentinck is demonstrated by a letter his lordship wrote to him in the summer of 1845. 'We must try to do something to pull Epsom racecourse together. Now if *you* would get complete control, Mr Dorling, I should feel that the future was better assured.'[7] The reforms Bentinck proposed aimed at reducing the opportunities for foul play to a minimum, and included improved starting regulations, the proper weighing-in of jockeys, and an official saddling area. When Henry suggested that the most convenient and advantageous place for a saddling area would be in front of the Grand Stand, where it could be witnessed not only by the stewards but also by the spectators, he replied that in his view the best thing would be for Henry to lease the Stand.

Had it not been for Bentinck's authority, and the fact that it suffered from a chronic shortage of funds, the Grand Stand Association would probably have done its best to quash this idea. But the depressing state of its finances had already driven some of the members to ponder over the possibility of finding a tenant, and when Henry made an offer of a thousand pounds a year for twenty-one years in return for five per cent of the takings, it was accepted. That he was able to offer so much bears witness to the enormous profitability of the race cards. From Henry's point of view, no investment could have been better calculated, for as clerk of the course he was in control of both the racing and the spectators and was ideally placed to maximize his percentage. Under his aegis the organization and prestige of the racing benefited enormously, and Henry made a great deal of money out of his double position. The most profitable and controversial of his manoeuvres was to lay out a new course with the starting-line visible from the Stand instead of being hidden by the slope, which, with a characteristically apt sense of timing, he had ready for the Derby of 1847—the first year the race day was made a national holiday. Dickens noted rather drily that to accommodate

the ever-increasing influx of spectators, he had added a new wing
to the Stand and fitted out two ladies' rooms. But the advantages
of his tenure of the Stand were not merely directly financial, for
his family increased as swiftly as his income, and he was able to
use it as a very convenient solution to his domestic problems.

MR MAYSON

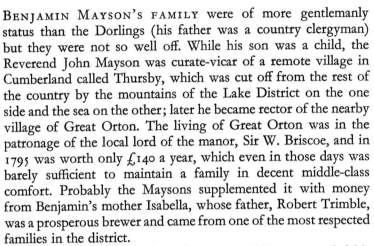

BENJAMIN MAYSON'S FAMILY were of more gentlemanly status than the Dorlings (his father was a country clergyman) but they were not so well off. While his son was a child, the Reverend John Mayson was curate-vicar of a remote village in Cumberland called Thursby, which was cut off from the rest of the country by the mountains of the Lake District on the one side and the sea on the other; later he became rector of the nearby village of Great Orton. The living of Great Orton was in the patronage of the local lord of the manor, Sir W. Briscoe, and in 1795 was worth only £140 a year, which even in those days was barely sufficient to maintain a family in decent middle-class comfort. Probably the Maysons supplemented it with money from Benjamin's mother Isabella, whose father, Robert Trimble, was a prosperous brewer and came from one of the most respected families in the district.

Benjamin, who was their only son, would have attended his father's little parish school until he was old enough to go either to St Bees, a nearby public school, or a private school called Greenrow Academy. The latter was the more likely, since it was part of this school's charter that the sons of the neighbouring clergy could be educated free. When he grew up, he faced the same problem as every young man of his class born in such an outlying spot: either he left home in search of a job or he went into the church. By the time he met Elizabeth, he was running a small linen business from a house in a drapers' street in London, No. 24 Milk Street near St Paul's, and it was here, following the custom of the time (for this was before the days of commuting), that they went to live when they were married.

Only two further pieces of information about Benjamin Mayson have survived—the fact that a year or so after his marriage he was able to buy his house, which he had begun by renting for sixty pounds a year[1] (about the average for the street); and the announcement of his death. There is no indication as to what he was like as a person; neither Elizabeth nor Isabella, who was their first child, and the only one old enough to be able to remember him meaningfully, mentioned him in any of the letters which have come down to us.

There is every reason to suppose that Benjamin and Elizabeth's marriage turned out very satisfactorily. The purchase of the house suggests that business prospered, and Elizabeth, though very young, was sensible and realistic and became a careful and economic housewife. Milk Street was dark and narrow, and must have been a rather oppressive place to live, but it came to life at weekends, when a street-market was held in Honey Lane, an alley at the far end. London street-markets had something of the atmosphere of fairs, with singers, organ-grinders, acrobats, peepshows, and other entertainments; on Saturday nights the whole street was bright with the glow of grease-lamps and candles, which illuminated the animated faces of the coster-mongers, the rags of the children darting about hawking fruit and nuts, and here and there the agonized grimace of a beggar. Shopping amid the confusion required a level head and a firm grasp on the purse, but Elizabeth was capable of both, and no doubt enjoyed the excitement and festive atmosphere.

Isabella, who was named after her paternal grandmother, was born on 12 March 1836, scarcely nine months after her parents' marriage, and was followed in swift succession by Bessie and John (who was named after his paternal grandfather). Then, in the summer of 1840, when Elizabeth was pregnant with her fourth child, Esther, came the trauma of Benjamin's unexpected death. The notice appeared in the 'Deaths' column of the *Carlisle Journal*, presumably inserted by his father: 'Suddenly, Mr. B. Mayson, linen factor, Milk Street, London, son of the Rev. John Mayson, aged 39 years.'[2] What he died of is unknown, but it was probably fever, perhaps cholera, which had reached London a few years before.

Isabella was four, an unfortunate age, for she was too young to comprehend what had happened but old enough to have formed a deep attachment to him, which, in the face of her mother's lack of understanding, may have been even more important to her than is usually the case with small girls. It is very unlikely that Elizabeth gave her much help in coming to terms with her bereavement, for even if she had been a more sympathetic sort of person, she had her own problems to face— namely, the prospect of another confinement and having to support and care for a family of four on her own. Indeed, she probably paid her less attention than formerly, simply because Bessie and John were still almost babies, and she was the only one of the family old enough to do things for herself. Isabella was thus thrown on her own resources from infancy, and although she was surrounded by brothers and sisters throughout her childhood, was always in a slightly special, isolated position.

Her mother's only assets, so far as is known, were the house and her husband's business, and for several years she kept up both as best she could, greatly helped and encouraged by a good-natured neighbour who lived down the street, a young woman called Eliza Beeton, the wife of the local tavern-keeper. The Beetons also had four small children, of much the same age as Elizabeth's, and the two mothers formed a friendship which lasted for many years. But even with Eliza's assistance, Elizabeth found that she could not cope with her children, her house, and the business simultaneously, and after a year or so, almost inevitably, the business deteriorated. Knowing her, it may be assumed that things had got pretty bad by the time she appealed to her father-in-law, whom she did not know very well and had not seen for several years; but eventually she was driven to write to him saying that she needed money, and was planning to sell Milk Street and rent premises for a new business (probably she proposed to follow her mother's example and take in lodgers). John Mayson, who was by now almost an invalid and wrote in a weak, shaky hand, was naturally very upset at the idea of her selling her house, which was now the only security she had.

August 8th, 1842

My dear Bessie,

I am sorry the business you entered upon did not answer your expectations. Of the one you are going to begin I can form no opinion, as I am totally ignorant about it. You say you have seen a House which might answer your purpose. You do not mention the Rent, but I understand the first

Quarter's Rent is to be paid in advance, and if the rent be
high you will observe another Quarter's Rent will soon be
due. Do you suppose you will be able to meet it at the time,
as he requires a Qr. in advance? I am afraid he will be a sharp
landlord.

You say you want a little money. I think I can advance you
50£, if that will do. Since last Christmas I have had a great
deal to do. As I was not able to do any Duty, I was obliged to
engage a curate. I think I shall never be able to attend the
Church again to do Duty. If 50£ will be of any service to you,
after you receive it you must send me a Note, as I wish at
my Decease to have something made up for your children,
and the above 50£ was a part of it. I intended to make you an
allowance yearly. But if I do too much there will be less
afterwards. I assure you I am anxious to save something for
my little grandchildren. I have my curate to pay quarterly. I
do not wish you to sell your house, and also not to lay out
your money extravagantly. I hope to hear that you are doing
well. Carefulness will do a great deal.

I am sorry to say I do not improve much, I cannot leave
Home. I do not enjoy Company. I am best when alone. I was
glad to hear that you and the little ones were well. Make my
love to Isabella and Bessy. The other 2 do not know me. They
are very well at Thursby. I have not seen them lately except
Anne who was at our House yesterday. I have not had much
of Anne's Company lately. I want to know when Esther was
born. I have forgot. Write soon.

With kind regards I subscribe myself,

Yours sincerely,

JOHN MAYSON

Fifty pounds was hardly a fortune, though it would have been
just about enough to cover the first year of the rent he was so
concerned about; but apparently this was not the only letter
Elizabeth wrote at this difficult time. Another made its way to
Epsom, to her husband's old friend Henry Dorling; what it
said, and whether she had kept in touch with him over the years
or whether it came to him completely out of the blue, we do not
know. It may have been simply a conventional letter of con-
dolence, for at about this time his wife Emily died, and he too

was left to bring up four small children. Untimely deaths were so common in the absence of modern medical resources that there was nothing remarkable about this coincidence—but it turned out to be a fortunate one for Elizabeth. The upshot of it was that she married Henry on 24 March 1843, and took her children and her mother (henceforth known as Granny Jerram) to Epsom.

From Henry's point of view, it was no less than a brilliant match. In the first place, he was clearly genuinely in love with his wife, and remained so for the rest of his life; and in the second, he acquired in her a social asset and fount of morale and intelligence which were invaluable to him throughout his career. Their partnership lasted for nearly thirty years, and when Elizabeth died at the age of fifty-four, bloated and worn out with excessive child-bearing, Henry outlived her by only two years. Their grandson Edward, admittedly a romantic, declared that he died because he could not live without her;[3] and in his case, it was probably true.

If for Elizabeth it was a marriage of need, she did very well out of it. So far her life had not been luxurious at the best of times, but as Mrs Dorling she lived to enjoy wealth and a social position such as her mother, Henry's former landlady, had never dreamt of. But it was no sinecure: she began with a combined family of eight children and ended with twenty-one, which was an alarming total even by the standards of the time.

For Isabella, her mother's marriage was not quite the unqualified blessing it may have appeared at first sight. True, it gave her a secure, prosperous home and the advantage of an unusually good education, which she certainly would not otherwise have had; and at this period such worldly considerations were all anyone was concerned with, so that by contemporary standards she was to be accounted very lucky. But from a more modern point of view her situation as the eldest girl in a large family, and, for a time, as something like an interloper in her own home, was neither very happy nor very fortunate.

CHILDHOOD

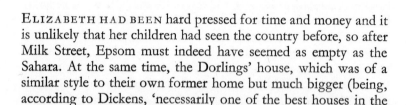

ELIZABETH HAD BEEN hard pressed for time and money and it is unlikely that her children had seen the country before, so after Milk Street, Epsom must indeed have seemed as empty as the Sahara. At the same time, the Dorlings' house, which was of a similar style to their own former home but much bigger (being, according to Dickens, 'necessarily one of the best houses in the place'), and with the four children who already lived there and the bookshop underneath, represented an oasis of activity.

They had a hard time settling down with their new family. Their stepbrothers and sisters were uncomfortably close to them in age: Henry Mayson, their father's namesake, was a few months older than Isabella, his brother Edward slightly younger and the two girls, Jane and Mary, approximately matched Bessie and Esther. Also, the Dorlings had only recently lost their mother and were in just as unsettled a state as the newcomers, so that they could not have been expected to assimilate them easily. They were not a particularly quiescent bunch at the best of times; Henry Mayson, though an exceptionally kind man, was notorious for his autocratic behaviour when he succeeded to his father's position on the race course,[1] and Sam Beeton commented rather drily on Jane's 'sharp little ways'. There is no reason to suppose that they were any different as children; nor were the three Mayson girls exactly lacking in character. Arguments, fighting, and quarrelling were the natural outcome of the situation, and Isabella, as the eldest of her faction, automatically found herself their leader and champion.

Elizabeth too must have had a difficult time at first, for to half her family she was in the invidious position of the traditional, unwanted stepmother, a role her unbending manner was not calculated to dispel; unsurprisingly, she was never really accepted by the elder Dorlings, just as Isabella and Bessie, at any rate, could never quite accept Henry as their father. Both sets of children always remained separate cliques within the household, and Elizabeth made no attempt to unite them. She was too preoccupied with a strange household, another pregnancy, and, above all, the complexities of Henry's life (the Running Rein scandal took place the year after her marriage). There is no doubt that she took an active part in his affairs; Edward Dorling, who knew the stresses and strains of Henry's job all too well as a result of his own experience as managing director of the Grand Stand Association, said: 'He relied very much on her judgement and good business sense'.[2] Rather than relaxing once her new responsibilities were sorted out, she grew steadily busier as her family and the annual tide of racegoers increased, and the Maysons in consequence were pushed further and further into the background of her life.

Even if the children had been more peaceable, the house, which had been ample for William Dorling's family of five and in turn for Emily's of four, was by no means large enough for all of them, particularly when the new baby and Granny Jerram were added to the total. After a year of noise, tension, and strife, Henry's tenure of the Grand Stand came as a timely deliverance. Elizabeth, quick to seize the opportunity it offered, at once proposed that all the children should be sent to live there, remarking casually, 'Isabella and Bessie and Granny can all look after them'.[3]

Granny Jerram's reaction to this suggestion is not recorded, but if Elizabeth, who was not yet thirty, found nine children wearing, it can be imagined how exhausting they must have seemed to her at nearly fifty. But she was a neat, spry-looking woman, surprisingly well preserved after a life of hard work, and proved an excellent nanny; all the children remembered her with the greatest affection, and she was still at her post looking after the younger ones ten years later. The children, who were not of an age to resent the idea as a sentence of banishment, nor to regard it as in any way out of the ordinary, went, by all accounts, cheerfully enough. Isabella took the role assigned to her by her mother as literally as any eager, serious-minded little girl of nine, and was extremely helpful to her grandmother. She was by this time a bright, brisk, impatient, perhaps somewhat nervous child, not necessarily as self-confident as she tried to appear to her younger brothers and sisters, who—especially Bessie—idolized her; and of all the children, she perhaps was most grateful for Mrs Jerram's kindness, which she never forgot. Years later, just before her marriage, she wrote:

> Jane and I have been doing the charitable to Granny. Poor old lady, she complained sadly it was so dull in the evening sitting all alone so we posted up there to gossip with her. You can well imagine *you* furnished a large subject for conversation, for every now and then she would burst forth and say I wonder what your dear Sam is doing etc.

The Grand Stand must have been one of the most bizarre nurseries of all time. It had even less of a domestic atmosphere than a boarding school during the holidays, which is probably the nearest parallel one can draw in trying to imagine what it was like to live in. It was a vast, four-square structure in the classical style, its size and elegance having given rise to much admiring comment in the press when it was first completed, and was generally agreed to be the crowning glory to the greatest race in the world. It was fifty yards long and twenty yards wide, and was designed to accommodate five thousand spectators. It was encircled on three sides by balconies supported by magnificent Doric columns, and the races could also be watched from the roof, which was tiered like an auditorium. Huge as it was, it seemed even larger, being situated on the highest point of the Downs so that it dominated the course from every direction. The inside was no less impressive: there was an immense, pillared hall, a great stone staircase, a thirty-yard-long saloon, four refreshment rooms, and a warren of committee and retiring rooms.[4] During the races, half the first floor was given over to an impromptu magistrates' court, where thugs and pickpockets could be sentenced on the spot.[5] The principal areas had been redecorated a few years before for the Queen, who paid her one and only visit to the Derby in 1840 (apparently she did not return because she was offended by the lack of enthusiasm shown for Albert). The Association, on the assumption that she would attend regularly, somewhat grudgingly spent two hundred pounds on luxurious carpets and 'figured paper of a splendid and appropriate pattern on a ground of white satin'.[6] It was literally true to say that the children's new home was fit for a queen.

To them, however, its chief advantage was the space, both indoors and out, where they could work off their energy in other ways than on each other—though they did not stop quarrelling.

'For Heaven's sake, Elizabeth, what is all that noise about?' Henry yelled down one of the corridors one day.

'That, Henry, is your children and my children fighting our children,'[7] she replied calmly.

In summer, they were able to play unrestrictedly on the race course, go for long rambles in the surrounding woods, and watch the horses taking their early morning gallops. Henry and Elizabeth's sixth child, Lucy, loved the outdoor life, and attributed the whole family's excellent health to it. 'If the Downs are good for young horses, they're good for young children,' she once remarked. Isabella too grew up with a passion for the open air; she lavished a great deal of time and money on her gardens, which were always laid out and looked after with loving care, and her greatest joy when she went on holiday was going for long country walks and mountain-climbing.

Another great advantage of the family living in the Grand Stand was that they escaped the strict discipline imposed on most Victorian children, who were expected to be seen and not heard, and were punished with what now seems almost inhuman severity. If they had continued to live with their parents in the High Street, they would certainly have been brought up with no less than the usual rigour—and as their parents grew older, with considerably more; but Granny Jerram, Isabella, and Bessie did no more than mop up the tears, supervise bedtimes, and preside over their simple, starchy nursery meals. They ate in one of the refreshment rooms and slept in the smaller committee rooms and offices, presumably on truckle beds that could be taken away or folded out of sight when race day came round.

The Stand was at its least agreeable in winter, when it was cold and eerie. No matter how many fires they had, it was impossible to thaw the enormous rooms, and the balconies, which kept the interior pleasantly cool and shady in summer, made it correspondingly gloomy and depressing later in the year.

The wind shrieked and whistled down the roof and round the columns with unnerving ferocity, and when it snowed the slopes of the Downs seemed as remote as a mountain-side. If they had been fanciful children they might well have imagined themselves abandoned in an ogre's castle; but fortunately they were not— far from it—and one and all accepted their surroundings with complete unconcern.

They were by no means abandoned by their parents. Elizabeth paid periodic, sometimes unexpected, visits to the Stand, among other things to inspect the Queen's wallpaper and the china (Dickens's three thousand plates, which presumably they used, were specially designed with a picture of the Stand in the middle and a border of the wild flowers of the Downs round the edge). Henry, as clerk of the course, had his offices there, and moved his printing presses from the High Street to the basement, so he saw the children every day, and was able to observe them rather more closely than his wife. It seems that he felt uneasy, perhaps even slightly guilty, about his stepchildren, and perceived that they were rather unsettled; there must have been some reason why he decided to send them away to school in preference to his own two elder daughters. It is possible that he also recognized Isabella as a girl of exceptional promise.

It was impossible for the children to remain in the Stand over the frantic period of the Derby, when it reverted to its proper use, and they were either sent back into the town or to Brighton, over the Downs, where Henry held a second office as clerk of the course. 'I am going to the Stand this afternoon to assist in bringing down that living cargo of children into the town, where they will remain ten days,' Isabella wrote one year; another time, she said, 'If you can manage to get away tomorrow evening to Brighton I shall be so pleased as I am going down there with the parents some time in the morning. Granny and the smaller members of the family are quartered at yr. Marine Parade. . . .'

She thoroughly enjoyed these enforced holidays, despite the ordeal of packing up to go—for every trace of their habitation had to be hidden away or taken with them. Toys and games of all kinds—the beautifully made Victorian dolls, kaleidoscopes, cards, draughts, and dominoes (many years later, their sets of the latter were sold)—got mixed up with Bibles and spelling books and the complicated, confusing paraphernalia of boots and slippers, underclothes and nightclothes, hats, caps, ribbons, and curling rags. The piles of trunks and boxes, plus the crowd of passengers, called for a small procession of carriages into the town—a spectacle which was watched and commented on by the townspeople every year with unflagging interest.

Someone, (perhaps Elizabeth herself, since it was inscribed 'Many happy returns of the day from Elizabeth') did a sketch of the whole family to commemorate Lucy's birth in 1848, in which they look a remarkably happy and wholesome group. Isabella, who was twelve, was depicted as if she were virtually grown up, dressed in a dark dress and white cap like her mother's, with a pantalooned infant in her arms; her parents, on the other hand, appear unexpectedly young. To anyone familiar with photographs of Henry as a dignified, portly old gentleman, this version of him—slim, swarthy, even slightly untidy—is quite unrecognizable; Elizabeth was evidently as beautiful as ever.

Youthful as they still looked, however, Henry and Elizabeth were already slipping into an early middle age; and the price they paid for their conspicuous fertility and success was not cheap, at any rate so far as their offspring were concerned. Elizabeth had always been somewhat unapproachable, but Henry in the early years of his marriage seems to have been a relatively sympathetic father. But as time went by he degenerated into a typically stern, authoritarian Victorian parent; by the time Isabella was engaged and the family consisted of about seventeen, he had lost all trace of humour and was fiery and impatient, despite the family motto, which presumably he himself invented, 'Place a curb on your anger'. He and Elizabeth made a formidable pair. Isabella was less affected by them than the younger children were, no doubt partly as a result of the early independence that had been thrust on her, but the rest of the household, not to mention Sam Beeton, were completely dominated by them. Later still, when Isabella had left home, it seems from various family stories that Elizabeth and Henry were truly terrifying.

The tale of Alfred, the twelfth child, does not do Henry much credit, though its sad ending was not directly his fault. Alfred, so the legend goes, committed the unforgivable sin of playing a dirty joke on his father. When he was twelve, he sent him a contraceptive, wrapped anonymously in an envelope. It was, admittedly, a strange thing to do; although it is hard to believe that he did not know what it was, he probably did not understand its full implications, as at that time birth control was only practised by prostitutes and men about town (who used it chiefly as a means of trying to avoid venereal disease). No one ever discovered how Alfred got it, but presumably it was sold or given to him by one of the many disreputable characters hanging about the race course. Having discovered who the culprit was, Henry was so outraged that he packed him off to sea as an apprentice in the merchant navy, despite the fact that he was officially several years too young. He never returned, for he was drowned in Sydney Harbour.

The force of Elizabeth's personality was described by her grandson Edward, who said that he had always been very much in awe of her, and told of a strange incident with a peculiarly Victorian ring. One day as a small boy he was playing in Elizabeth's garden when a grown-up came and picked a large bunch of pinks, which on a sudden impulse he stuffed into the child's shoes. 'I strutted round, proudly regarding my beflowered feet, when my grandmother appeared. She took in at a glance how her garden had been desecrated. To this day I can remember her towering annoyance, as of an angry queen.'[8]

Nancy Spain, her great-niece, also described her as 'imperious', sitting majestically in her drawing room 'ruling with her slightest whim twenty-one young lives'.[9] This is exactly the popular image of Mrs Beeton, the archetypal lady, stern, forbidding, and elderly —except that nothing would have offended Elizabeth's sense of propriety more at this time of her life than to pick up a saucepan. If Isabella had lived longer, she would almost certainly have developed a similar presence; the ingredients were there, for of all her sisters she bore most resemblance to her mother. But she was dead even before she had reached Elizabeth's age at the time of the birthday sketch.

IV

EDUCATION

———————— ◇ ————————

No mention of a school in Epsom was ever made by any of the Dorlings, nor was a governess employed for the elder children, though it may be presumed that the younger ones had one—at any rate, there was a well equipped schoolroom in the house they later moved to near Croydon. In the earlier stages of their career, Henry and Elizabeth were not of high enough social status to feel able to take on such a classy appendage, convenient though it might have been; governesses, though often themselves under educated (by governesses), invariably came from so-called 'good' families and were aggressively conscious of their genteel position. Granny Jerram, at any rate, could never have been mistaken for a lady, and it must have taken even Elizabeth a few years to qualify; meanwhile, the family did not wish to be thought of as giving themselves airs. Nevertheless, Henry was as anxious as any ambitious parent that all his children should be educated as ladies and gentlemen, and this was the most obvious reason for his sending some of his daughters to boarding school.

In Victorian society, the conduct of ladies was modelled on what the middle classes believed (quite erroneously) to be the behaviour of the upper classes. Ladies were expected to be ethereal, not to say imbecile, beings who substituted intuition for intellect and did not soil their purity with any sort of work: menial work was left to the servants and earning a living to men. Ideally, they were never angry, never rude, never untidy, and (of course) absolutely chaste, notwithstanding the fact that their husbands might be openly licentious. The most admired feminine virtues were docility, submissiveness, and self-sacrifice (always provided that the sacrifice was of the right kind). Gentility thus confined women to their social and domestic roles, requiring them merely to have as many children as possible, organize the servants, and

2*

be ornamental—and at this time the elaborate, uncomfortable fashions made it more or less impossible for them to do anything useful anyway. Any other concerns were beyond their sphere of responsibility, particularly an interest in money (apart from the management of their dress and housekeeping allowance). It was logical enough in a way, since married women could not own anything and could not even claim the legal possession of their own children; hence the desirability of widowhood and the independent status it brought. Intellectual interests were also disapproved of, since it was feared that they would interfere with the more essential duties of wife and mother. As marriage was the only socially acceptable career for ladies, and men, then as now, generally had a horror of 'blues', few girls were prepared to jeopardize their chances by showing any obvious signs of intelligence. Unmarried women, unless very rich or brilliant, were doomed to a vicarious existence of aunty-ing and looking after aged parents, or when money was short, of governessing, which was their only respectable means of earning a living.

Girls' boarding schools existed for the specific purpose of teaching their pupils to be ladies, and their curricula were carefully tailored to this end. With the exception of languages, which were regarded as a valuable social asset, they glossed over academic learning and concentrated on social accomplishments such as music, dancing, embroidery, sketching, elegant hand-writing, and learning to wear corsets. Some fragmentary bits of general knowledge were imparted by means of question and answer books; and for exercise, instead of games, the girls went for walks in formal crocodiles, dressed up in hats and gloves as though they were going to church. The general intellectual standard can be gauged from the recommendations finished young ladies carried away with them, which were on the level of being able to write a good hand and spell accurately. Needless to say, unladylike domestic skills, especially cooking which was smelly and greasy, were avoided with as much conviction as science and philosophy. Not surprisingly, the 'Boarding-school Miss', as she was dubbed in the magazine of which Isabella was to become editress, was notorious for her uselessness. An article under this title, which was almost certainly written by her future husband, concluded gloomily:

. . . the young lady's peculiar talents consisted in dress and fancy-work, with some interludes of novel-reading and playing fantasias on the piano (in company), and, as we were forced to admit on seeing her with some of her particular friends, in a great faculty of talking and laughing about nothing. Our sketch is of *but one*, but that one, unfortunately, stands for a class; and woe to the father, mother, brothers and sisters, who number in their family a 'Boarding-school Miss'.[1]

This appeared in the very same year that Isabella must be presumed to have started school.

The school originally selected by Henry and Elizabeth was in Islington and run by a Miss Lucy Richardson, who, like Thackeray's Miss Pinkerton, was 'a very genteel lady indeed'.[2] Her name does not appear in either the 1841 or 1851 census, but she was probably the daughter or sister of a Mr Richardson, who ran a school for boys in a street of elegant houses called Colebrooke Row, and opened his doors to girls as well in 1852, when Isabella was sixteen. One can easily imagine how bored an eager, highly intelligent girl would have been at any typical school; apparently Isabella's reaction was no more favourable than Sam's, for she was taken away after a short time.

After this, Henry sent her to school in Germany, where girls' education tended to be taken more seriously than in England. This also had the advantage of being desirable from a social point of view, since it was fashionable to send girls abroad to perfect their languages and acquire a cosmopolitan gloss. The school he chose was in the old, picturesque university town of Heidelberg, run by two sisters, Auguste and Louisa Heidel. Their establishment was not a finishing school (these did not exist in Germany), but an ordinary school for girls of all ages, and had an outstanding reputation. All three Mayson girls went there in due course; Bessie and Esther were still pupils when Isabella was married. Probably Bessie and Isabella were sent out together, Esther joining Bessie a year or two later. At the Heidels', Isabella gained a thorough general academic training, learnt to speak French and German fluently, and became an exceptionally promising pianist. It sounds as if she also received culinary instruction, for we are told that 'The headmistress noted with approval her interest in cooking'.[3] This was considered permissible in Germany, since the rich cakes and puddings of the national cuisine demanded considerable skill, and were quite often made by the lady of the house. But patisserie would have been all that was taught, so that she was still left with virtually no knowledge of any other branch of cookery. On her return home, she endeavoured to follow up her interest by starting a course of lessons with a pastrycook in Epsom.

Even the Heidels, however, did not concentrate solely on the serious side of education; the conventional social element was not ignored, and there were dances and even, occasionally, balls. Esther wrote:

> Polly and I . . . enjoyed our first ball extremely. On Shrove Tuesday we girls got up a Mask Ball on a small scale, and invited the governesses and Miss Heidel to join us. It went off with great éclat and Miss Louisa was perfectly enchanted with our costumes. M^rs. Yattn or Miss Breidenbach is still here and sends her best love to you. Our school is increasing very fast. Two new girls came last Sunday and we are expecting 3 more this week. Happily for us 4 or 5 are going away at Easter but till then we shall be rather crouded [sic]. I must now say Good bye as the table is being laid for Tea.

Isabella was as fond of dancing as any other girl, but however much she enjoyed such gaieties, they were not her central interest at school. Her rejection of the Islington establishment, her prowess on the piano, and the remarkable intellectual discipline she exercised a year or two later, all suggest that she spent her time working extremely hard. It is also significant that the only lasting friendships she made were with her schoolmistresses, one of whom some years later sent her a German cookery book in response to her request for recipes for *Management*, and all of whom were very friendly towards the Mayson sisters. Her isolation was, of course, partly because most of the pupils were German, and she had Bessie for company. But she does not seem to have made many friends (as opposed to acquaintances) in later life either; all those known to have been intimate with the Beetons were her husband's or family's friends. Basically, she was not interested in other people's problems, and did not enter into the confidences of her schoolmates. As a result, she was still in some ways very immature and inexperienced when she met Samuel Beeton.

But if her schooldays did not help her in the matter of human relationships, they were invaluable to her in her professional career. If she acquired any knowledge of cookery, it was the least of the assets she gained. Her mastery of French was to prove invaluable to her in her role as reporter of the Paris fashions, and prior to that enabled her to translate a famous French book on gastronomy. Her studies taught her the value of diligence and a Germanically methodical approach to work. Also, she learnt down to the last subtle nuance how to be a lady. This enabled her to write what was in some ways the most interesting and important part of her book, and also to assess accurately the requirements of the genteel readers of her husband's women's magazines—for it was to her and not his editorial judgement that they owed the solid respectability for which they became known. No doubt she would have done all these things even if she had not gone to the Heidels', but she would not have been able to do them so well.

V

H. DORLING ESQ

———————— ◇ ————————

ALTHOUGH THE MÉNAGE in the Grand Stand continued until after Isabella's death, no sketch of her family background would be complete without a description of the Dorlings' opulence during the last few years of Henry's life. The size of the fortune he amassed (not without a certain amount of public comment) can be measured by his eventual purchase of a splendid eighteenth-century country house near Croydon, which he re-named Stroud Green House. Probably he had been on the look-out for a suitable property for some time, and would have made his purchase sooner if anything attractive had come up; as things were, he left it almost too late, for Stroud Green came on the market in 1869 and he died only four years later, leaving orders in his will that the house should be sold to provide equal portions for his eighteen surviving children.

Nancy Spain, unaware of the late date at which the house was bought, raises the question of why Isabella was excluded from these provisions, suggesting that she might have been driven by her husband's improvidence to ask her stepfather for her share of the money some time previously.[1] In fact, Isabella died four years before the will was drawn up. As Sam Beeton and Dorling had not been on speaking terms for some years, and Henry was smarting from an insulting article Sam had just written about his methods of money-making, it was hardly to be expected that he would have left him or Isabella's children anything. Even in other circumstances, there would have been no earthly reason why he should; indeed, if he wished to divide his estate impartially, he would have been foolish to consider his grand-children, in view of their potentially enormous number.

The house was large, white, and imposing, standing on a slope in some twenty acres of park, certainly fit to be a worthy partner to the Grand Stand, which Beeton once referred to as the 'White House' of Epsom.[2] It was designed in 1788 by an architect called Valentine Wright and was originally built in a severely classical style, but photographs taken in the Dorlings' day show circular, domed conservatories at either end of the façade, which somewhat spoilt its symmetry and gave it a deceptively Victorian appearance —as was doubtless the intention. These were added by Henry, who also re-laid the gardens and planted an avenue of fir trees down the drive.

The catalogue of sale gives a vivid, depressingly uninviting picture of the interior, which was almost a caricature of mid-Victorian magnificence. As in so many fashionably appointed houses of the period, the colour scheme of all the principal rooms was red: the drawing room had a crimson carpet with matching upholstered furniture and red tasselled silk curtains,[3] the morning room was curtained and carpeted in green and crimson, and the study also carpeted in crimson. Every available space was crammed with pieces of sculpture, costly china, knick-knacks, ornaments, and extravagant clocks: three faces symbolizing Sculpture, Painting, and Fame glowered over the dining table from a clock designed by Marc of Paris; a huge ormulu clock in the drawing room was entwined with the form of a voluptuous nymph, who was merely one among a dozen statues and statuettes disposed about the apartment, including a number of Venuses; the library clock, also by Marc, represented Richard I riding a galloping charger. The walls were chequered with sombre pictures, mostly copies of Old Masters, predominantly Titian and Rubens; and there were also portraits of Henry's patrons, Sir Gilbert Heathcote and Lord George Bentinck (both long since dead). Overall glittered gigantic gasoliers, hanging from the ceilings like monstrous pendants of diamonds.

Here, Elizabeth, now grossly obese after a life of continuous pregnancies, entertained on a scale in keeping with her surroundings. In Epsom, the Dorlings' acquaintance had been limited to the handful of professional people and other families of suitable standing who lived around; their circle was wider at Stroud Green and included visitors from London, where Henry had bought a house a few years previously—presumably to give the girls an entrée to London society. At this time he had at least four eligible daughters and three more still in the schoolroom.

Among those who received Mrs Dorling's discreet, elegant cards were the Smiles, another large, prosperous middle-class family, who lived at Blackheath. Samuel Smiles was the author of a little book called *Self-Help*, which had originally been written as an address to the working classes and was published in volume form just as Isabella was finishing *Management*. It preached the virtues of self-education, and in a sense was parallel to her work as it, too, came to represent a characteristic aspect of middle-class Victorian life. He had also written a biography of George Stephenson and *Lives of the Engineers* (his early life had been spent as a railway company administrator); among his later works were *Nasmyth, Autobiography*, and *Josiah Wedgwood*. His eldest son Willy married Lucy, who was the only sister to follow in her mother's footsteps and raise a large family.

The lavishness of the dinner parties at which the Smiles and other guests assembled can be judged from the contents of Henry's cellar. He died leaving no fewer than thirty-eight dozen bottles of port, sixteen dozen of sherry, twelve dozen Sauternes, and an impressive amount of claret, Madeira, and Champagne. The dining table on such occasions was embellished with azaleas, camellias, orchids, and other exotic flowers from the conservatories; home-grown luxuries included peaches, nectarines, oranges, and, in due season, footmen carried in whole cherry trees in ornamental tubs as part of the dessert.

On evenings when the family were alone, the brothers departed to the billiards room while their sisters sat in the drawing room drinking tea, making up their scrap-book—every family kept a scrap-book, but theirs was particularly lavish, bound in velvet and decorated with Austrian carvings—or playing genteel games such as draughts, chess, or cribbage. Isabella had commented on the desirability of such amusements years before when she wrote her book:

Where there are young people forming part of the evening circle, interesting and agreeable pastimes should especially be promoted. It is of incalculable benefit to them that their homes should possess all the attractions of healthful amusement, comfort, and happiness; for if they do not find pleasure there, they will seek it elsewhere.[4]

No serious card games were permitted, for to someone of Henry's occupation, gambling of any kind was anathema. Those who wanted to read could retire to the library (also furnished in crimson), which was stocked with a comprehensive selection of the classics—Shakespeare, Milton, Wordsworth, Scott, Byron, Longfellow, Macaulay, Dickens, Thackeray; of note also were Disraeli's biography of Bentinck, Smiles's *Lives*, and Beeton's *Dictionary of Universal Information* and *Illuminated Family Bible*. Henry had always kept a generous supply of books about him and it was this that enabled Isabella to become exceptionally well read, and scatter her work with an impressive list of literary references; the long, boring evenings in the Grand Stand paid their dividends.

It was just as well that she never saw Stroud Green, for she hated extravagance: much of her life was spent campaigning against it. The galaxy of *objets d'art* and oppressive gloom of the blood-sucking red went completely against her taste. Her own houses were as quiet, discreet, and cheerful as she could make them. Moreover, she would have found the tedium and ceremony of the Dorlings' elevated way of life almost insupportable. Sam Beeton would have reacted similarly, but the purchase of Stroud Green came at a time when his own fortunes were at their lowest, and though his ambition had never been for wealth, the vision of such splendour against his own poverty was naturally humiliating and irritating.

After the sale, the house was turned into a convent and eventually demolished in 1927. The unmarried daughters lived together in the London house until Lucy's marriage, which took place soon after Henry's death. The newly married pair went to Ireland, where Willy ran a ropeworks in Belfast, which was for a time the largest in the world. It cannot have been exactly a happy marriage: Willy was neurotic and tyrannical, they were frequently hard up, and they had eleven children. A typical story of their household was that in order to promote punctuality and economy, only ten eggs were boiled for breakfast every morning, so that the last child downstairs had to go without. But Lucy nevertheless always seemed to come up smiling and full of chatter. She was by far the most forthcoming of all the sisters on the subject of Isabella, and it is to her that we owe much of what is known of the Beetons personally.

Of the other girls, Amy, the youngest, who was described as
'a sweetie, small and attractive',[5] married a judge; Eliza, the next
up (whose son was the barrister 'Khaki' Roberts)[6] a solicitor; and
Charlotte, the eldest of Henry and Elizabeth's children, General
Charles McMahon. In describing her, her granddaughter Rosemary Fellowes remarked:

> Nancy Spain says she was known as 'the beautiful Mrs.
> MacMahon'.[7] I don't think I agree. I know my mother was
> very annoyed with Nancy. Charlotte when young was not
> beautiful, judging by all the photographs, but in her old age
> she became very good looking, with white hair piled high. She
> was certainly very musical.

Bessie and Esther Mayson's lives after the disbanding of the
paternal household sound something of an anticlimax. Neither of
them married (they were both over thirty by the time the Dorlings
moved to Stroud Green) and in many respects their lives followed
the usual depressing spinsterly pattern. With their inheritance they
were comfortably independent, with no incentive to follow
Isabella's example and compromise their respectability by working. Their relatives remember them as abrasive, unbending, well
intentioned, bountiful, and slightly eccentric—and it is all too
easy to see how like them Isabella might have become if she too
had remained single. Bessie's name was mentioned twice by Aileen
Smiles in her humorous, lively biography of Samuel, on both
occasions in connection with clothes: she was reported as 'a most
fashionable woman who said that no fashion was ugly'.[8] This
perhaps was as a result of her desire to live up to the standards
set by Isabella in her position as a fashion editor. But the most
telling description of both the sisters comes from Mrs Fellowes:

> I remember being taken to see them many times when I was
> a child during the 'Twenties. . . .
> They always wore long, old-fashioned silk dresses in blacks
> and mauves, with 'housewives' at their waists. They lived in a
> rather gloomy dark house in Warwick Road close to Nevern
> Square. . . .
> Their speech used to puzzle me, as they always said 'Ain't
> and dropped their aitches. This was the fashion in their youth

apparently. They referred to the 'laylock' tree in the garden, and yellow was always 'yaller'.

Before one of our visits, I grumbled to my brother about having to waste an afternoon in a dark over-furnished Victorian drawing room behaving myself. So he said, 'Don't be silly, don't you realize they will TIP us?' And they always did, a folded 10s. note would be taken from the little draw-string purse hanging from their belts. Once they pinched my brother's cheek, and said, 'Ain't 'e 'andsome?' He was furious! (They never said it about me.)

Another aunt tells a story of Aunt Esther in 1914 saying 'oh *por por* Edith' on hearing that my mother had just had another baby. So the aunt said, 'Aunt Esther, it's not as bad as all that, no worse than having measles.' Aunt Esther replied, 'Well I dunno I'm shor, I never 'ad either.'

◈

PART TWO

Mr Beeton

◈

\

ORIGINS

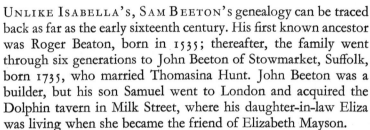

UNLIKE ISABELLA'S, SAM BEETON'S genealogy can be traced back as far as the early sixteenth century. His first known ancestor was Roger Beaton, born in 1535; thereafter, the family went through six generations to John Beeton of Stowmarket, Suffolk, born 1735, who married Thomasina Hunt. John Beeton was a builder, but his son Samuel went to London and acquired the Dolphin tavern in Milk Street, where his daughter-in-law Eliza was living when she became the friend of Elizabeth Mayson.

Samuel Beeton had two sons, Samuel Powell and Robert. Samuel Powell married Helen Orchart, the daughter of a rich baker in the next street, Wood Street, and in 1831 they had a son, Sam (Samuel Orchart), Isabella's husband. Soon after Sam's birth, Helen died of tuberculosis. The widower married again, this time Eliza, née Dowse, with whom in due course he had five daughters and two sons. At the death of his father in 1836, the same year that Isabella was born, Sam's father and Eliza took over the tavern.

Both Samuel Powell and his father were genial, cheerful, unintellectual characters, very much mine hosts, and they took an active part in City affairs: old Samuel Beeton was chairman of the Licensed Victuallers' Association in 1827, and both he and his son were members of the Worshipful Company of Patten-makers and the Common Council of the City of London for the ward of Cripplegate Within, wherein Milk Street lay. The branch of the family stemming from old Samuel's second son, Robert, however, was rather different, being more intellectual and artistic. Robert's son, also called Robert, was a manager of Beaumont's Philosophical Institution of Beaumont Street, whilst his son, Henry Coppinger, gained a silver medal from the Royal Society of Arts. In 1854 Henry Coppinger had a son called Henry Ramié, and his son, Alan, was an ARA. Sam seems to have taken after this side of the family rather than his father's, and always kept in touch with his cousins, regularly sending them signed copies of his books.

There is a possibility that the Beetons were connected with a Highland family, the Bethunes of Skye. The Bethunes' tree, in the writing of John, fifth laird (born 1539) has been handed down through Robert's descendants, and the two families used a very similar crest and arms—the crest of a lion and arms with three lozenges, or mascles, with the motto *Fortis in Arduis*. These arms, with the mascles, are identical to those of Cardinal Beaton, Abbot of Arbroath in France and Archbishop of St Andrew's in Scotland, who was assassinated in 1546 after having a number of Protestants burnt to death in front of his palace. Sam's cousins were using his insignia by about 1850, and Henry Ramié left a gold watch dating from about 1880 with the mascles engraved on the back. He also preserved a newspaper cutting (undated) recording the Bethunes' claim to a baronetcy, which says that the name 'came originally from Artois in France. The Bethunes were an old seigniorial [sic] family who flourished at the beginning of the 11th century. . . . It was a French poet, Quesnes, or Coesnes, de Bethune, who was the first to plant the Latin flag on the walls of Constantinople in 1204 as a soldier of Baldwin I.' The possibility of a connection between the French and English Bethunes was investigated by Sam and later taken up by his younger son Mayson, who wrote to Henry Ramié in 1893 to say that he had made no progress in his search for a link with the French line 'with wh. my father always used to claim kinship'. The College of Arms also observes that no relationship is proven, adding that in the absence of such proof, Henry Ramié had no proper authority for using the Bethune coat of arms.

Presumably Henry Ramié's interest, like Mayson's, originated with Sam. Sam's motivation was partly natural curiosity, perhaps shared by Robert, and partly his personal vanity, of which there are a number of other examples; one particularly silly one is his entry on himself in his *Dictionary of Universal Information*, somewhat fuller than the preceding paragraph on Beethoven and ending complacently: '. . . his "Boy's Own Magazine" and "The Englishwoman's Domestic Magazine" are amongst the most popular and successful periodicals now in the hands of the public.'[1] This would have looked better if it had appeared a few years later—but by then perhaps he would not have been bumptious enough to write it.

After Sam's mother died, he was looked after by his grandmother at the Dolphin until his grandfather died, when he was five. The widow then decided to leave London, either because she had had enough of the rough life of the tavern, which on Saturday nights was crowded out with the rowdy marketers, or because Sam was unhealthily pale and thin, and she felt that he ought to be taken to live in the country. She took him to Hadleigh, on the Thames estuary in Essex, where Constable immortalized the ruins of the castle in one of his most melancholy, romantic sketches. Over the bleak strip of sea rose Canvey Island, and beyond that were the Kent marshes, stretching into the mist to the inlet of the Medway, where the convict hulks featured by Dickens in *Great Expectations* rode to anchor. It was a wild, windswept, desolate spot, just the place to feed the fancy of an imaginative child; and Sam no doubt peopled it with his own cast of characters, or from tales the old woman told him in the evenings—for at this time there were scarcely any exciting children's storybooks likely to appeal to little boys (*Great Expectations* was not written until 1860). During the day he could play on the rock-strewn beach or go swimming; he was always an excellent swimmer, and still enjoyed the exercise when he was far advanced in illness. All in all, despite being separated from his family, he was probably better off than Isabella, for he not only had the freedom of the country and the seaside, but his grandmother's undivided love and attention.

When he was twelve, his father sent him to a school called Pilgrim's Hall Academy, near Brentwood, one of the many private schools which grew up at around this time alongside the new railways. A large advertisement for it in the *Illustrated London News* announced that it prepared pupils for public schools, Oxford and Cambridge, business, and the professions—in other words, everything likely to appeal to the prosperous, up-and-coming type of middle-class parent. It seemed ideal for Sam, firstly because of its convenient position between his grandmother's house and the new Brentwood station which was only an hour's ride from London on the Eastern Counties line, and

secondly because of the stress the proprietors laid on its healthy
situation: 'This Establishment is delightfully situated in one of
the healthiest parts of Essex, and offers, from the very com-
modious arrangement of the mansion, and its exterior play and
pleasure grounds (comprising more than twenty acres) one of the
most eligible localities in England for studious retirement and
healthful recreation.'[2] This was accompanied by a large, handsome
engraving showing a house with a clock tower and weathercock
surrounded by trees.

Enticing as the picture looked, it gave no idea of how beautiful
the place actually was. When the Beetons went to see it, they
found one of the most perfect Regency houses imaginable, set on
a gentle slope in the midst of deep woods, so that as the carriage
approached it was revealed to them by degrees, in tantalizing
glimpses through the trees. The front was embroidered with
wrought-iron balconies wreathed in foliage, and to one side lay
an ornamental lily pond. The inside was no less welcoming; even
if they did not recognize the elegant Adam fireplaces and ceilings,
as Samuel's brother might have done, they could not have failed
to appreciate the airy rooms and cheerful views from the large,
low windows. By amazing luck, the house has escaped any
significant alterations, and is still almost exactly as it was when
Sam was there, even down to traces of its use as a school.[3] A
letter from a subsequent occupant written in the early 1900s said
that there was a 'persistent rumour' of its being haunted by the
ghost of a priest,[4] but there is no previous reference to it, and
certainly no indication that any of the pupils was ever troubled
by it.

According to the 1851 census, the establishment consisted of
twenty-eight boys between the ages of eight and sixteen, three
teachers and a student, four servants, and the headmaster's
family. The teachers were the headmaster, W. Alexander Watson,
who presumably taught classics, a French master, Louis Morell,
who was actually French, and an English master. They were all
young, Watson being only twenty-eight when he started the
school in 1843 (Sam was one of the original pupils). On the whole,
this can be taken as a good sign, though Watson's wife, who
apparently acted as matron, was considerably older, and had two
daughters by a previous marriage. The English and French
masters were something of a luxury in a school of that size in

those days, when two masters were often considered adequate, and this suggests that Watson had ambitious, even liberal, ideas. All too often, classics were virtually the only subjects studied; literature in particular was neglected, and if taught at all was treated in the same manner as the classics, as an exercise in grammar. It was further circumscribed by contemporary views on what was suitable for children to read, which by and large was just what would now be considered most unsuitable: educative tracts, moral tales, and long, complicated histories and biographies. Fiction, except of an improving kind, was frowned on, for fear it should put improper ideas into their heads, or divert them from more profitable studies, just as it was feared that intellectual activities would distract girls.

Whether or not the teaching of literature at Pilgrim's Hall rose above these constraints, it was in an endeavour to change this situation that Sam devoted a large part of his career; and it was during his schooldays that the need to do so first became obvious to him. Apart from literature, he evidently enjoyed French, for he won *Une Histoire de Napoléon le Grand* as a prize (perhaps Louis Morell, like Becky Sharp in *Vanity Fair*, lent him French novels to improve his fluency). He also became, in the course of his two years there, a competent classical scholar.

It seems clear, from the promising nature of the staff, the attractive surroundings, and the generous accommodation (forty people altogether lived in the house in 1851, and it is now spaciously fitted up for thirty-five guests) that whatever may have been the limitations of his education, Sam had a better time at school than the majority of his contemporaries—for boys at this period were frequently subjected to the most frightful ordeals in the name of education, and learnt little more than how to endure pain and smoke cigars; it is quite likely that Sam's taste for cigars, constantly regretted by Isabella on account of his health, originated from his schooldays. His personality must also have been a great help to him, for he was easy and outgoing, and in spite of his bumptiousness, popular with almost everyone he met. Also, he had a regrettably schoolboyish sense of humour, later extremely useful to him in his writing, and a total lack of respect for authority—this being doubtless partly the fault of his doting grandmother. Without question, he came in for his share of caning, but he does not seem to have remembered it with any particular dread, for although in the course of a discussion he said he thought it seldom did much good,[5] he was not absolutely against it.[6]

By the time he was fourteen, he had informed his father that he did not wish to succeed to the tavern, as was his right as the eldest son, but wanted to make his career in publishing. This announcement probably came as no surprise to his parents, and Samuel, perhaps after consulting Robert, came up with the proposal that he should serve out an apprenticeship in a suitable trade, and when he came of age receive a sufficient sum of money to enable him to set up in business. Very possibly the money in question was a legacy from his mother. He thus emerged, after only two years in his gentlemanly retreat, into the tougher world of a City paper-merchant's office.

VII

APPRENTICESHIP

———————◆———————

THERE IS VERY little documentation on the seven years of Sam's life as an apprentice, and what there is refers only to his private exploits; but whatever else he did, he must have used them as a period of intensive journalistic training, for by the time he had completed them he had planned the most adventurous, and in many ways the cleverest magazine of the day. His apprenticeship enabled him to gain a thorough grounding in the technical aspects of publishing, which was of course very necessary to him, but the most important part of his programme was carried out in the evenings, when the day's work was over.

Then, he could settle down to read everything he could lay hands on. It was an active time in the literary world: *Vanity Fair, Pendennis, Dombey and Son, David Copperfield, Jane Eyre* and *Wuthering Heights* all came out over this period, and Longfellow's poems and Hawthorne's *The Scarlet Letter*, which Sam later serialized, appeared in this country for the first time. In addition to books, he studied every available newspaper, journal, and periodical—and tried out his own hand as a writer; it is impossible to say whether any of his early efforts appeared in print as almost all such contributions were published anonymously—but by no other means could he have become an editor and journalist of such accomplished skill by the time he was twenty-one. The habit of early rising and late nights never left him, and it enabled him to get through more work in his limited life-span than at first sight seems possible. As soon as they were married, Isabella, already prepared by her spell in Germany, followed his example.

Despite his dedication, his study of literature was not so lonely as might be supposed, for he had a number of friends with similar or allied ambitions, some of whom were apprentices like himself in the printing and paper trades. Among them were two brothers,

Frederick and James Greenwood, who were printer's apprentices with the same firm as another young man, James Wade, who duly became a printer and printed many of Sam's magazines. Frederick Greenwood, as is evident from scattered references in these magazines, worked for Beeton as general assistant, deputy, and editor for thirteen years. His early youth and subsequent career as editor of the *Pall Mall Gazette* are chronicled by J. W. Robertson Scott in *The Story of the Pall Mall Gazette*,[1] but apart from two years with Sam as the first editor of *The Queen*, shortly before he took over the *Gazette*, Mr Scott leaves the years he spent in the anonymity of Beeton's offices a blank. He married, perhaps because he had to, before his apprenticeship was over, after which he kept himself and his wife as best he could by journalism, at one time having some connection with a smart women's magazine, the *New Monthly Belle Assemblée*; the steady income Beeton provided was undoubtedly very welcome to him. As an apprentice, he was quite a colourful character, with red hair and (allegedly) the temper to go with it, a taste for fancy cravats, and a passionate desire to be a novelist. He did indeed publish two or three not very successful novels;[2] it is interesting to note that fiction was almost the only form of writing that Sam never attempted, though his imagination and adaptability indicate that he might have been rather better at it than his friend. As business partners, the two young men were ideally suited to each other, Greenwood being precisely what Beeton needed as an adviser—for underneath his adolescent mannerisms, he was responsible and sensible, besides being a journalist of distinction; apart from Isabella, Sam never found anyone on whom he could rely so implicitly, nor was there anyone who had so much influence over him. Before he married her, it was Greenwood who restrained him from indiscretion, Greenwood who helped him to recruit his staff (a difficult task in the case of his second magazine), and probably, as is suggested by later events, Greenwood who advised him over financial matters. He became a figure of some political as well as literary consequence as editor of the *Gazette*, and as a supporter of Disraeli was able to perform the considerable service of passing on the news of the Khedive's willingness to sell his shares in the Suez Canal.[3]

His younger brother James was a more erratic, slightly bizarre character, with a taste for exciting living and low company. He

wrote travel books and adventure stories for boys, but was best
known for a series commissioned by his brother, 'The Amateur
Casual', about the appalling conditions in the workhouses, which
he was one of the first journalists to inspect personally. He and a
friend dressed up in rags and went to spend the night in the casual
ward of the Lambeth workhouse, an experience so lurid that
even Dickens could scarcely have done justice to it; the editor
of the *Morning Post*'s comment that they deserved the Victoria
Cross for bravery was not altogether an exaggeration.[4]

While he was working for the paper merchant, Sam also met
the artists Birket Foster and Harrison Weir, and a young man
called Charles Clarke, with whom he went into partnership as
soon as his apprenticeship was over. Weir, who did the pictures
for the first edition of *Household Management*, restricted his career
almost entirely to illustrating, whereas Foster became one of the
most popular artists of the period, painting idyllic rustic scenes
with thatched cottages, woodland stiles, and spreading elms. At
this time, however, he was known chiefly for his engravings for
the *Illustrated London News*, the first illustrated newspaper, which
had been co-founded by an editor called Vizetelly, whom Clarke
also knew.

It is easy to envisage how, like students—as indeed in effect
they were—this group of friends, plus perhaps others who were
to contribute in some way to Sam's publications, would meet in
the evenings in pubs or each other's lodgings and analyse,
criticize, and comment upon the latest books and magazines;
they may sometimes have retired to the Dolphin, where Sam's
stepsisters, who adored him, welcomed him rapturously.

Sometimes, as the natural consequence of what they read, their
discussion may have veered towards political topics, radicalism
being the predominant view among such young men at that time.
Sam was seventeen in the year of the final Chartist demonstration,
and despite its failure, it left a residue of socialist feeling and
writing that apparently made a deep impression on him; at any
rate, he always had socialistic leanings, though he did not become
politically articulate until the end of his life. Earlier, it seems that
he had not thought out all the implications of his position, but
simply seized on several issues he felt strongly about and which
had a direct bearing on what he was doing.

He held unorthodox religious views and refused to enter a

church except purely as a sightseer (except on the occasion of
his wedding); nor, after her marriage, did Isabella. Yet he believed
very sincerely in some sort of God; it was not Christianity he
rejected, but only the hypocrisy, extravagance, and Popery that
he felt attended it:

> The English Church our serious thought bespeaks—
>   We write as friend to it, and not as foeman;
> We write to save it from the trait'rous sneaks
>   Who, English-named, at heart are wholly Roman;
> We write, unfettered, with a pen that seeks
>   Fair field from all, favour undue from no man;
> We write because a thousand blots besmear
> Th'eschutcheon of the Church we hold so dear.
>
> Blots of all kinds and colours, sorts and sizes—
>   Blots Evangelical and Ritualistic;
> Blots so pronounced that indignation rises;
>   Blots hidden carefully in language mystic;
> Blots publicly exhibited as prizes;
>   Blots to all usefulness antagonistic—
> Blots so diffuse, in fact, that without doubt
> They threaten soon to blot the Church right out.[5]

But according to Nancy Spain, not all their evenings ended in
mere talk. In his latter years, Sam pointed out a window that he
used to climb out of at night (which obviously did not belong
to the Dolphin) to Myra Browne, who looked after his children
and wrote for one of his magazines for nearly ten years. 'He had
quite a gay time until he was married,' she is reported to have
said. 'He was apprenticed to a paper merchant . . . then he joined
a man in partnership who he said tried to poison him and caused
his first illness.'[6] Miss Spain's source for this conversation cannot
be found, and it seems most likely that she was quoting from
spoken information, either from someone in the family or from
Mrs Browne herself. It is therefore impossible to verify; but there
seems no need to query the first part of it. It would have been
surprising if a youth like Sam had not had a gay time, for he
was extremely good looking, relatively well off and could afford
to take girls out in style. The trouble was that the girls who

were available were not stylish, since those of his own age and class were still shut away in the schoolroom, and like all others in his position, he had to make do with whoever he could find. Nevertheless, he must have had a certain amount to do with women, for right from the outset of his publishing career he was able to gauge their needs with absolute accuracy and a remarkable amount of imagination, and in his writing hit exactly the right note of flirtatiousness, even suggestiveness. This was partly due to sheer verbal dexterity, and was easier for him than most because he had an instinctive sympathy with and understanding of them which sprang from a pronounced feminine element in his own personality.

The second part of the statement attributed to Mrs Browne is open to a number of interpretations, though in view of the lack of corroboration it should not be taken too seriously. Miss Spain commented:

Whether it was Clarke or Salisbury [a printer who worked for Clarke and Beeton] who was the 'poisoner' and whether the 'poison' was some form of moral corruption we do not really know. But . . . it is fair to assume that this illness was contracted as a result of licentious London life. He always said that he began this sort of life 'too soon'.[7]

In fact the poisoner was certainly not Salisbury—he was not Beeton's partner, as Miss Spain states, but a middle-aged, happily married, highly respectable independent tradesman; the partner referred to must therefore have been Clarke. Very little is known of Clarke beyond the fact that his father had sufficient means to establish him in business, and that he was not especially able, though he seems to have been a competent partner to Sam.

The obvious assumption about the poison is that Sam caught VD soon after his apprenticeship was over; it is not unlikely on the face of things, since a large proportion of all classes of the population suffered from it. It was as much the result of bad luck as bad judgement, 'the Russian roulette of Victorian sex', as Ronald Pearsall puts it in his excellent book *The Worm in the Bud*.[8] All that can be said is that until he died of pulmonary tuberculosis twenty-five years later, Sam never showed any symptoms of it, and there is no reason to associate the deaths of the Beetons' first two babies with the disease, since the illnesses from which they died are sufficient explanation in themselves.

More probably, Sam said something of this kind in jest or as a form of showing off—which would have been very like him —or that he simply meant that Clarke encouraged him in his liking for sex, which by and large the Victorians looked on as a very potent kind of poison; and as his own conduct after he had met Isabella, even following her death (when the remark was made) was absolutely undeviating, he may well have come to look on his youthful activities in this light. He certainly had no particular personal interest in either of the mild perversions later discussed in one of his magazines, which surprised him as much as they did the majority of his readers.

Even though Sam found time to have what was no more than a normal amount of fun for a young man in London during his apprenticeship, these years of his life can be regarded as the most fruitful from a professional point of view that he could ever have spent. He ended up far better qualified for his career than he would have done if he had continued his gentlemanly upbringing and gone to Oxford or Cambridge, or to work for an established publisher, for he attained complete mastery of the practicalities of his vocation, as is shown by the efficiency with which he responded to his initial stroke of good luck; and as the result of his own efforts was better educated in the academic, or at least literary, sense than most of his social superiors. In addition, he knew his public, the people he had been living among, as no confirmed gentleman could hope to do. He had a ready-made set of friends prepared to work for him, and was well acquainted with the journalistic scene, if not, as Greenwood came to be, with any of the great literary personages of the day; and last, but perhaps most important of all, he learnt the value of hard work. Knowing himself ready, he must have been chafing to go into business for some time before his dependence ended. No one can have welcomed their twenty-first birthday more eagerly than he, nor put their ideas into practice more swiftly.

VIII

PUBLISHING

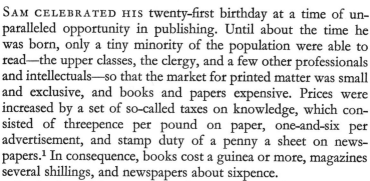

SAM CELEBRATED HIS twenty-first birthday at a time of unparalleled opportunity in publishing. Until about the time he was born, only a tiny minority of the population were able to read—the upper classes, the clergy, and a few other professionals and intellectuals—so that the market for printed matter was small and exclusive, and books and papers expensive. Prices were increased by a set of so-called taxes on knowledge, which consisted of threepence per pound on paper, one-and-six per advertisement, and stamp duty of a penny a sheet on newspapers.[1] In consequence, books cost a guinea or more, magazines several shillings, and newspapers about sixpence.

By the time of the 1851 census, however, the reading population had expanded by millions: over half the adults in the country could sign their names (which for the purposes of the census was accepted as proof of literacy) and nearly half the children went to school (though not necessarily regularly or for long). But the millions were still far too poor and under-educated to be able either to afford or understand the old-style publications, and needed something which had never existed before—easy, unsophisticated, relatively entertaining texts which would hold their interest—and at very low prices.

The need for cheapness was recognized early on, but it was longer before it was realized that a new approach was also required. Some of the first attempts to satisfy the needs of a mass public were unsuccessful as it was naturally difficult for publishers and editors, themselves educated men, to come to terms with the untutored minds of the lower classes, of whom they knew next to nothing except that they were ignorant and in need of instruction. They produced long-winded, close-printed, scholarly works, which, although marvellous bargains in terms of the amount of information per square inch, were so dull that nobody, educated or not, could have been expected to get through them.

One such pioneer was Charles Knight of the Society for the Diffusion of Useful Knowledge, an organization founded, as its name suggests, by a group of earnest, upper-class intellectuals. He published two extremely worthy but virtually unreadable serials, the *Penny Cyclopedia*, which lost an immense amount of money, and the *Penny Magazine*, which, surprisingly, kept going for eleven years—perhaps a proof of the very genuine spirit of self-improvement prevailing at the time. In spite of their failure, they earned him great personal prestige, and he came to be looked on by everyone in publishing, no doubt Sam included, as a kind of Grand Old Man of popular education, and he continued to edit learned tomes for the rest of his life. Another pioneering venture was *Chambers's Edinburgh Journal*, a lively publication which contained pictures and fiction as well as information and, in contrast to Knight's papers, was still in circulation at the turn of the century. In retrospect, the moral seems obvious, but it was some time before anyone followed *Chambers's* example, partly because of the inhibiting effect of the advertisement tax.

One highly successful experiment was made in the field of cheap book publishing, and this was the publication in 1836 of *Pickwick Papers* as a serial in unbound parts, which brought in a vogue for publishing new books of all kinds as serials at a few pence a time. It was an extremely practical idea, since it cut out binding costs and spread both publishers' and purchasers' outlay over a conveniently long period; if all went well, the book was brought out as a bound volume when the parts were completed. Sam initiated all his longer books in this fashion, including *Household Management*.

Cheap books as volumes soon appeared from some of the conventional publishers, whose main business continued to be prestigious, high-priced works, and from a handful of enterprising newcomers. Both groups were extremely cautious, and limited their lists to reprints of classics and other established works which they could be sure would have wide sales, and which in most cases they could appropriate without copyright fees. The result was a dearth of new titles in the lower price range. It was in an attempt to provide something more stimulating that Henry Vizetelly of the *Illustrated London News* entered the field, at almost the same time as Sam.

Vizetelly, egotistical, individualistic, and unusually imaginative, was one of the few who understood the needs of poorer readers, and spent most of his life trying to promote their interests. Later, he started another popular newspaper; later still, he was imprisoned for publishing Zola. Early in 1852 he planned a series of books called, appropriately, Readable Books, which was intended to be lively and entertaining as well as improving, and to introduce works which had not appeared in Britain before for a minimal price. He selected six titles, including Edgar Allan Poe's *Tales of Mystery, Imagination, and Horror; and Poems*; a translation of an amusing book by the French writer Arsène Houssaye, *Philosophers and Actresses, or, Scenes Vivid and Picturesque from the Hundred and One Dramas of Art and Passion*; and a biography of Wellington. He planned to bring out one a month at the price of one shilling; the series was very successful—but it was not Vizetelly who reaped the profits.

After *Chambers's Edinburgh Journal*, there was a conspicuous lack of popular periodicals, and in the decade before Sam's coming of age only half a dozen others survived for a significant length of time. Of these, three were scurrilous penny weeklies for the working classes, and the others—an interesting trio for various reasons—were impeccably respectable middle-class journals: Dickens's *Household Words*, which was a purely personal creation; the *Mirror of Literature, Amusement, and Instruction*, run by John Limbird, which folded in 1849; and the *Family Friend*, launched that same year. All cost twopence and provided general family reading. There was nothing at a comparable price for more specific groups of readers, of whom the most obvious were women and children. For women there were only expensive upper-class fashion journals like the *New Monthly Belle Assemblée*, which had little relevance to ordinary housewives, and for children virtually nothing but one or two prim columns in their parents' magazines.

These gaps must have been obvious to anyone who had analysed the situation, and it was not surprising that Sam determined to fill them, making up his mind to publish cheap magazines for children, of whose deprivation he had himself been conscious, and for women, whom he liked and understood so well. It is hard to assess the extent to which his inclination and recognition of his particular talents, as opposed to objective reasoning, influenced his decision. They almost certainly did not influence his order of action: he began with a women's magazine because it commanded a bigger market and was more likely to show a profit than a children's periodical; he does not seem to have expected, nor even intended, to make money with his boys' publications. Also a women's magazine was easier to set up from a technical point of view. It is of course possible that he did not conceive the idea of the second magazine until the first was proving a success, but this is unlikely because it was the second which inspired his chief interest and enthusiasm.

More remarkable than his initial decision to cater for these groups was the way in which he set out to do so. A less imaginative man would either have produced conventional, educative magazines, larded, if he had any sense, with enough entertaining matter to make them sell, or gone in for commercial rubbish and turned out an up-graded, watered-down version of the penny press. But Sam, with something of Vizetelly's instinct, did neither. Like Knight, and in very much the same pioneering spirit, he set out to instruct—but in a totally different way. He was concerned to inculcate ideas rather than facts, and his mode of presentation was light rather than heavy: he aimed to make learning fun. This went against the prevailing mood of the period; also, the ideas he was trying to put over were progressive and un-Victorian, in the generally accepted sense of the word. His magazines therefore invited the disapproval of the more staid and conforming elements in society, and relied to an exceptional degree on his attractive personality and skill as a journalist.

His birthday fell in April or May 1852, the year following the Great Exhibition, at the beginning of more than a decade of general prosperity and expansion. In publishing, the existence of a mass market was beginning to make itself felt: W. H. Smith's bookstalls were springing up on the new railway stations as fast as they were built; Mudie established his lending library in Oxford Street, which was soon patronized by practically every lady in London; and a novel became a best-seller on a scale which took the whole civilized world by surprise. This was *Uncle Tom's Cabin* by a hitherto unknown American writer, Harriet Beecher Stowe, an impassioned story about the sufferings of the slaves in the southern states. By pure luck, Sam managed to be in the right place at the right time.

As soon as he had been given his money, he bought a partnership with Clarke, who was trying, in a rather hopeless, haphazard manner, to build up a business as a publisher and bookseller. He had persuaded Vizetelly to give him the job of publishing the Readable Books series, but that seems to have been more or less the only work he had. A month or so before Sam joined him, Vizetelly appeared with an obscure novel he had just received from America, and was considering for the series—*Uncle Tom's Cabin*. Frederick Greenwood and the printer of the series, Salisbury, were asked to read it, and on the strength of their recommendation Clarke, Salisbury, and Vizetelly decided to bring it out as a joint venture (hence the misapprehension that Salisbury, as well as Clarke, went into partnership with Sam). At first it was a complete flop, and Vizetelly, who had never been very optimistic about it, went abroad with Birket Foster.

The book was originally priced at 2s 6d, but shortly after Sam's arrival it was reduced to one shilling, presumably at his suggestion. As a result, it began to sell, slowly at first, but with increasing momentum. By the summer it had become such a hit that no fewer than a dozen other British publishers hastened to jump on the bandwagon. Clarke and Beeton moved to offices at 148 Fleet Street, where they claimed to be employing four hundred people and seventeen printing presses to keep up with the demand,[2] and brought out at least nine different editions, ranging from a penny serial to a *de luxe* volume containing 'Forty Magnificent Engravings'. Some had a preface and explanatory headings by Greenwood,[3] others a specially written preface by the author. Altogether, it was estimated that a million and a half copies were sold in Britain and the colonies alone.[4] The story made such an impact that even *The Times*, fearful of its repercussions in America, devoted two long, annihilating reviews to it.[5] In political terms these were quite justified, since the book certainly played its part in hastening the outbreak of civil war.

For Sam, the affair had several consequences. In the first place, most significantly, he and Clarke made a considerable amount of money, a proportion of which they lost very soon afterwards on a sequel, *The Key to Uncle Tom's Cabin*, which was not another novel but a compilation of the documentary evidence on which the original had been based. Mrs Stowe was convinced that it would be even more successful than the first book, saying confidently, 'My Key will be stronger than the Cabin';[6] but the issue of slavery was too remote in England to justify the publication of a mere compilation of facts, which if Sam had had a little more experience he would have realized. In spite of this miscalculation, however, he was still sufficiently well set up financially to be able to pursue his journalistic ambitions much more freely than he could otherwise have done over the next few years. He had no need to worry if his magazines were slow in taking off, and was able to afford extravagances to help establish them which, if they caused adverse comment at the time, paid off in the long run. A by-product of the fiasco of *The Key* may have been the break-up of his partnership with Clarke,[7] but as Clarke, so far as one can see, never had anything to do with his magazines, this caused him little inconvenience, and in fact was probably a relief to him.

Largely as a result of good luck, he also inherited Readable Books from Vizetelly. On his return from Europe, the latter was surprised to find *Uncle Tom's Cabin*, which he had thought a non-starter, selling tolerably well (this was before it had really got under way) and called unexpectedly on Clarke to demand his share of the profits. He was somewhat put out to be confronted by Sam, and instantaneously took a violent dislike to him, probably because of his lively manner—for Vizetelly had a somewhat swollen idea of his own importance and would certainly have expected a younger man to treat him with respect. His reaction was very similar to that of Henry Dorling a few years later, and though it did not have the same lasting consequences, it was a pity, since in terms of talent and interest he and Sam had a great deal in common. As it was, he accused Beeton of making fun of him, flew into a rage, in the course of which he threatened (apparently quite unjustifiably) to go to law, and finally walked out with five hundred pounds in return for his share of *Uncle Tom's Cabin*, with the Readable Books series thrown in. He had still not got over his bitterness at having thrown away a fortune nearly forty years later, when he came to write his autobiography.[8]

Sam took up Readable Books with enthusiasm and added seven more enterprising and profitable titles, including *The Life of Nelson* by Robert Southey and *Reveries of a Bachelor* by an American writer, Ik Marvel.[9]

In terms of his personal life, the most interesting outcome of *Uncle Tom's Cabin* was a visit to America in the autumn of 1852 to persuade Mrs Stowe to give him preference as publisher of *The Key to Uncle Tom's Cabin*, and to present her with five hundred pounds as a token author's payment, since in the absence of copyright laws between England and America[10] (a source of much indignation among leading authors on both sides of the Atlantic), she had no legal right to gain anything from her English sales. This was his first trip abroad and his only visit to America; naturally, it made an indelible impression on him, and he harked back to it as a landmark for the rest of his life. He arrived characteristically full of optimism about his meeting with the authoress and eager to find out as much as he could about American writers, whose work was being borrowed on an increasingly wide scale in England because it could be used free, and also because it was more suitable for a mass readership than that of more conservative British authors.

His meeting with Mrs Stowe must be accounted a personal triumph, for she began by refusing to see him and ended by being completely captivated by him. As well as the promise of an early copy of *The Key to Uncle Tom's Cabin* and other favours, she supplied him with several introductions, including one to her brother, the well-known (later notorious) preacher, Henry Ward Beecher, to whom she wrote: 'You will, I think, find pleasure in his conversation.' Other letters she gave him were probably to Longfellow and Whittier, with whom she corresponded; Sam certainly met them, and also a young man called Mr Fields, who later started an American boys' magazine.

He was no less enchanted with her than she with him, despite the fact that she was middle-aged, rigidly Puritan, and, by her own description, 'never very much to look at in my best days, and looking like a used-up article now'.[11] An engraving showed a strong, bony face surrounded by an incongruous coiffure of ringlets. But she represented a type of woman Sam had never met in England, of formidable intellectual strength and passionate emotions, neither of which she had the least hesitation in displaying, utterly dedicated to her cause, yet at the same time a conscientious wife and mother. Until he met Isabella, she seems to have represented the nearest he found to his feminine ideal; when he returned, he wrote an adulatory article about her in his magazine[12]:

There are hearts which are not all contained in themselves—whose chords put out delicate shoots and fibres into the hearts of all humanity, instantly and painfully responsive to the sorrow of all. Such a heart has Mrs. Stowe. . . .

THE MAGAZINES

SAM'S FIRST MAGAZINE, the *Englishwoman's Domestic Magazine*, appeared on the bookstalls within a few days of his arrival at Clarke's offices. It was very modest looking, about the size of an ordinary paperback, with a plain, drab grey cover, and thirty-two pages of such small type that at first sight it seems almost unreadable (thanks to the paper tax, however, the contemporary public were used to it). It was to be a key factor in Isabella's life, for she worked on it continuously from her marriage to her death, and *Household Management* was its offspring. It was also the forerunner of the vast industry of cheap women's magazines. Though Sam is not generally credited with having originated them, at least five of its novel features—essay competitions, problem pages, prize distributions, medical columns, and paper dress patterns, (this was not, strictly speaking, Sam's idea but a notion he introduced from France)—have come to be taken for granted in modern journalism. To its readers, however, the most important thing about it was the price, for like *Household Words* and the *Family Friend*, it cost only twopence.

Its most obvious prototypes were the expensive ladies' fashion journals, of which there were about half a dozen at the beginning of 1852 (three of them merged together in the course of the year). Because of the restricted sphere of interest thought proper for ladies, they were all prudish and trivial, clearly intended for the drawing-room table rather than actual reading. For the most part, they consisted of sentimental stories and verse and reports on the Paris fashions, usually illustrated with hand-coloured fashion engravings, which were sometimes very pleasing; the magazine Frederick Greenwood had worked for, the *New Monthly Belle Assemblée*, had particularly attractive, lavish fashion plates. The only one of these magazines to contain anything practical was *The Ladies' Companion*, which had a column on servants, outstandingly good cookery articles by Eliza Acton, whose book *Modern Cookery* had appeared a few years before, and a generously illustrated embroidery feature called 'The Work-table', which was probably the inspiration for a similar feature with the same name in Sam's magazine. Otherwise, however, the *Englishwoman's Domestic Magazine* owed nothing to any of them; it had no fashion feature as its readers were of a class who could not possibly afford to buy clothes from Paris, it was brisk and practical rather than sentimental, and above all, thanks to its editor's personality, it was the very opposite of prudish.

It seems that instead of using the ladies' magazines as models, Sam had turned to the twopenny journal, the *Family Friend*, for ideas; indeed, it was probably the *Family Friend*'s dramatic success that originally drew his attention to the cheap magazine field. It started as a monthly, had soon become fortnightly, and then turned weekly, claiming the amazing sales figures of two and a half million.[1] In contrast to the ladies' magazines, it set out to be useful, with columns on domestic subjects such as cooking, gardening, and nature study, under the co-ordinated headings 'The Housewife's Friend', 'The Gardener's Friend', 'The Naturalist's Friend'. The cookery articles, though hardly in the same class as Eliza Acton's, were presented in what was at that time an exceptionally practical way, with lists of food in season, straightforward recipes, simple directions, and explanatory illustrations. There were also a couple of educational features for children, 'Grandfather Whitehead's Lectures for Littlefolk' and 'Aunt Mary's Cabinet Pictures', which were so successful that a separate magazine was set up for tutorial purposes. To balance all this information, there was a roughly equal amount of amusement—the usual romantic fiction and poetry,[2] games, puzzles, and a nauseating pair of columns called 'Trifles' and 'Treasures', which were lists of puns and aphorisms—always useful, among other things, as aids to witty conversation.

Although the editor, R. K. Philps, cultivated a smug, rather schoolmasterish image, in accordance with the prevailing taste for self-improvement, his aims were in essence scarcely different from Vizetelly's: 'Is it necessary for good principle to be ever shrouded in gloom? For instruction to be presented in ambiguous and oppressive shapes? For the schoolmaster to increasingly flourish his rod? We think not. Our book is an experiment in illustration of this opinion.'[3] He went on to declare that he would have nothing to do with foolish intellectual theories or frivolities such as romance, and was invariably scrupulously careful to avoid anything which could possibly have been considered improper or controversial. He also expressed the utmost contempt for the usual custom in magazines of correspondents adopting pseudonyms, saying that an honest letter could be signed with an honest signature; he had 'a huge "WASTEBASKET" to which the Absurd, the Ambiguous, the Indiscreet, and the Irregular, are unceremoniously consigned'.[4]

Sam openly appropriated his approach to domestic subjects, and copied the Treasures and Trifles idea with equivalent columns of 'Wit' and 'Wisdom'; but that was as far as the similarity between the two magazines went, for his aims in the remainder of the *Englishwoman's Domestic Magazine* were diametrically opposed to Philps'. In spite of its reassuringly conventional name, the *EDM* was full of controversial ideas, and deliberately set out to encourage its readers to use their minds and extend their interests beyond the limits of the home. This was evident from the carefully worded preface: 'When introducing the ENGLISHWOMAN'S DOMESTIC MAGAZINE to the public, we stated that our object was to produce a work which should tend to the improvement of the intellect, the cultivation of the morals, and the cherishing of domestic virtues.' Sam certainly did not avoid the topic of romance—he himself conducted a correspondence page devoted exclusively to lovers' problems. These differences, plus the striking contrast in style between the two editors, effectively concealed the fact that there was anything in common between their publications, and it is unlikely that in the early days Philps was even aware of the existence of the *Englishwoman's Domestic Magazine*.

Sam's condemnation of girls' education was on both the practical and the theoretical level: he deplored the impracticality of teaching girls nothing relevant to their adult lives as wives, but he also challenged the assumption that girls would not benefit from a similar intellectual training to boys, to which he believed they had an equal right. This belief he carried to its logical conclusion—female emancipation; but he could not say so in the magazine yet, for like other progressive notions (such as birth control) it inspired everyone with any pretence to respectability with disgust, and no paper openly supporting it could have survived more than a few months; this had already been proved once, and was to be confirmed several times over the next two decades. It was not until the end of the 'sixties that the 'Woman Question' came to be freely debated in magazines and newspapers, and then the *EDM* played its part fully; but until that time Sam left the central topic alone and concentrated on the side issues of education, employment, and women's achievements in the arts and medicine. The latter were spotlighted in an occasional series of profiles of women who had been successful in some professional calling, most of the earlier subjects being writers: the first was of Maria Edgeworth, the author of *Castle Rackrent* and a number of moralistic (though even now by no means unreadable) children's tales, rather of the kind he tried to supplant in his boys' publications. The second, written the winter after he returned from America, was his eulogy on Mrs Stowe.

He also tried to broaden his readers' minds by publishing stimulating fiction, his most adventurous experiment in this direction being the serialization of Hawthorne's mysterious, heart-rending novel *The Scarlet Letter*, which not only featured an unfaithful wife as its heroine, but questioned the whole structure of a society based on the subordinate role of women.[5] When the book first appeared in England a few years before, it caused great indignation, but apparently it attracted no adverse comment from the magazine readers—at least, no letters of complaint were published—which perhaps says something for the influence Sam had by then established over them. A more conventional serial was Frederick Greenwood's *The Path of Roses*, which had a faintly Wilkie Collins-ish ring about it. Much of the fiction, regrettably but perhaps inevitably, was as bad as that which appeared in the ladies' journals and the *Family Friend*— for Sam had to admit that even his public could not do without their ration of tears and tragedy.

The essay competitions were the most constructive part of his educative policy, though he did not announce them until after he had been to America, when the magazine had been in circulation for six months; possibly, he came across the idea while he was away. He introduced them with some excellent advice on how to write (which probably he later repeated to Isabella): 'The most illiterate of our readers will find that she is able to write something worthy of being published, if she will only sit down with the determination to communicate something worth knowing in the fewest possible words.'[6] The winning essays were published in the magazine every month, with a commentary on the runners-up, from which it is clear that he not only thoroughly enjoyed his role as tutor, but also had considerable flair for it.

At first the subjects set were cautiously conventional, such as the Duke of Wellington's funeral, 'Christmas Day in England, its Observances and Customs', and 'On the Influence of a Mother's Teaching in After-Life'. After a while, however, he grew bored, for which he can hardly be blamed because the essays, though competent, were uniformly serious and pedantic, and he must have found the chore of reading them month after month almost insupportably dull. Once, in an attempt to break the monotony, he put the question, 'Do Married Rakes Make the Best Husbands?' but even this failed to produce the slightest spark of humour or originality. But the next topic, 'The Rights of Women', proved more inflammable, for among the usual pile of unexceptionable discourses was an entry advocating total emancipation. That month's commentary makes amusing reading, for although Sam had presumably been angling for something of the kind, he was at a loss to know what to do having got it; unable to support it, but equally unwilling to condemn it, he was obliged to hedge: 'As we cannot print it—the too discursive treatment of the subject alone forbidding that—it would be unfair to offer an opinion of the arguments. . . .'[7]

Given the purified, unrealistic Victorian attitude to love (sex was as far as possible denied recognition, and certainly not openly discussed), 'Cupid's Letter-Bag'— Sam's page of love problems— was a daring, not to say progressive, idea. Correspondence pages of a general nature were usual enough, but romance had not featured on them within memory, so that Cupid came as a complete novelty, and can fairly be said to be the ancestor of the modern agony column. Sam was in his element as an expert on romance, for his experience as a man of the world, his liking for the opposite sex, and his sense of humour were all drawn into play; altogether, he probably got more fun out of Cupid, at any rate for the first year or so, than from anything else he ever attempted. The silliness of some of the problems submitted must have reduced the whole of his staff to helpless laughter, but others were genuinely pathetic; in all cases, his replies were models of rectitude and prudence:

MINNIE looks cold. Gentleman sends presents; MINNIE refuses them. Nevertheless, the gentleman perseveres—sends his presents in such a manner that they cannot be returned, and otherwise continues his assaults upon the heart of MINNIE. But business calls him away; he still writes to MINNIE, but says not a word of love. Meanwhile, she says, she had found that 'absence makes the heart grow fonder' and now she is 'deeply in love with him.' What is to be done? MINNIE has a wilful mind; she must now tarry till the gentleman renews his attentions, and smile upon him—when she gets an opportunity.[8]

At times he showed a degree of common sense almost worthy of Isabella. 'Henrietta' had the older woman's classic problem:

'I have been married some years, and to the best of my knowledge have always acted the part of an affectionate, prudent wife—only one thing mars my happiness. My husband, who is kind and considerate in other respects, always leaves home until quite late. Would it be wise to question him as to the cause of this?' We think not. Let HENRIETTA make her home a happy one, let her endeavour to engage her husband in some amusement or occupation for the evening in which she can share, without, at the same time, appearing to force his inclinations; and if he be kind and considerate, as she says he is, he will no doubt yield to her wishes. On no account employ remonstrance or upbraiding.[9]

Presumably, Henrietta's husband, in company with a surprising number of other kind-hearted, considerate gentlemen, spent his evenings with his mistress in a luxuriously appointed maisonette in North London.

Coelebs of Gray's Inn Lane wrote to complain that the essay competitions had turned his girlfriend into a 'blue'. (Was she, one wonders, the girl who wrote the essay in favour of emancipation?)

Up to the last two years I have been most happy in the affections of a young lady, whom I have fondly pictured as my wife. I am now most deeply concerned to find that she has taken to authorship, and has gained a prize from you for composition. If there is one thing I hate more than another it is a blue. I would rather marry a woman that [sic] could not write her name than one who could pen the best essay ever produced. How can such an one be presumed to attend to household matters? Instead of darning stockings, I shall find her writing essays on the 'Rights of Woman'. Can I expect her to descend from her Pegasus, think you, to make my tea? Altogether, my prospect appears very inky, and should I not be justified in according, in my own person, a true subject for an essay 'On the Inconstancy of Man?'

This was an attack on the basic principles on which the magazine was founded and naturally provoked Sam to an indignant rebuke—but still he did not allow himself to be carried away, and his reply was just within the popularly acceptable limits:

COELEBS can never be so prejudiced or narrow-minded as he would lead us to suppose! Are we to infer from what he says that he thinks ignorance qualifies a woman better for the performance of her complicated duties than intelligence? What companionship, what sympathy, what co-operation can a well-educated man, or man of the world, find in a partner of contracted ideas or confined education; a partner without judgement, without general information or refined tastes? We pity COELEBS. . . . The really well-educated never think any duty beneath them. For our part, we consider the sympathy of an intelligent woman one of the greatest boons heaven has bestowed on man.[10]

One of the funniest correspondences in the Letter-Bag was the enigma of Albert, who wrote asking Cupid to help him find a wife. Sam, although by no means convinced that he was genuine, could not resist the temptation of publishing his letter, whereupon no fewer than nine young ladies, all, according to their own descriptions, extremely eligible, expressed an interest. One, who sounded particularly arch, described herself as having eyes like the Sphinx; another claimed to be the victim of a heartless father who was trying to force her to marry a rich man she detested; a third, a shade more sensible than the rest, wanted to know why Albert could not find a wife for himself—a question which was destined to remain unanswered. In due course, Albert sent in a personal description of himself, which was not published, but forwarded direct to the candidates. All nine immediately withdrew: whatever handicap poor Albert suffered from (if he existed), his case was clearly most unfortunate. However, one more belated offer arrived from a girl called Nettie, who sounded much jollier and nicer than the rest: 'Now I must tell Albert, first of all, a *terrible* little secret before I go on in the least to recommend myself—Oh, Albert: this must, I fear, prove a deathblow to all my hopes—I am (I must say so) very *very* untidy!' She was eighteen, with blue eyes and curly hair, and wanted nothing more than to live in the country and keep a pony. Whether she too rejected Albert was never revealed.[11]

Sam continued Cupid until the year of his marriage and the launching of his third magazine, the *Boy's Own Journal*. It is conceivable that he gave it up under pressure from Henry, whose disgust goes without saying; probably Isabella too did not altogether approve of it, though she was ready to assist with its more sedate successor; possibly, he merely grew bored with it, as he had with the essays. Later, he started a second correspondence page, the 'Englishwoman's Conversazione', which had a (slightly) more serious tone and dealt with an unlimited range of topics, from which romance was by no means excluded—and from the number of love problems printed, it is clear that whatever may have been the reason for Cupid's demise it was not lack of popularity. Ironically, it was the Conversazione which gained a dubious reputation.

Despite the attraction of Cupid, it was the domestic section of the *EDM*, like that of the *Family Friend*, which was its strongest selling point, especially at first, when there were no other women's magazines offering a similar service; and its usefulness was the first thing Sam stressed in his Address to the first issue:

The ENGLISHWOMAN'S DOMESTIC MAGAZINE will doubtless be found an encouraging friend to those of our countrywomen already initiated into the secret of making 'home happy;' and to the uninitiated, who sometimes from carelessness, but oftener from want of a guiding master, have failed in this great particular, we shall offer hints and advice by which they may overcome every difficulty. . . . With this in view, we propose, in the first place, to treat of domestic management, embracing as it does actions minute and insignificant in detail, but each one tending to swell the amount of happiness *if performed*, of misery *if neglected*.

This, apart from its echo of Utilitarianism, amounted to much the same as Isabella's introduction to *Household Management* nearly a decade later:

What moved me, in the first instance, to attempt a work like this, was the discomfort and suffering which I had seen brought upon men and women by household mismanagement. I have always thought that there is no more fruitful source of family discontent than a housewife's badly-cooked dinners and untidy ways.

There is no need to say more to show that the foundations for the book were laid when the *EDM* was planned; Isabella had only to carry out the intention.

There were columns on child and invalid care, beauty, cookery, pets, gardening, embroidery, dressmaking, and a medical column written by a surgeon. For the first year or so, the cookery was laid out in much the same manner as in the *Family Friend*, with lists of food in season accompanied by recipes, which were simple enough for the ordinary small household. The dressmaking feature was an inspiration, for in the absence of ready-made clothes, women had either to employ a dressmaker, or, if they could not afford one, make their own. It was not illustrated with plates, which would have been an impossible expense in a magazine costing twopence, but with diagrams from which a full-sized pattern could be worked out. Ready-cut, full-sized patterns as we know them were not introduced for some years. But it was not the practical value of the magazine, nor the educational or entertainment value of the other parts of it, which attracted most attention at the time. Contemporary comment centred largely on Sam's promotional device of an annual 'Golden Prize' raffle, for which the entry qualification was a year's worth of the special coupons printed in each issue of the magazine. The prizes were substantial: the first year he offered twenty-five gold watches from Bennet's of Cheapside, a shop he must have known well since it was only a few steps down the road from the Dolphin; the next year, a hundred gold chains were presented. The value of the prizes over four years totalled the astonishing sum of 1,645 guineas, and in seven years three thousand guineas; though Sam could not have foreseen the profits from *Uncle Tom's Cabin* when the first year's prizes were announced, he would not have been able to spend anything like as much without them. The main gifts were always gold watches or jewellery, but after two or three years subsidiary items such as cheques or dressing cases were added. Sam was not giving away rubbishy products: a second supplier of jewellery was J. W. Benson of Ludgate Hill, whose watches were praised in the *Morning Post* for their 'exquisite artistic feeling' and 'perfection of mechanism'.[12] Both Benson and Bennet advertised in the magazine (luckily for Sam, the advertisement tax was lifted soon after it began) and though there is no record that he offered them reduced rates in return for a discount on their goods, it seems likely that he made some agreement of this kind.

Even at this date, it was not unheard of for advertisers to make give-away offers, but so far it had only been done in a small way, and no one had ever come across such a display of generosity before. The provincial papers, when they came to review the magazine (it was years before it was noticed by the national press) were extremely suspicious, and Sam was obliged to defend himself against accusations of fraud:

When, on the establishment of the ENGLISHWOMAN'S DOMESTIC MAGAZINE, in May, 1852, it was promised that valuable gifts should be distributed among the purchasers, it was not, perhaps, generally believed. The announcement, however, was made in good faith—proof being that it has been honestly and literally fulfilled. . . . Formal receipts for all the prizes may also be seen at the Office. . . .[13]

In the excitement caused by the gift hand-outs, most other aspects of the magazine were ignored, though several reviewers praised the illustrations, and it was generally agreed that it was a marvellous bargain for twopence.

Like Vizetelly, but unlike Philps, who was sparing with pictures and on the whole used them only for explanatory purposes, Sam was a firm believer in the importance of illustration in popular journalism, and used it freely in all his publications. Many of the engravings in the *EDM* were by his friends Harrison Weir and Birket Foster; their chocolate-box style was ideally suited to a woman's magazine, and both were pioneers in the new methods of block-making. Sam used steel plates, which were cheaper than the old wooden ones, and enabled him to be more generous with his illustrations than would otherwise have been possible.

As Isabella's book was to do later, the magazine made its way unspectacularly but surely. At the end of its first year (1852) Sam declared that it had been 'liberally' patronized; at the end of the second its circulation had reached 25,000; at the end of the fourth (at the time of his marriage) 37,000; and by 1860, when Isabella joined the staff, 60,000, which if not sensational was a very respectable figure and far exceeded that of the lady's magazines. That year, at the beginning of its ninth volume, Sam and Isabella between them transformed it into something very much more like them, adding coloured fashion plates and needlework patterns and raising the price to the half-way mark, sixpence. Thereafter, she had nearly as much influence over it as he did.

In January 1855, when the *EDM* was two and a half years old, Sam launched his second magazine, the *Boy's Own Magazine*. Isabella never had anything directly to do with it, but she was able to make use of its contributors when she came to write her book, and it deserves a little discussion because it was the most courageous and praiseworthy of all Sam's projects, and the one which above all inspired him with a sense of mission. 'I can hardly imagine a more responsible task for a man than undertaking to answer for the matter and manner of literature intended for the youth of one's country,' he wrote a few years later. 'No small thing I count it to help form the taste and influence the mind of a youth whose glorious heritage it is to possess the empire that their fathers have founded or preserved. . . .'[14] From the first, he was even more personally involved in it than in the *EDM*, and was constantly trying to extend and improve it, and establish further publications.

It came at exactly the right moment, for in the years since Sam had been at school the refreshing influence of Hans Andersen and others had brought about a slackening of the restrictions on children's literature, and children were allowed a somewhat livelier, more varied range of books. It was also at about this time, with the enormous increase in the number of juvenile readers, that publishers and editors began to realize that children were not just children, to be lumped together into an amorphous mass, but boys and girls of different ages, with widely varying tastes and interests. The advances in children's books, however, had not yet extended into journalism; the very few existing periodicals—such as the *Family Friend*'s offshoot, the *Family Tutor* (which did not share the success of the parent publication) and Charlotte Yonge's *Monthly Packet*—were founded with educative aims. The first was intended for the schoolroom, and the second for Sunday school, and primarily for girls—fairly well off girls at that, for it cost eightpence. The *Boy's Own Magazine* was not only the first magazine aimed specifically at boys, aged roughly from eight to twelve, but also the first magazine for children clearly intended to be read for amusement as well as instruction. Although it is seldom credited for it, perhaps because it has been overshadowed by the much later *Boy's Own Paper*, it was the pioneer of a new genre of literature, and with the classic *Tom Brown's Schooldays* set the tone of writing for boys for the rest of the century.

It was constructed along similar lines to the *EDM*: 'The pages of the BOY'S OWN MAGAZINE . . . will contain . . . matters of interest, amusement, and healthful and moral excitement, calculated at once to produce pleasure and convey instruction.'[15] The contents were as exciting as Sam could make them, and presumably contained all the things he himself would have enjoyed as a boy: travel and adventure features, biographies of famous men, articles on sport and nature study, and various games and puzzles. There were essay competitions and prize raffles as before, the only difference being that the prizes were silver rather than gold; twenty silver watches were given away in the first year. The price, format, and artists were also the same, Foster and Weir being regular contributors. The title page was an intricate symbolic design incorporating books labelled Story, Biography, and Travels, rabbits to represent the study of nature, a globe, compass, and ship to indicate adventure, and a cricket bat for sport.

The opening article in the first issue was about Benjamin Franklin, whose career was an outstanding example of how a man could get to the top by means of sheer hard work—one of the virtues Sam was especially at pains to instil. Some of the famous men featured in subsequent issues were Christopher Columbus, Captain Cook, William Hogarth, and James Watt. After the feature on Benjamin Franklin came a gripping account of catching a crocodile, with an illustration of a crocodile chasing a terrified woman up a river bank. This was followed by an article on war weapons, another on famous places, a story by Edgar Allan Poe called 'The Thousand and Second Tale', and an Old English ballad of Robin Hood, which was held up by Sam as an example to be emulated of plain, straightforward, unembellished narrative writing. The rest of the issue included a history of the Gunpowder Plot and the equivalent of Wit and Wisdom, 'Facts, Fancies, and Phenomena', which consisted of snippets of curious and unusual information such as the oldest tree in the world.

To the modern reader, this may look as if the balance was still heavily weighted in favour of instruction, but at the time it represented something of a revolution, for although most of the subject matter was intrinsically informative, such a wide range of topics had never been attempted before; also, determined to avoid the usual 'Goody-Two-Shoes style of composition', Sam made a point of presenting the magazine in a much brisker, more adult style, which he felt was more worthy of children's intelligence.

The real challenge which faced him was not finding the right formula, but suitable contributors, who could write about the adventurous topics he planned to include and present them in the desired manner. A great many of those he took on were not writers at all, but travellers, adventurers, and ex-soldiers, who had actually been to far-flung parts of the world, and could draw on their own knowledge and experience. Some in due course made extremely lucrative careers in boys' literature: one was

Captain Mayne Reid, who had spent his youth in America, where he fought in the war with Mexico and had many other adventures which he was subsequently able to turn to excellent account in a string of around forty authentic, exciting tales. Several of these characters were, or became, personal friends of the Greenwood brothers, who probably originally introduced them to Sam. Whether they also became intimate with the Beetons, and knew Isabella, is not recorded; the only writers she certainly knew well were Frederick Greenwood and two other members of Sam's staff, John Tillotson and Christopher Weldon—neither of whom, however, were on the original *BOM* staff, but joined later.

Inevitably, the *BOM* gave rise to a good deal of scepticism when it first started, and parents and others who had been used on the one hand to such writers as Charlotte Yonge and Maria Edgeworth, and on the other to penny-dreadful-type rubbish, alike predicted its rapid demise. But it sold in spite of them, and at the end of its first year Sam reported, imprecisely but optimistically: 'Our readers, instead of remaining a few, as was predicted, increased by thousands, and went on increasing. We then pitched the tone . . . a little higher; and more Boys—more thousands of Boys—rushed to buy.'[16] He was helped by the provincial press, who at this time, because it was an obviously worthy enterprise and fulfilled an undeniable need, managed to look beyond the prizes and were wildly enthusiastic. During the second year, the readership increased by seven thousand; since an absolute figure was still not given, it is impossible to know whether Sam had any justification for setting up a second venture at such an early stage, but it was probably merely an impulsive gesture inspired by wishful thinking and the spate of laudatory notices; at any rate, he launched a companion paper, the *Boy's Own Journal*, less than a month before the upheaval of his wedding. Even initially, it did not do as well as he expected:

> The 'Boy's Own Journal' has gone off pretty well—not quite so well as I had anticipated by Wednesday's sale—however, it promises exceedingly well and will require a longer nursing (that is all) than I had intended to have given it. My quality of obstinacy will have to be brought forth.

It lasted scarcely longer than a year.

It was not long before rivals of both the *BOM* and the *EDM* appeared, though, surprisingly in a way, the *EDM* suffered less from direct competition than the former. In 1856 a magazine called *The Ladies' Treasury* was founded, which carried some of the *EDM*'s domestic features but was much staider and more conventional, and probably did not noticeably affect the Beeton readership; furthermore, it looks as if the Beetons got their own back a few years later by borrowing several ideas from it in their turn. But a paper called *The Youth's Instructor*, launched two years later, was so obviously a copy of the *BOM* that Sam declared that if he had not been 'the best-tempered fellow in the world'[17] he would have sued. More charitably, and certainly more profitably, he was able to buy it up and merge it with his own magazine, the proprietors finding themselves in financial difficulties and unable to fulfil their promises of prizes after only eight months. It was not until the middle of the next decade that he had cause to be seriously worried by competitors, and by the time they came, in 1866, he had other matters to distract his attention. In that year, however, two magazines were founded by rival publishers, *Chatterbox* and *Boys of England*, the second of which constituted a very real threat: among the extraordinary array of prizes announced with the first issue were two ponies, sundry other pets, books, and cricket sets, as well as watches,[18] which although they probably did not add up to a great deal in monetary terms, looked extremely attractive.

With its narrower readership, it was perhaps not to be expected that the *BOM* should achieve such a large circulation as the *EDM*; nevertheless, the year fashion plates were added to the latter, Sam raised the number of the pages in the *Boy's Own Magazine* to half as much again, and when it had completed its first eight-year series doubled them, as well as adding coloured plates. The first set of increases, in 1860, were made in anticipation of the repeal of the paper tax, but in the event this did not take place until the following year, which lost Sam a considerable sum—a thousand pounds in the case of the *EDM*, and no doubt something comparable in that of the *BOM*. When coloured plates were introduced, the price, as with the older magazine, was raised to sixpence, but for those who could not afford the increase, he launched a second penny publication, the *Boy's Penny Magazine*. Despite wonderful reviews, it proved no more viable than the

Journal, and, sadly, he was obliged to withdraw this too after a short time.

By this time, he had moved offices twice. He ended his partnership with Clarke shortly before his marriage, whereupon he moved from Fleet Street to Bouverie Street, which was where the printer Salisbury, who still did much of Sam's printing, had his works. At first he called his firm 'Samuel O. Beeton', but after a few months this was contracted to 'S. O. Beeton', which it remained for the rest of its existence. Its symbol was the sign of the beehive, which stood for industriousness, but was also, for those sharp enough to notice, a pun on his own name, 'Bee-town'. In 1860 he took larger premises at 248 Strand, where he had a handsome house with 'BOY'S OWN MAGAZINE' and 'THE ENGLISHWOMAN' emblazoned over the walls in huge letters. It was here that Isabella worked and even, for a short, unhappy period, lived. The building was eventually demolished to make way for the new law courts, but his former offices in Bouverie Street are now part of Northcliffe House—very appropriately, since Lord Northcliffe was, by his own acknowledgement, the inheritor of many of his ideas.

X

THE MEETING

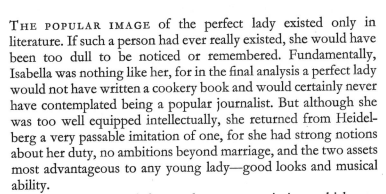

THE POPULAR IMAGE of the perfect lady existed only in literature. If such a person had ever really existed, she would have been too dull to be noticed or remembered. Fundamentally, Isabella was nothing like her, for in the final analysis a perfect lady would not have written a cookery book and would certainly never have contemplated being a popular journalist. But although she was too well equipped intellectually, she returned from Heidelberg a very passable imitation of one, for she had strong notions about her duty, no ambitions beyond marriage, and the two assets most advantageous to any young lady—good looks and musical ability.

Allowing for the difference between a painting, which was probably flattering, and a photograph taken in the earliest days of photography, a studio photograph of her at about twenty-one shows that she was no less good-looking than her mother at a comparable age. The most striking difference between them in these portraits was that Isabella was fatter, and for this reason looked softer, prettier, and altogether more human than Elizabeth. But in a later snapshot, when her face was thinner, she was severely beautiful, and bore a strong resemblance to her. Her full figure in the first picture may have been because she had a baby at around this time, but she must have been plump during her engagement for she signed one of her letters to Sam, 'Your affectionate Fatty' (presumably he had been teasing her). However, voluptuous curves, especially big bosoms, were fashionable, and altogether she would have been an ideal model for the fashion-plate artists, whose women were invariably like her, with large eyes and thick brown hair (blondes did not have their innings until the advent of fashion photography, perhaps because they were more difficult to draw).

But it was not until she became the *EDM*'s fashion editor that she learned to dress like the fashion-plate ladies. Until her marriage, her clothes, including her trousseau, were made in Epsom by a Miss Findlay.

Yesterday and today I have been sitting a great deal with Miss Findlay, and scarcely seem to have an idea beyond needle and thread. There is one thing to be said if you feel at all dull she amuses you much with all sorts of poetry, as well as tales in prose, which by the way are not of the most delicate nature.

In her portrait, she was dressed too fussily for elegance even at that period, with loud plaid, elaborate lace, a large cameo brooch, a pendant, and a braided shawl. Later, when she had become more sophisticated, she still treated her clothes with cheerful disregard, and had no hesitation in going for muddy walks, climbing mountains, and even riding in her everyday dress, despite the grease and smell. She never bothered particularly about her appearance; in her diary she records waking at half past six and being ready to leave for a week's holiday within an hour, which considering the number of layers women wore, the corsets, the complicated hairstyles, and the large breakfast she always ate, meant that she must have made a remarkably swift *toilette*. Cosmetics were anathema to her; not needing them herself, she heartily disapproved of them as unladylike and a waste of time, as was demonstrated by a crushing reply to a reader who wrote innocently inquiring about rouge.

Next to her looks, her greatest social asset was her skill on the piano, for in the days when people had to supply their own entertainment, young ladies who could play or sing inevitably stole the limelight. Most families boasted of their daughters' musical prowess, and the Dorlings were no exception, but in their case there seems to have been some justification, since several of the girls had genuine talent. Henry, only too eager to encourage Isabella, sent her to take lessons with a fashionable London teacher, Julius Benedict, who had recently accompanied the celebrated Swedish soprano Jenny Lind on a concert tour of New York, where Harriet Beecher Stowe became one of her most ardent fans.[1] Later (he was already in his fifties) he rose to fame as the composer of the opera *The Lily of Killarney*; but even before that, to be accepted as his pupil was no small compliment to Isabella's talent.

Henry Dorling, having given her all the advantages money could buy, had every reason to congratulate himself on the way his eldest stepdaughter had turned out, and it is obvious from his subsequent behaviour that he was extremely proud of her, seemingly more so than of any of his other daughters. This may have been partly because she was the first of the girls to grow up; it may also have had something to do with her resemblance to Elizabeth—in which, however, she was not alone, since Bessie too was very like her. Nor were they the only sisters who were attractive, for several of the others in their turn, notably Lucy and Amy, were said to be extremely pretty—indeed, the 'girls on the hill', as they were called, were celebrated for their looks throughout Epsom. But no one remembers Henry being difficult about any of his other daughters' marriages; and although the direct cause of his objection to Isabella's was Sam, his feelings were surely rooted in his exceptionally strong attachment to her.

From his point of view, it was sad that, like so many stepchildren, she could not return his affection. She did not actually resent him—she was simply indifferent and looked on him rather as if he were a necessary piece of furniture. Whenever she mentioned him in the letters she wrote during her engagement, it was in some more or less disagreeable context (one must remember, however, that by this time her attitude was to some extent coloured by Sam's). In the circumstances, it is greatly to her credit that although she often found him irritating and narrowminded, she never faltered in her loyalty and obedience to him right up to the day of her marriage.

But if she held Henry at bay, she saw more of Elizabeth than she had as a child, for as a fully fledged young woman she was expected to go into society, which meant accompanying her mother on rounds of calls and attending dances and dinner parties. This was the time most girls spent their adolescence waiting for, and Isabella was greatly envied by her sisters—as, no doubt, to a lesser extent, was Jane, who was busily occupied in finding herself a husband throughout the year of Sam and Isabella's courtship. One of her suitors was a Mr Wood: 'Jane has been treating Mr. Wood with German songs to a vast extent which to all appearances he has been enjoying immensely,' Isabella

observed; and Sam asked several times how the affair was going.
'Is Mr. Wood progressing towards Jane? If so . . . she would then
understand the seeming selfishness of affection. He's a good
fellow, I think. . . .' But Mr Wood was swiftly superseded by Mr
White, who was a lawyer and evidently fairly well off, since he
gave several parties which were the only social occasions in
Epsom Isabella admitted to enjoying.

But after the stimulating, purposeful atmosphere of the Heidels'
school, being a young lady in a small town, far from being an
enviable situation, was a frustrating anticlimax. The local company held nothing for her, and having to attend dinner parties
she found 'a terrible ordeal . . . I do so hate it; a good dance
somewhere is much more my line'. The dinners she hated most
were those given by her parents, when she was usually the only
young person present and had to sit at table for four hours on
end listening to 'old men' droning on about politics or race-horses
(several of the Dorlings' friends were trainers). The inordinate
length of time such meals took was due to the number of courses
served—usually five—and the immense variety of dishes in each,
which had to be laboriously served and cleared away in succession; at a party of any size there would be ten to twenty choices
of entrée and pudding. It was not considered genteel for ladies to
display a hearty appetite, however, and they were usually too
tightly corseted to eat much. Many must have felt like Tom
Hood's hostess:

> How *shall* I get through it!
> I never can do it.
> I'm quite looking to it,
> To sink by and by.
> Oh! would I were dead now,
> Or up in my bed now,
> To cover my head now,
> And have a good cry![2]

Isabella's sufferings were reflected by her detailed suggestions for
keeping guests amused in *Household Management*, where she was
particularly emphatic about the importance of ensuring that
everyone had someone congenial to talk to.

She complained continually about the dullness of Epsom: 'I

wish I had some news to tell you; it is rather a scarce article in Epsom'. . . . 'Your sisters are dragging on a miserable existence here, doing plenty of embroidery and going out for gigantic walks and coming home covered with mud. I am afraid they must find it rather dull'. . . . 'I wish, my dearest, I had something to tell you that I thought would interest you, but as nothing of importance has occurred, you must put up with this news-bare epistle.' Her days were lost in a round of trivialities: apart from walks, sewing, and the tedious socializing, she continued to help with her brothers and sisters—probably the liveliest aspect of her life— read whenever she could find the time, and practised the piano conscientiously—for before she met Sam, her music was her only personal outlet. She seems to have got on well with Benedict '. . . had a very nice music lesson . . .'; but during her engagement, her enthusiasm waned, and on one occasion she skipped her lesson altogether.

The lessons took place in Manchester Square in the West End, which provided a welcome break for Isabella and also for whoever acted as her chaperone (it was not thought proper for a well brought up young lady to travel alone). Sometimes her mother accompanied her, taking advantage of the opportunity to call on her friend Eliza Beeton, whose husband had died and had left her with seven children to provide for. Her decision to stay on as landlady of the Dolphin was almost certainly prompted by the financial necessity of giving her children a proper education, and she remained there until her second marriage some years later. As her children were older than Elizabeth's had been, two being virtually grown up, she was able to solve her chief problem by sending the next three away to school. Apparently she consulted her friend, for instead of choosing somewhere modest and convenient—Islington, for instance, which was within walking distance—she sent her daughters to the Heidels' in Germany and her son Edward, then about thirteen, to a German boys' school close by.

Eliza was a much warmer personality than Elizabeth, and enjoyed a closer relationship with Sam than Mrs Dorling had with any of her children—though one must admit that Sam was more responsive—and after her husband's death she saw her stepson more or less daily; all Isabella's letters were addressed to the Dolphin, so he must either have been living there or called regularly. One day, he happened to be there when Isabella and her mother were visiting.

Neither of the Beetons ever made any reference to their first meeting. Though Sam was unusually handsome in a pale, aesthetic way, Isabella, like Harriet Beecher Stowe, was probably struck more by his loquacity than by his appearance; she was soon teasing him about his 'large catalogue of words', and acknowledged his personality by observing, 'If you choose, you can do anything you like either with boys or girls'. Not surprisingly, in view of her inhibitions, she was extremely reticent at the beginning of their relationship; even after they had been engaged six months, she would not commit herself to signing her letters more fondly than 'affectionately' (though three months later she was sending him a million kisses and wishing him happy dreams). To Sam, her beauty was of course one of her main attractions, but perceiving at the outset that to compliment her on it would probably offend her, he never mentioned it. Instead, he professed 'a vast deal of admiration' for her 'most excellent abilities'— which was very sincerely meant, for her intelligence and serious-mindedness must have stood in startling contrast to the silliness of the majority of the Letter-Bag correspondents; it did not take him long to realize that she was the living embodiment of his belief in women's intellectual ability, and had a far more rational, business-like mind than he possessed. This, and her apparently impenetrable poise and reserve, confounded him, and (for once) he was very far from confident of his chances of success. 'It seems to me impossible. No one can tell how grateful I feel and am to the "Great Good" for having brought me thus near to the point of earthly felicity, which, twelve little months ago, I dared not have hoped for,' he wrote shortly before the wedding. Nevertheless, it did not take him long, relatively speaking, to prevail, for by about June 1855 they were engaged, less than a year after Isabella left school.

They continued to meet at the Dolphin on music-lesson days; both their mothers therefore had the opportunity of observing what was going on, though Isabella was sometimes accompanied to London by Jane, and a friendship sprang up with the two elder Beeton girls, Lizzie and Viccie. Eliza watched the affair developing with the greatest satisfaction: whatever she may have made of the life Sam had been leading, she must have been pleased at the prospect of his settling down, especially in view of his delicate health, which she watched the more anxiously as a fellow-sufferer from coughs and colds; and she welcomed Isabella as a girl after her own heart—sensible, steady, and well able to look after her son. On several occasions she tried to arrange for them to go out together, usually unsuccessfully, but Isabella nevertheless appreciated her efforts, and thanked her profusely; after her marriage, lacking the sympathy of her own family, she had further reason to be grateful to her.

XI

COURTSHIP

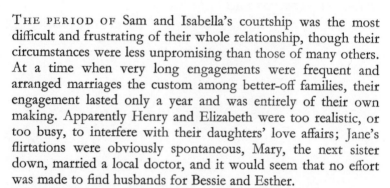

THE PERIOD OF Sam and Isabella's courtship was the most difficult and frustrating of their whole relationship, though their circumstances were less unpromising than those of many others. At a time when very long engagements were frequent and arranged marriages the custom among better-off families, their engagement lasted only a year and was entirely of their own making. Apparently Henry and Elizabeth were too realistic, or too busy, to interfere with their daughters' love affairs; Jane's flirtations were obviously spontaneous, Mary, the next sister down, married a local doctor, and it would seem that no effort was made to find husbands for Bessie and Esther.

Certainly, if the choice had been Henry's, Isabella would not have fallen to Sam for the marriage was a lasting source of grievance to him. His disapproval eventually resulted in a complete schism between the Dorlings and the Beetons, but during Isabella's lifetime it gave rise to little more than awkwardness and unpleasantness. Inevitably, however, his reaction communicated itself to the children, and encouraged the Mayson sisters in their instinctive jealousy of their brother-in-law and resentment against him for the kind of life Isabella led, which they did not consider to be that of a lady. According to Lucy (whose opinion of Sam was at least as low as Henry's), part of the family accused Sam of being in some measure responsible for Isabella's death by failing to ensure that sufficient care was taken over her last confinement and disobeying the doctor's orders. Furthermore, Henry refused to offer him assistance in his subsequent financial trouble. A year or so later, Sam took a stinging revenge in a strange publication called *The Derby Carnival*. After this, it would hardly have been possible for the Dorlings to maintain any communication with him; time heightened their animosity and for nearly a century he was looked on as an outcast, the black sheep of the family—a tradition vigorously upheld by Nancy Spain (whose grandmother was a Dorling).

Initially, all this stemmed simply from a clash of personality. Henry reacted to Sam in much the same way as Vizetelly had, but there was the added disadvantage that he had nothing whatsoever in common with him. The two were diametrically opposed in ideals, outlook, character, and manner, and lack of understanding produced not merely dislike, but contempt, though Sam's, at least to start with, was merely defensive. If only he could have swallowed his pride and tried a little humility, or if he had had the courage to confront Henry openly, their relationship might have been better; but he dropped the challenge half way through the engagement, which only confirmed Dorling's unfavourable opinion.

Henry's antagonism was no doubt augmented by a sense of disappointment, because Isabella, with her superior education and accomplishments, had not selected someone more eligible. Apparently the Beetons' claims to distinguished ancestry did not impress him, and so far as he was concerned, Sam was merely a tavern-keeper's son; it is surely not without significance that Sam described his father as a wine-merchant on the marriage certificate (which neatly matched the designation of hers as linen merchant). Very likely Henry's feelings were also clouded by the vague resentment of any father against the man who takes away his daughter. It would of course have been easier for him if he had had faith in Sam's ability to make a success of his career, but at this stage he can hardly be blamed for being somewhat sceptical about his future son-in-law's publishing activities. If he bothered to look with any attention at the *EDM*, there was plenty besides Cupid that he could have found to object to; moral or aesthetic scruples, however, were less likely to have troubled him than the impression he gained of Sam's financial irresponsibility from the losses on *The Key to Uncle Tom's Cabin* and the vast sum spent on prizes. As Isabella's guardian, he was more or less obliged to make inquiries into his business affairs, and Sam's income from the magazines was depressingly modest. This, however, did not trouble Isabella, who said cheerfully, 'I don't believe things will be as bad as people try to make out: as long as you have a head on your shoulders, I think you will be able to scrape a living together somehow.'

Considering his hostility, it may perhaps seem surprising that Henry consented to the engagement at all; the fact that he did so says much for his genuine affection and respect for Isabella, his sense of fairness, which prevented him from acting on feelings which he no doubt recognized as being in some degree personal, and his regard for Elizabeth, whose powers of persuasion were probably the ultimate reason for his acquiescence. Elizabeth, if only on account of her friend, was not against the match and may even from her own point of view have welcomed it; at any rate, having done nothing to discourage it at the beginning, she showed a cautious degree of friendliness towards Sam, joining her daughter in pressing him to visit them and readily assisting in such practical matters as buying furniture. But once the engagement had been announced, she does not seem to have exerted her influence further over Henry for she supported him over various tedious points of propriety and made no noticeable effort to shield the couple from his annoyance.

For the first half of their engagement, their courtship followed the usual formal, restrictive pattern and Sam visited his fiancée and her family regularly, usually on Sundays. There was scant, if any, opportunity for privacy on these occasions; Sam could only have Isabella to himself if he took her to concerts or exhibitions and even then some other member of the family had to be present as an escort, and it was only by great good luck or ingenuity that he could snatch a few moments alone with her. Naturally, he was as familiar with these conventions as she (almost more so, perhaps, after his experience as Cupid), but after his relatively free and easy life, it was more difficult for him to accept them and his impatience with the limitations they imposed mounted as the months passed. Furthermore, the tension between himself and Henry increased to the point where Sam found the mere presence of the other an intolerable embarrassment. Over Christmas he developed an ominous cough, and was unable to visit Epsom for some little time; it was probably while he was laid up that he decided that his weekly attendance was too great a strain, and that in future he would go to the Dorlings only when forced by the dictates of politeness, which meant in practice that he cut his visits down by about half. He did not tell Isabella of his decision and she was hurt and greatly perplexed by his desertion, being unable to perceive, as others would have done, how deeply her stepfather disturbed him. 'Anyone would think our house was some Ogre's Castle, you want so much pressing to come!' she once exclaimed, with unwitting accuracy (perhaps she had read Dickens's article).

You are sadly tiring my patience; consider it is ten days since I saw you. Anyone would think you lived in Londonderry instead of London, you are so very sparing of your company. There is one consolation to look forward to, namely that we shall see each other more than *once* a fortnight as is the case now.

In your next note, pray tell me how you feel, whether you have kept your resolution of not smoking, and when it is likely I shall behold you. Answer these questions and oblige,
Your loving and affectionate deserted one,
ISABELLA

Obviously, by this time he was sufficiently sure of her to be certain that his policy would not endanger the success of his suit—and, as usual in such matters, he was right. 'I am coming up to Benedict on the 11th. How I am looking forward to that day; it will then be a fortnight since I have seen you. Absence &c. &c. &c. I don't know whether you have found that out. I have for one. . . .'

As they had ceased to meet regularly, she and Sam resorted to letters, the only other means of communication open to them. Despite Isabella's self-consciousness, which prompted her to ask Sam to burn a number of her letters, he kept most of them for the rest of his life together with a selection of his replies—which can be looked on as some measure of his devotion (and, perhaps, of his sentimentality). Nearly forty were found in one of his pockets after his death—his in a careless, flowing scrawl, hers in the flat, stylized script girls were taught at school, many of them neatly crossed.[1] The correspondence—or as much of it as survives, for it is almost certainly not complete—is less revealing than might be hoped, being for various reasons somewhat constrained, especially on Isabella's side, and mostly restricted to unexceptional, day-to-day trivialities. They had a series of burning rows, but if they committed hot feelings to paper, Sam did not care to preserve those outpourings, perhaps following her frequent injunctions and burning them; for only the penitent aftermaths remain. Nor did they discuss Isabella's career—which at this stage

it is most unlikely that either of them could have foreseen; Sam
said several times that he wanted her to be her own master, but
went no further than that, and she had no ideas beyond being his
wife.

These letters nevertheless bring us closer to them than any
other existing documents, and give a valid, if understated, picture
of their relationship. In terms of personality, they were about
evenly matched, Sam's persuasiveness being easily balanced by
her determination—indeed, on occasion she was already almost as
imperious as her mother. They constantly teased and needled
each other, never allowing any point to pass, which must have
made their marriage always lively and sometimes exhausting, and
might have been disastrous had it not been for their respective
senses of humour. Isabella's was dry, even wry, as is discernible
here and there in *Management*; in emulation of Sam, she made
some rather dreadful, schoolgirl-type jokes in her letters, but
apparently grew out of them fairly soon as there is nothing of
this sort to be found in anything she wrote later.

Their contrasting characters were reflected in their styles of
writing: hers was brisk, his effusive even by contemporary
journalistic standards, and without her repeated protests would
have been even more fanciful and high-flown than it was; but
because she distrusted any display of feeling, and probably also
because she was embarrassed by her own inability to return it—a
deficiency to which she readily admitted in a moment of stress—
she begged him not to write too demonstratively. Nevertheless,
he could not help slipping in a few picturesque sentences now and
again, usually with an apology:

No more Brute,—in future, there shall be the r taken away,
and then the proper title, 'Beauty,' will remain, and if you
please, the other title of the fairy tale I'll take unto myself.
I have not, Bella darling, been certainly sober all this day—
not drunken with Malt or the more refined juice of the grape,—
but a mysterious wool-gathering, and such prettily color'd,
sweetly tinted, charmingly textured wool it is and has full
possession of me, and refuses to surrender its sway. Oh—what
would I not resign to see you now for just one short half-hour?
That sweet, short preface that I have read and studied during
the past few days,—what a joyous volume does it not foretell?

—a book of bliss, with many pages to smile and be glad over. Now then, business, and no more nonsense! Attention! Shoulder, etc. . . .

The letters also remind one of the difference in their ages and situations; Sam was twenty-four and an experienced writer, probably experienced with women, whereas she, around her twentieth birthday, was in many ways little more than a schoolgirl. One of the most interesting aspects of the correspondence is that it shows her growing up, responding for the first time to adult problems and emotions—nervously and somewhat clumsily, but with an enviable conviction in the rightness of her principles. In the face of Sam's professionalism, her confidence in her ability as a correspondent was nil, but as her confidence in him increased so did her courage on paper. Her first letter, written after a dreary Christmas spent tending the children, who were ill, was remarkable as a masterpiece of banality (the family had another Christmas celebration a fortnight later, when the children had recovered).

Epsom

Decbᵣ 26th/55

My dearest Sam,
    Your kind letter I did not receive till this morning, so of course was unable to answer it before. I trust however this will reach you in time. I do not know how to thank you enough for your kind invitation, the more delightful because so unexpected; to hear Jenny Lind again was a treat I never anticipated, so if you come down tonight I shall be quite ready to go back with you tomorrow. Walter I am happy to say is much better, as also the other children on the Hill. Frank is also progressing towards recovery, but still wants a deal of nursing, and this morning Lucy has made up her mind to be ill, so you may imagine we are not in a very healthy condition taking us altogether. I cannot say I spent a happy Christmas Day, *you* can well guess the reason and besides that Frank being so poorly, we were not in spirits to enjoy ourselves. I should very much have liked to have sent you as long a letter as you sent me but Frank is impatient to be dressed, and you know invalids are not the most patient people in the world.

Hoping to see you this evening as soon as you can, with best love,

Believe me, dearest Sam,
Yours most affectionately
ISABELLA

Her second was scarcely less tentative and self-conscious, yet she was desperately anxious lest Sam's young stepbrother Edward should read it and think her '*soft*' (to her, the worst sort of condemnation). There was no conceivable reason for her desire to have it destroyed except sheer sensitivity and perhaps the fear that Edward might spread her not very offensive comments around the family. Saying that she was not in a writing mood, or very busy, were her standard excuses for brevity and imagined inadequacy. Her first remark indicates that she had been criticizing Sam (who had arranged to go to Suffolk to recuperate from his own illness) for being too wordy.

Epsom
Decbr 31st/55.

My dear Sam,
Many thanks for the *few* lines you so kindly sent me yesterday. I certainly cannot complain of the length of your epistle; however, it was to the purpose. I was very glad to hear your cold was so much better, only mind and take care of yourself, as you promised you would, for I certainly was terribly afraid you were going to be seriously ill when I left you on Friday night. I enjoyed my half hour's tête à tête with your respected uncle very much indeed; seldom has he been so agreeable to me before. When I arrived home I found the girls had gone to Mr. Sherwood's to tea and turn out, so the old birds are quite alone. This week I do not come to town for a music lesson as I have not worked at all for him, also, as the children say, do not know my lesson, so it would be useless to come up. When do you start for Suffolk? I should like to know because then I can fancy what you are doing. Much to my annoyance I discovered this morning that I was invited to Mr. White's tomorrow evening, so shall have to go through that terrible ordeal, a dinner party. . . .
Our children I found much better on my return; Lucy is

quite recovered in everything but her temper, and that I am sorry to say is considerably worse than before her illness. . . . I have no desire that your Edward . . . should see all this nonsense. I am sure he would think me so very *soft* and so will you also I am afraid; the fact is I do not feel in a writing mood this morning, so the sooner I bring this scribble to a conclusion the better it will be for dear Sam's patience. Wish everybody a very happy new Year for me and tell your sisters I hope they will spend a pleasant evening at Bow. John thinks of coming out in his tail coat for the occasion. I am afraid he will look more like a monkey than a man; however, chacun à son goût.

Give my best love to all and accept the same share as Sam from,

Your affectionate Fatty
Isabella

Please burn this as soon as read. I hope your Mama is better than when I last saw her, and that she has quite got rid of her troublesome cough.

Compare these first efforts, with the affectation of the French phrases, to this, fifteen letters later:

My dearly beloved Sam,

I take advantage of this after dinner opportunity to enjoy myself and have a small chat with you on paper, although I really have nothing to say, and looking at it in a mercenary point of view my letter will not be worth the postage. I am so continually thinking of you that it seems to do me a vast amount of good even to do a little black and white business, knowing very well that a few lines of nonsense are always acceptable to a certain mutable gentleman, be they ever so short or stupid. How have you been amusing yourself today? Have you been rusticating solo at Pinner or enjoying the society of Milk Street, Cheapside? You cannot imagine how I have missed you, and have been wishing all day that I were a bird that I might fly away and be at rest with you, my own precious one. . . . 1000000 kisses. Goodbye, my darling.

Sam's holiday in Suffolk is sufficient indication that his attack
4*

had been unusually severe, for although he suffered from coughs
nearly every winter, he allowed himself to be parted from his
work on only one other occasion (with disastrous consequences).
Both these illnesses were contracted when he was living in
London, at this time at its smelliest and most insanitary: 1858
was the year of the Great Stink, which almost drove even
Parliament into retreat. It was largely on account of his health
that he and Isabella elected to live in the country. For this reason,
and no doubt also because he was leading a more regular life,
his chest improved noticeably after his marriage; until then, to
judge from remarks about his bachelor style of life, he not only
deprived himself of sleep, but did not bother to eat properly. The
wonder is, if he was already consumptive, that his strength stood
up as well as it did.

He did not keep his own earlier letters, but it is clear from
Isabella's next that he had succumbed to depression following his
illness, which was not at all typical of him; he showed the same
symptom when prostrated after the launching of the *Boy's Own
Journal* later that year, and one may guess that both instances were
caused by the mounting strain of the engagement. The end of
this letter described the kind of dig at Sam Henry was liable to
make; too late, Isabella realized that she would have done better
not to mention it.

Epsom
Jan.ʸ 3rd/56.

My dear Sam,
    I cannot say I read your note with any degree of satisfaction;
it was so full of the miserables. I was indeed sorry to hear you
had been such a sufferer; now your enemy has departed you
will be able to enjoy yourself in the country, and come back
looking as jolly as a fat farmer. You know very well that is how
I should like you to appear on your return. I intended writing
to invite you to join our family circle on Saturday. . . . I see
however by your note that we are not to have the pleasure of
your company. I am not disappointed in one respect, for I
think change of air and Suffolk living will do you more good
than romping with the children. . . . I enjoyed myself very much
indeed at Mr. White's, more than I anticipated; we had a good
dance after dinner which exactly suited me.

I hope you will not be offended with me for sending you a few envelopes: Father said this morning he supposed your passion for advertising was such that you could not resist sending these stamped affairs. Pray do not think me rude, but I cannot bear for all the world to know who my letter comes from. I can assure you I look upon *your* letters as far too sacred to lighten. That you will return in better health and think sometimes of somebody residing at Epsom, is the sincere wish of your own

ISABELLA

Pray excuse this scribble, as I am very busy, I do not really know what I have said, so you must excuse the composition.

Her apologetic postscript was one of a long series which caused Sam in later life to observe that the postscript was the only part of a woman's letter that revealed her true state of mind. Understanding her confusion, he responded promptly and sympathetically, to which she replied with breathless relief: 'Many, many thanks for your kind note, which I received with much pleasure yesterday morning. . . .'

Then began a battle of wills over a dinner party, to which Sam was resolutely determined not to go; history does not relate who won, since the party was not mentioned after the event, but one suspects that on this occasion it was Isabella:

Now for business. Will you be so good as to arrange your affairs, so that you will be home by Monday night or Tuesday morning, as we are to have a few friends to dinner and you are to be one of the dozen if you can manage to be home by that time. I hope you will not disappoint me because you know very well these formal *feeds* I abominate, and if you come of course it will be much pleasanter for me. I am the only one of the girls going to dine with them so pray do not leave me to sit three or four hours with some old man I do not care a straw about. . . .

Sam at once declared that he would not be back until Thursday, whereupon she persuaded her mother to postpone the date of the party.

Epsom
Jan.ʸ 12th/56.

My dear Sam,

You say you intend returning home on Thursday evening,
but as our dinner party is put off till *that* day perhaps you will
have the kindness to favour us with your company. One day I
am sure cannot make much difference to you, and besides you
have had such a nice long holiday you will be quite ready to
come home by that time. Mama sends her kind regards and
says she cannot hear of a refusal, and the girls say they are
quite sure you would not think of refusing now you have been
pressed so much.

I cannot tell you how disappointed I was in reading your last
letter that you were not coming home so soon as I expected.
We do not dine till 6 o. c. so I beg *once* more that you will come,
and if you do not, I shall begin to think you a little bit
unkind. . . . It seems such an age since I have seen you I am
really quite longing for Thursday now you are coming. I shall
expect to see you grown quite jolly, for you really looked very
queer before you left. . . .

Hoping you will not refuse my *first* request, with love of the
very best quality,

Believe me, dearest Sam,
Yours devotedly,
Isabella

I hope you will reach your journey's end safely and that I shall
see you on Thursday. I think I shall feel desperate if you refuse
to come.

By this time one begins to feel thoroughly sorry for her. She
continued with quite astonishing tenacity to exhort him to visit
her throughout the whole of the rest of their engagement, never
ceasing to upbraid him for his heartlessness and relentlessly
counting the days between their meetings. This, and the tug of
war with her parents, were the chief reasons for their rows.

About three weeks after the dinner party, when Sam's sisters
were paying their thankless visit to the Dorlings, he was induced
by the combined pressure of both families to make his appearance
on Sunday as formerly. It was a disaster, for he was so on edge and

eager to escape that he deeply offended Isabella, who even forgot to date her letter in her agitation (in contrast to her usual punctiliousness, he hardly ever dated his).

My dear Sam,
    Your sisters have kindly invited me to come up with them on Friday to the Concert, but as you said nothing about it on Sunday to *me*, I thought I would write and ascertain your intentions on the subject so if you will not object to letting me know about it I shall feel much obliged.
    You went off in such a hurry the other morning, I have scarcely recovered from the shock yet. Your reason for doing so I suppose was business. Before this you will have received an invitation from Mr. White for the 6th. I am very sorry you will not be able to go, for I think you would enjoy yourself. . . .
                            Ever yours,
                            Isabella Mayson
Epsom.
Wednesday morning.
I shall expect a note by return of post, so please don't disappoint.

All their quarrels were patched up in turn by Sam's conciliatory replies; one is tempted to wonder what would have become of their affair if he had not been so skilled in diplomacy and penmanship. This is the first of his letters to have survived.

                                    London, Jany. 31, 1856
My dear Bella,
    I am very delighted to think I am going to see you tomorrow, and can only say that I consider I owe a large debt of gratitude to my sisters, in prevailing on you to come to London, to Sig. Opertz concert: the suggestions of your most humble and loving servant have been latterly so unfortunately received that I have not had the courage to utter my notions with respect to your going anywhere or doing anything. I had *heard* nothing decidedly and distinctly from any quarter on the concert subject, and that was the simple reason why I *said* nothing to you about it on Sunday. You write 'you say', to ascertain my intentions—they are on this point as they always are on every matter connected with you, (whom I prize and love beyond all

other things) to do precisely and exactly as you wish. It will gratify me greatly to see you tomorrow, and if you can find means to let me know by what train you will arrive in town, I will meet you at London Bridge. Mr. White's very kind, informal invitation reached me here this morning. I shall reply to it, after I have finished my devoir to you, and I undoubtedly feel very vexed not to be able to be there—you will enjoy yourself, very much, I hope, and find some good partners. I did not get your letter till 10 o'c last night, or I would have posted to you before this.

I have been exceedingly busy all week,—was at Covent Garden on Monday, Dalston on Tuesday, and Holloway on Wednesday, and tonight I go again to Perkes' Manor House Hotel. I like immensely the walk up to and from town morning and evening, with a cold bath before a good breakfast. If you can come up, dear Bella, to-morrow in time to go for a short walk with me, I shall be very glad, and if I can't hear from Epsom what time you will come to town, tell them at Milk St. to send down to Bouverie, the moment you are there, and on the wings of—but I had forgotten—no namby pamby nonsense, so dearest Bella, I am,

Yours with fondest love,
S. O. Beeton

In May Isabella was so angry that for some time she refused to write at all; it was when she did that she acknowledged her undemonstrative disposition.

I know I have been a very cruel, cold, and neglectful naughty girl for not having written to you for so many days and cannot sufficiently reproach myself for the sad omission. I acknowledge my transgression and my sin is ever before Thee. What a contrast is my frigid disposition to your generous, warm-hearted dear self; it often strikes me, but you know I cannot help it, it is my nature. Forgive me this once my own dear Sam, and rest assured you shall not have occasion to find fault with me on the aforesaid score again. You have guessed my weak point, for if there is one thing more than others I detest, it is to be chafed in that quiet manner as you did in the note I received this morning. You have made me feel much

more unhappy than if you had given me a downright good
scolding which I well merited and am very penitent, so let us
forgive and forget, be friends again, and don't think any more
of my thoughtlessness.

And three weeks later, in the middle of the preparations for
the Derby, came another clash, clearly brought about more or
less directly by her parents.

Epsom
May 26th/56

My own darling Sam,
    As I have here two or three little matters in your note of
yesterday which rather puzzled me, I thought I must write and
ask an explanation; very stupid of me you will say, as I am
going to see you on Wednesday morning, no doubt you will
think I could just as well have *my say* then as trouble you with
one of my unintelligible epistles. In the first place in what does
Bella *sometimes now* pain Sam just a little? Why does he not
wish to be near her? Secondly; what right has he to conjure
up in his fertile imagination any such nasty things as rough
corners to smooth down, when there is one who loves him
better and more fondly than ever one being did another on *this*
earth at least. Oh Sam I think it so wrong of you to fancy such
dreadful things. You also say you don't think I shall be able to
guide myself when I am left to my own exertions. I must
certainly say I have always looked up to, and respected, both
parents and perhaps been *too* mindful of what they say (I
mean regarding certain matters), but then in a very short time
you will have the entire management of me and I can assure
you that you will find in me a most docile and willing pupil.
Pray don't imagine when I am yours—that things will continue
the same way as they are now. God forbid. Better would it be
to put an end to this matter altogether if we thought there was
the slightest possibility of *that*, so pray don't tremble for our
future happiness. Look at things in a more rosy point of view,
and I have no doubt with the love *I am sure* there is existing
between us we shall get on as merrily as crickets, with only an
occasional sharp point to soften down, and not many, as you
fancy. I am very tired indeed tonight, as I have been at the Stand

all day long, and of course have not sat down all day. I wish I
had you near me that I might just love you a very little bit. On
Wednesday you will have a nice talk with me and can tell me
all about matters; I certainly wish they were come to a conclusion. I could not sleep without writing to you, so you must
excuse this nonsense. Good night, my precious pet, may angels
guard and watch over you and give you pleasant dreams, not
drab colours, and accept the fondest and most sincere love of,
                    Your devoted
                    BELLA MAYSON
Burn this as soon as perused.

It was hardly the moment for a long speech on his views about
women, and Sam couched his plea for independence in firm but
gentle terms at the end of a very tender reply. Isabella did not
refer to it thereafter, but it was probably by means of an accumulation of such hints that he gradually enlightened her as to his way
of thinking, so that by the time of their marriage she was unknow-
ingly half converted; this is one explanation for her swift rejection
of the way of life she had been brought up to. His opening remark
was one of several which suggest that they wrote other, more
outspoken letters besides the ones he kept.

                                            Bouverie.
                                            Tuesday aft.ⁿ
My dearest Bella,
    I was most delighted with your kindest of notes, so con-
siderably better than *some* sharp-keel'd cutters that have sailed
thro' the post to the Milk St. Haven.
    You're a dear little brick, and blessed must have been the
earth of which you were baked. I could not find the slightest
spec of a fault in any one of your remarks, for there exists no
one more mindful of the respect and love due to a parent than
your cavaliero, who is now writing to you.
    Well, my own loved one, you have made me so much happier
and more comfortable today as I see you write so firmly, yet so
prettily, upon that dreaded subject of interference, that I now
do quite hope that matters will not remain as they *now* are. I
don't desire, I assure you, to *manage* you—*you* can do that quite
well yourself—my only desire, my sweetest darling, is that no

one else should manage you. You, as you know, can do anything with me—anyone else, on your a/c, nothing! . . .

I have written you this, with many people in and out of the Office so if anything is particularly absurd, consider it not there.

S. O. B.

This cleared the air considerably, and they had no more quarrels, the wedding being now only six weeks away. Sam's relief tumbled out into several letters of the kind that until then Isabella would have objected to—but by this time she was in no mood to complain.

London, Bouverie.
Friday aftr.

My dearest Bella,

How shall I thank you enough for your kind note—in what way can I pour forth my appreciation of your thoughtfulness and goodness in writing me in so fond a manner? I give up the sweet task in despair, for if one were to search out all the most telling words of gratitude from all the vocabularies, written and unwritten, of all the nations—the mystic Chaldean, the classic Latin, the pure Greek, the rare Hindustanee, the trenchant Saxon, the modern French, the mellifluous Italian—yet would all these fall far short of expressing that sentiment of thankfulness which I so strongly feel. . . .

You are right in your supposition that we have been very busy in Bouverie St.—and now, to lay aside irony, I have to tell you that I have now commenced preparations for launching the new Barque—"Beeton's Boy's Own Journal"—(so to be christened) and shall have, consequently, much on my hands until it is fairly before the public on Saturday, June 14. I am sanguine of success, and I *know* you would write me a line or two, (be they never so short, or even scolding) if you had a notion, my dearest one, of the cheering influence, the fresh life, the new vigour and increased strength which your most valued lines ever impart. The reason is simply this—I can think and work and do so much better and so much more when I can see and feel that it is not for myself (about whom I care nothing) I am labouring, but for her whom I so ardently prize, and so lovingly cherish in my inmost heart—my own dear Bella! I

believe most surely in her truth and troth, and I do like to see
the words written by her 'My dear Sam.'

I shall have so much to do to-morrow and on Sunday
morning, prospectus writing, and arranging for the B.O.J. that
I don't think I shall be able to see you this week. . . . will you
write a line, if you *can* spare the time, to your suppliant,

S. O. B.

This serves as a reminder that while Isabella languished in the
country with little to think about besides him and their letters
(though she had evidently been kept busy with the preparations
for race week), Sam, now with three magazines on his hands, was
working at higher pressure than ever before, planning, editing,
writing, visiting booksellers, publicizing the new magazine, and
trying to keep abreast of the rest of his post, which in the days
before the telephone presented an overwhelming volume of
paper-work. '. . . a thousand thanks for your note, which was to
me a sweet oasis in the huge and dreary desert of notepaper and
Envelopes, at which I had been working all day—A thousand to
twelve hundred horrid epistles do I receive every twelve hours
from the P.O. which have to be attended to all at once.' He
worked not only late into the night and all Saturday, but usually
most of Sunday as well; visiting Isabella represented a very real
sacrifice of his time, which, as the last proper letter she wrote
before the wedding shows, she was quite unable to appreciate. It
was no wonder that he was played out after the launching of the
BOJ, which forced him to rest for several days. 'Poor dear, I
suppose you felt so poorly, and not equal to climbing the great
hill of Ludgate. . . . I must give you a little piece of advice,' she
wrote—no doubt she repeated the same thing many times over
the next years—'That is, for the next three weeks to take things
quietly, and not fume and fret yourself about trifles. You will find
it much better for yourself and me also.' The remedy she
prescribed was rest and fresh air at their new house at Pinner.

This house, 2, Chandos Villas, Woodridings, was a further
drain on his overtaxed energies. He moved in around Easter to
oversee the finishings and decoration, which of course turned out
to be time-consuming and complicated, the more so as Isabella
was extremely exacting about what she wanted, and neither of
them would have tolerated for a moment the idea of leaving

anything unfinished until after the wedding. But for them more than most, after the Grand Stand and what Sam called his 'wanderings', it was a source of especial pride and pleasure, serving perhaps as some compensation for their other difficulties. Though totally inexperienced in such matters, he lavished ungrudging care on it, interviewing the various workmen, worrying about the plumbing, and living in considerable discomfort amid the rubble and sawdust.

In itself, the house was extremely ordinary, being a typical, moderate-sized, semi-detached suburban villa on a new estate, apparently selected by Sam simply because it happened to be available at the right time, and was relatively cheap—fifty pounds a year, with the added bonus of a free railway season ticket for the seven years' duration of the lease—'long enough, I think, to look forward to,' he said cheerfully. (It is worth observing that he does not seem to have considered buying at this stage, presumably because he did not have the capital.) The best feature about it was the garden, which they laid out and planted with the lawn, shrubs, vegetables—including a marrow Sam had been given—and various flowers, in particular roses, sweet peas, and mignonette. 'I have no partiality for anything particular but mignonette, and I think that would look best planted at the edge of the Border; however, please yourself and you please me, my dear.' She was, however, very anxious to hide the rawness of the new red brick: 'Honeysuckle, Jasmine, Clematis, Canaryanthus are all very pretty creepers. The first named grows very quickly and soon covers a place, and that I think is very desirable at Pinner.'

Beyond their decision to live out of London, which in view of Sam's health and Isabella's liking for the country was an obvious one, the choice of Pinner was probably as fortuitous as that of the house. It was less convenient for Sam than somewhere further east—since it took him nearly half an hour to get to the office—and not at all fashionable. Its chief attraction was that it was still a small village surrounded by woods and fields, and except for the estate they lived on, virtually unspoilt. Sam, at any rate, revelled in his rustic surroundings after ten years of living in the City; to begin with, he also rather enjoyed the novelty of camping out. This is his account of his first weekend there.

I commenced the day badly, I fear, for I was *violating* the

Sabbath by *violetting* in the fields and woods, this morning, round Pinner. Fred P. went down with me last night, and we 'made out,' as the Yankees say, tolerably. I had excessively interesting interviews with the band of Pinner tradesmen and handicraftsmen—your bricklayer commences making the place a mess on Tuesday morning, your carpenter commences his cupboards on the same day, and your painter follows them up closely at the end of the week.

Mr. Cutbush, the Nursery*man*—not woman—of your establishment is going to run down to Pinner to-morrow afternoon to see what Shrubs, Creepers, etc., are the best to plant. I have to go and choose the Chimney Piece to-morrow —I do heartily wish you were here to go with me—I've no doubt I shall make a terrible mess over this and other matters. What colour are your Venetian blinds to be? Green or drab? They will have to be made, I apprehend—Do your parents know any good man? Messrs. Green & Co., 25 Baker S^t., you can purchase some furniture of, if you like. I have £120-worth to come from there, as per agreement—Will you ask your Mama if she knows them—from all I can learn, they are first rate people. Our bachelor bedroom is quite comfy—the bed and bedstead are capital, and the chest of drawers, complete with toilet cover, with my old buffalo rug before the fireplace, and a washing stand, borrowed from Mrs. Scott, constitute the furniture—I had forgotten—the sheet nailed in front of the window, so as not to expose us too much to Mrs. Browne's ken—We took down Coffee, and Sugar and Sausages, and had a good tea last night, and a first rate breakfast this morning— went last night to Pinner village, which was quite in commotion, being Saturday—I really believe I saw 10 people altogether. The butcher's shop near the Church was driving a tremendous trade, and vice versa, this morning the Church was doing all the business.

I am going into the Ash-leaf Kidney (early potatoe) market to-morrow. Oh! what a curious, quaint road this is—to become a Benedict—you truly said—I didn't know what I had to do, and I certainly didn't, for what with pots and potatoes, and Gravel and Carpets, and Crockery and Creepers, Grates and Greens, Fenders and Scrapers, and other his's and her's, it certainly keeps a fellow up to the mark. Have you seen or heard more of your domestic? My old lady gets on for us in the rough and ready style very well—now my dear girl, don't get in a fume and think I'm suggesting her for a continuance. . . .

But as the work progressed, his humour grew a little heavier:

The Carpenter has finished your cupboard in the passage—and its a grand place,—there'll be room for 4 people to sleep, if we're hard up for beds. The nice fresh smell of the wholesome paint, as you observed in a portion of your letter, still obtains as much as ever, only more so. I am told this will gradually increase until a most healthful climax is reached; I can only add I'm exceedingly grateful—The weather, as you imagined, has been bitterly cold, but then one doesn't feel it much, because there are no blinds to any of the windows, or carpets on the floor, and a lack of furniture to the beds—in addition to which I may name, as an extra advantage, the fact of the sashes and frames being in such order that they freely admit a very large amount of the chilly exterior atmosphere—and the doors are usually all wide open.

Isabella was totally impervious to physical discomfort and not at all sympathetic—especially as she, too, had had to put up with the smell of paint as the Grand Stand had just been redecorated for the Derby. As she said several times, she would have liked nothing better than to be able to live at Pinner herself; but, as propriety demanded, she was permitted to do no more than give advice and instructions and pay the occasional, formal visit.

What a famous cupboard that will be for domestic purposes, particularly if you should happen to be in the same predicament as a certain lady of your acquaintance, who shall be nameless, fancy what a number you could stow away there. Not a very open prospect for the animals in question.

I am afraid I am going a little too far so must stop myself or you will be thinking me a very rude as well as forgetful girl. Pray take good care of yourself in that airy place of yours. . . .

Three weeks before the wedding, he sent her a last breezy, mischievous letter, to which, as always, she did not fail to rise, although she got her own back in her pay-off line. After that, they were too taken up with preparations for the ceremony to exchange more than scribbled notes.

Pinner
Sunday Eveng.

My beloved Bella,

I have been wandering through the fields, full of the newly cut hay, for the last hour or so, and have returned perfectly envious and full of bile—for I can assure you I was the only unhappy mortal who was alone. I met many happy maidens with many happy men, sometimes one male with two females; at other times the animal and panniers were reversed, but there was always somebody with somebody else, so to this fact do you owe, my dearest, this letter, as I have made up my mind to be even with the people I have seen in some way or another, and if they are *with* those they love, they cannot, at any rate, be experiencing this pleasure now felt by me of writing to her, 'in whose hands are all the corners of my heart'. You must have had a lovely day at Brighton, for it has been charmingly sunshiny—the moon is electrotyping at this moment with its beautiful silvery light all around, and I instinctively am walking with you on Brighton Pier, and almost hear you ejaculate 'Oh! Sam, if you only knew.' I don't know why it is, Bella mia, but you never get any further than that. But I am getting into Cabs again—am I not, darling? and I shall be leaving something again at the Opera, and be obliged, reluctantly, to return for it, and then, perhaps, you will be cross at my carelessness in leaving anything behind—but then it's so like the thoughtlessness of that chap Sam, you will reflect, and pardon me. Now, down to Earth again, and let Furniture act on us as attention! on a regiment on parade. What colour are the Cord Tassles to be? These Blinds, Oh, these blinds, I can't get along with them at all. The plumber and carpenter have departed the house at last—peace go with them!—pieces they've left behind. The rooms are all cleaned—the stoves polished—I took the brushes down—quite ready for carpets and blinds, and all the rest of your property. I have written a note to your friend, Mr. Green, that he can send down the food for Chandos as soon as he pleases, as its quite ready to be lined.

Been manipulating severely any people to-day, Bella! Have Father and Mamma been using you today as of old monarchs used the man who stood behind their chair, ornamented with cap and bells—to wit—trot him out, and then laugh at his stepping. I hope not. . . .

Bella dearest, 3 Sundays more, and then the holidays, as school-phrase has it. . . . None can tell how grateful I feel and am to the 'Great Good'. . . . May He bless and protect you, my own dearest one, and make us happy, and contented in each other's true and ardent love.

Je t'embrasse de tout mon coeur.
Yours, in all things,
S. O. BEETON.

Epsom.
June 22nd 1856.

My own darling Sam,

You cannot imagine how grateful I felt this morning when I received your note telling me you were so much better, and although some parts of the letter were a little bit unkind and cool, that small sentence quite made up for everything sharp although I have no doubt you did not mean it to be so. You have written me so very many loving letters lately that if I receive one only two pages and those pages very matter-of-fact, I imagine you are cross with me and don't care so much about me. Now you are better, I am going to ask you a question about the rest of the furniture. I did not like to ask you on Wednesday evening as you seemed so poorly. When shall I come to finish, because as you well know there are several things to do yet. You can write and let me know what time will suit you best. . . . Of course during Church time this morning, instead of listening to the sound of the Gospel and profiting thereby, I have been giving my imagination full play. I have been thinking how nice it will be at Pinner with the only being I at this moment care for on earth; how kind you will be to poor little me, and how you will say sometimes, 'I don't think I shall go to town this morning but stay and have a quiet day in the country'. You will arrange matters so, won't you dear? I am so very sorry you are not here to-day. I seem quite lost without you now. Don't you think I shall have a great deal to answer for, I mean thinking so much about you, always saying to myself, I wonder what Sam is doing and what he is thinking about, &c. &c. &c. &c. The time is fast approaching, my precious pet, for our affair. God grant that nothing may happen now to prevent our union, may he give you health and strength to enjoy many years of happiness with my heart's best love,

Believe me, darling Sam,

Yours with all love's devotion,

BELLA MAYSON

Your Uncle Tom has written to say he shall be happy to come on the 8th. of July instead of on the 10th.. The next time you see him just inform him of his mistake, as it would be rather funny to come two days before the Fair.

Oh Sam if you only knew.

PART THREE

The Beetons

XII

MARRIAGE

THE WEDDING WAS fixed by the Dorlings to take place on Thursday 10 July, as soon as was practicable after the Derby. 'I did not write you our final decisions as I thought it would make no difference to you whether it was Wednesday or Thursday,' Isabella wrote to Sam (who with magazine copy-dates to consider was probably the only person concerned to whom it might have made some difference). The invitations were sent out on 17 June, and the guests, obligingly, replied with astonishing promptness, for five days later she was able to report, 'All our friends invited have accepted; our numbers bid fair to be very strong.' Only one or two of Sam's guests did not respond in a perfectly desirable manner, for besides Uncle Tom there was Mr Perkins, who delivered 'a very dirty scrawl in pencil', and several others whose addresses he had omitted to supply. As the day approached, a series of messengers scurried to and fro between London and Epsom with a stream of parcels and packages, one of which contained a pair of gilt earrings and other jewellery. Three days before the event, Isabella was subjected to a drive from London in the company of her stepfather, which she described as 'very tedious'.

With all the organizational expertise of the race course behind it, it would hardly have been possible for the ceremony not to go off according to plan. The service was conducted by the Rev. B. Bradney Brockett at Epsom parish church; a week or so later formal notices appeared in three local papers and *The Times*.[1] There were no fewer than eight bridesmaids, the two eldest and the youngest of Sam's stepsisters, Lizzie, Viccie, and Jessie, and all the Dorling girls who were old enough—Jane, Mary, Charlotte, Helen, and Lucy. Sam's two middle sisters and Bessie and Esther Mayson were still at school and did not come back for the occasion, which was particularly hard on Bessie, to whom the wedding held far more significance than to any of the bridesmaids. It was probably not much consolation to her that a special cake was ordered for them from Gunther's, and was delivered in person by Sam's mother and the bride and groom on the way back from their honeymoon.

The six eldest bridesmaids wore flounced dresses of pale green or pale mauve, according to family, and bonnets sprigged with tiny flowers; Jessie and Lucy, the youngest, wore white dresses with straw hats and beige boots. 'I got my first corn from those boots,' said Lucy, adding that had it not been for that distraction, she might have remembered more about the wedding. Even so, eighty years later she could still clearly recall the scene although she had been only eight at the time: 'It was a gorgeous day just after the summer meeting. . . . I can still remember how picturesque the guests looked out on the course in front—the big skirts and the fringed parasols.'[2] She herself was the cause of the only untoward incident, when she burst into tears in the church vestry because, as one of the bridesmaids, she was asked to sign the register but could not write—not the best advertisement for the family's system of education.

The bride wore white silk tiered to the waist, held out by a petticoat Lucy could describe in detail, since each flounce had been embroidered in a different design by one of her sisters. Isabella, alone of all the family, remained quite unaffected by the excitement, and did not suffer in the least from nerves or doubts: 'Trusting you are perfectly serene and happy as your humble servant and that I shall see you jolly on Thursday morning,' she said to Sam on the Monday. It would have been quite untypical if her tranquillity had not lasted.

The wedding breakfast and presents were laid out in the Stand, the presents arranged between garlands of flowers. Lucy had been occupied all spring in making her sister a mat, which she duly finished several months ahead of time—'very pretty it looks; I am sure you will be very pleased with it,' Isabella told Sam loyally. At the other extreme, Henry gave her a white piano. The breakfast would have been along the lines laid down in her book,[3] which represented the standard spread for such occasions—and incredibly lavish it was: about a dozen different preparations of cold meat and fish, including salmon and lobster, the Grand Stand

pigeon pie, and joints of beef for the men, in case they needed
'something substantial' on the side (strictly speaking, beef was
considered too ordinary to serve at celebrations); followed by a
dazzling assortment of sweets and desserts, of which the most
spectacular was Charlotte Russe. The Champagne was praised, but
besides this there would have been other wines, liqueurs, and
possibly tea and coffee, which Isabella listed but which were not,
like beef, considered acceptable in the highest circles.

At the appointed hour, the newly married couple whirled away
in a carriage and pair in the direction of Reigate, on the railway
line to Folkestone. Probably they pressed on to Boulogne before
breaking their journey for their first night together—the first of
nearly nine exceptionally happy years. The success of other aspects
of their partnership would be enough to indicate that they had a
good relationship in bed, but besides this they let slip numerous
little remarks which all point the same way. Many of the entries in
Isabella's diaries ended with the statement 'went to bed' as though
it were a matter of significance. Before she was married, she was of
course as ignorant of the facts of life as any other young lady, but
once she had gained confidence in Sam, she had no false modesty.
'I should like to pop down to Pinner some evening and surprise
you at your devotions; it would be such capital fun, what do you
say? . . .' 'I am looking forward with great pleasure to that evening
at the Opera, that is to say, if we go by ourselves; rather a bold
expression for a maiden of twenty. . . .' 'I am sure if you were near
me I should feel inclined to hug you to pieces. . . .' And just before
the wedding, something took place which caused Sam to exclaim
that he was 'still in a state of electricity'. Unlike many girls,
nurtured on the idea that sex was an unpleasant necessity, and to
whom the thought of being seen by a man in a nightdress was
terrifying, she had no more qualms about her honeymoon than
about the wedding itself, and was furious almost to the point of
insulting her future mother-in-law when it was suggested that
Eliza might accompany the couple to Europe (this was not such
an outrageous suggestion as it seems now). Isabella returned from
the honeymoon pregnant.

They were away three weeks, most of which—their honeymoon
proper—was spent in France, the last few days being taken up
with the journey to Heidelberg. A lawyer called Frederick
Weaklin had given Sam a set of Murray's guide books, and Sam

wrote to thank him in a rather self-conscious man-of-the-world style, referring to his wife ('I cannot get used to that word as yet') as his 'business' for the trip—which was certainly planned with her interests in mind.

Isabella never forgot her first experience of Paris and harked back to it wistfully the next time they went when, instead of strolling down the Champs Elysées on a hot summer evening, she battled against wind and snow and marvelled, Spartan as she was herself, at the courage of the Parisians braving the weather to take their weekend airing. After Paris they went via Tours to Bordeaux, which marked the highlight of the holiday for Sam, who pronounced it the finest commercial city he had ever seen. From here they proceeded down the coast to 'your *funny, queer, droll, end-of-the-world* little "Bassin d'Arcachon" ', which 'much amused' him, went on to Bayonne, and ended up at Biarritz, already a fashionable resort. Five years later, *The Queen* ran what must have been one of the most unflattering pictures ever published of the Empress Eugenie, who was shown sitting bolt upright on the beach with a horrible scowl;[4] Isabella, however, liked the town so much that they stayed four days, which was apparently longer than they had planned.

Just as at home they were impatient, easily bored, and, as was soon to be proved, alike untiring in their work, so they were indefatigable on holiday. On their next one four years later they were scarcely ever still, determined to see as much as possible, never wasting a moment, and in the south of France, despite the heat, we may be sure they were the same. Two of their four days at Biarritz were spent driving to the neighbouring towns of Cambo and Bidart and exploring the countryside, and the rest of their time would have been taken up with a series of energetic walks, punctuated with expeditions to the beach, where Sam went swimming (bathing for women was a ludicrous performance involving complicated costumes and bathing machines, which did not appeal to Isabella at all). In spite of being extremely insular about food, they got indigestion, probably as a result of drinking more wine than they were used to; it was a luxury that for some years they seldom allowed themselves at home. They blamed their hangovers on garlic, to which they were also unaccustomed, for it was virtually taboo in Victorian England.

It was a pity that they did not have time to go on to Lourdes and into the Pyrenees, which Isabella would have loved, but even as it was they scarcely had time to take in everything they saw; Sam rather ruefully called the trip a race, and after the turmoil of the past months would really rather have gone straight to Pinner. 'How glad I shall be to get you to our quiet home at Pinner after the race on the Continent, and commence in right good earnest a settled life, for which after all my wanderings and vagaries I yearn immensely.' Being what he was, he also found it impossible to quite shake off thoughts of the *BOJ* and the other magazines he had abandoned; this was the only holiday he ever took (barring an enforced stay abroad when he was very ill) which was not undertaken in the name of business or constantly interrupted with work.

This was a compliment Isabella was not yet in a position to appreciate. Though she had all too often had to accept his work as his reason for not seeing her, she still had no idea of the strength of his commitment to it or she could never have written, less than a month before, 'I have been thinking . . . how you will say sometimes, "I don't think I shall go to town this morning, but stay and have a quiet day in the country." ' Like most Victorian brides, she knew alarmingly little about men in general, the pressures of a business, or the nature of the man she had married. More surprising, perhaps, is that from Sam's remark about wanderings and vagaries it sounds as though he had told her a certain amount about his bachelor life (which suggests that it was not really very sensational); on another occasion, too, he referred to 'what you are pleased to call my roving nature'.

In the whirl and excitement of France, she probably did not find out much more—indeed, it is unlikely that she ever plumbed all the multifarious facets of his nature. A few of his more obvious characteristics must have caught her notice: his carelessness with money, for instance, of which she had already had warning—and knew how to deal with. 'I am sorry to hear you are not likely to get out of your Lottery mess nicely. Certainly £200 per annum is not to be *sneezed* at, but if you have it not, why the only way is to make yourself happy and contented without it and do as well as you can. You must smoke one or two cigars less a day, and I must economize as much as possible.'

Before their return to England came the journey to Heidelberg with Jessie and Sam's stepmother, Eliza, who dreaded the thought of travelling abroad unescorted. She had already pressed Sam into service once, when Edward went to school, and had ventured to propose taking advantage of the young couple's plans by starting out at the same time and going to Heidelberg with Sam before he proceeded south. Isabella, in her annoyance, had said that she did not want to go to Germany—despite the fact that her sisters were there—and so Eliza apparently expected her to wait for Sam somewhere *en route*, presumably in Paris. The whole plan was untypically tactless, obviously made out of desperation on Eliza's part; Isabella was by this time obsessed with her desire to be with Sam and understandably could not bear the thought of a separation, or even of a few days' delay in the time before she would have him to herself, and reacted with equally uncharacteristic heat:

> Two things in your note annoyed me very much indeed, first of all Aunt Eliza being so very stupid. . . . That Germany business also I cannot get out of my head. My notions on the subject are that it would be very disagreeable to have a third party with us on our journey, and that it would be wrong and very unkind of you to leave me so soon after—you say it is a matter of duty. Do you think it would be dutiful to me, to go away so soon looking at it in that point. You ought certainly to consider me first in that respect because after a man marries he is supposed to look first to his better or worse half as the case may be. Now don't be angry, I am afraid I have said too much; however, we will talk the matter over on Thursday evening. . . . The horse is waiting, so please excuse this scribble. . . .

Sam, thus caught between his duties, as she had so often been, and in one way delighted at the back-handed compliment to him, smoothed over the situation by agreeing to meet his stepmother in Paris on the way home, whence they could all go to Heidelberg together—the chief sufferer from this arrangement being himself, to whom the long train journey at the end of their holiday away from Pinner and his work was far from welcome. But Eliza's gratitude and the rapturous welcome from both his and Isabella's sisters was doubtless sufficient compensation; on a previous visit, made in almost equally irksome circumstances, he wrote, 'I have certainly had a great pleasure in seeing the delight of my much loved sisters, and your own. . . . Squeezing soon commenced, and suffocation nearly ensued, and after some small chat, I took the four girls to the Prince Carl, where they have stayed devouring eggs and honey and chocolate . . .'—evidently, the wedding cake was not destined to be wasted. Isabella was no doubt subjected to a similar welcome, and received the congratulations of her former schoolmistresses.

Then, their obligations fulfilled, the Beetons at last set out for Pinner, and entered their own front door as man and wife on 2 August 1856.

XIII

PARTNERSHIP

THEY RETURNED TO find their wedding presents delivered
and set in place, including the piano, which looked very elegant in
their shady drawing room, and the newly-engaged servants—a
cook, kitchen-maid, and housemaid, the respectable minimum for
a middle-class household—standing at the door to greet them;
they also had a gardener, the only one who could be accounted a
luxury. Isabella's first task as mistress of her own home would be
to order the dinner.

After all their pains, the inside of the house was extremely
comfortable and convenient. Probably as a reaction against her
former surroundings, Isabella endeavoured to make it as restful
and intimate as possible, the predominant colours being beige and
green. The furniture came from a shop recommended by Elizabeth:

I asked Mama this morning about Messrs. Green's furniture
place. Curiously enough she went there yesterday and was
delighted with the shop. She saw some very pretty chairs she
felt much inclined to purchase and *very reasonable*. Smith's
somewhere between the City Road and the Angel at Islington
Mama recommends you to buy your Venetian blind of. . . . You
asked me which colour I preferred. Green decidedly as it looks
more subdued in the summer and much warmer than that in the
winter.

Altogether, they spent £320 at Green's, which bearing in mind
that a luxuriously upholstered sofa could be bought for £10, was
enough to provide a houseful of very handsome furniture. They
had a bath with running hot water, a notable luxury at this date
but one on which Isabella set great store, being a great believer in

the beneficial effects of hot baths; Sam, conversely, was in the habit of taking cold ones every morning, presumably also for reasons of health, though he always professed to enjoy them. The house was heated wherever possible with stoves, which were cleaner and more efficient than open fires, while the main purpose of the blinds was to minimize draughts. Isabella did not discuss the kitchen; unless she had read Soyer before her marriage, it may not quite have come up to the ideals of size and convenience laid down in *Household Management*, though she certainly equipped it with all the latest appliances. The stove was probably the Improved Leamington Kitchener, 'said to surpass any other range in use, for easy cooking by one fire',[1] which won an award at the Great Exhibition. It had a hot-plate, boiler, plate-warmer, and an open roasting compartment which could be converted into a closed oven, and cost £5 15s–£20, according to size.

Needless to say, this unaccustomed background of luxury did not alter Sam's habits a jot; as soon as he returned to his office in Bouverie Street, any intention he may have had of regularizing his working hours was buried under three weeks' accumulation of 'Ledgers, Cash Books, etc.,' in his 'den'—never to re-surface. Every morning he rose at six and had his cold bath, and, at Isabella's insistence, a substantial breakfast. Then he hurried to the station, which was only a couple of minutes' walk down the road, and caught the early train to the City, probably savouring his first cigar of the day *en route*. He returned late, frequently not until after dinner—but for this one can hardly blame him as they dined at 5.30, which was early even by English middle-class standards (the Dorlings, for example, dined around six). Once, he was so late that he missed the last train and, with a characteristically masochistic instinct, walked all the way home—which was all very well for him, but one feels that it would have shown more consideration for Isabella if he had taken a cab. His early departure and late return were among the things which caused Lucy, who went to stay with them a year or so later, to declare him the most selfish man she had ever met.

And indeed, from Sam's point of view, married life was pretty well idyllic. As Lucy reported, in tones of great surprise, Isabella did not mind his long hours; once the exigencies of his work were revealed to her, she accepted them in the same spirit as she soon came to share them, and organized her daily routine around

them. Everyone in the house got up early—as she would have
insisted on in any case—and the cook was instructed always to
leave a supper prepared in case Sam should be late. He had seen to
it that the kitchen grate was properly fixed, 'so as to be useful in
case of much fire being required for our "petits-diners" ', so we
can take it that they entertained fairly regularly; the Greenwoods
and Sam's other business friends would have been among their
first guests; Isabella might have found them a trifle unrefined but
she must also have granted that they were a great deal livelier than
her father and mother's acquaintances.

Nevertheless, for her the situation was not quite so perfect. Her
intense interest in the details of the house shows how passionately
she had been looking forward to running her own establishment,
but for a girl of her intelligence, organizing three servants for
two people was hardly demanding—less so, perhaps, than she had
imagined. She was left alone all day and most of the evening six
days a week in a neighbourhood where she did not know anybody, which, although she minded loneliness less than most, must
have taken some getting used to after a life of constant company.
After her childhood, even her pregnancy lacked the excitement it
might have held for others, and such immediate proof of her
fecundity must have made her wonder whether she would end up
with as many children as her mother. It does not follow that she
was bored or disillusioned—but she still had a good deal of time
on her hands, which she was not disposed to fill with lengthy
toilettes, endless embroidery, sewing for the baby, or playing the
piano. For anyone living with Sam, the obvious and natural
thing to do was to participate in some way with his work;
and sure enough, eight months after her arrival at Pinner, she
was writing the household and cookery columns for the *EDM*,
and she is also said to have translated French novels for the
magazine.[2]

The change from the ladylike notions of her upbringing that
this signified was radical, but she had never been swayed by considerations of mere convention. The combination of Sam's
influence over her, the ruthlessness which had always been latent
in her character (and without which neither she, nor any woman,
could have made a career), her impatience with her family's ideals
and her dread of boredom made her conversion inevitable. Its
speed was a little breathtaking, though, as it seems that the

decision to start writing for the *EDM* was made about five months before she actually began, and possibly within three months of settling at Pinner.

The cookery articles by the original contributor stopped in October and the household hints column, 'Things Worth Knowing', a month or two after that. We can only guess exactly what happened: Sam may have suggested that Isabella should take them over straight away, or perhaps she did not agree to do them until he had tried and failed to find someone else. Professional female journalists were an unknown species at this date, and although there was never any shortage of correspondents to the ladies' magazines, a vacancy for a practical writer on subjects neither men nor ladies much cared to tackle could have been very difficult to fill.

The magazine was left without domestic articles for six months. There were two obvious reasons for Isabella's hesitation: her diffidence as a writer and her ignorance of cooking. Judging by her first articles, she must have required a great deal of encouragement to get started, and since no prior announcement was made, it appears that Sam was uncertain as to when she would begin until the very last moment. Never having tried to write before, she was agonizingly nervous, though the symptoms were the opposite to those in her first letter to him. As for her qualifications, she was too principled, as well as too inexperienced, to say anything that she could not vouch for personally—from which sprang many of the greatest merits of her book. The thoroughness of her preparation for that leaves no doubt that the appearance of her early articles was preceded by many weeks of studying cookery books, questioning her own cook, and experimenting in her kitchen, which must have considerably startled her domestics. Understandably, she wrote with more confidence at this stage on the management of children (which she later preferred to leave to professionals) than on cooking.

She began writing the month before the baby was due and so absorbed was she in her new-found activity that the birth of the baby apparently took her unawares. Taking her cue from her mother, she was in any case inclined to belittle the event of a birth, and as she never suffered any inconvenience or illness during her pregnancies, she had no cause to take much notice of them. Her attitude to her babies once born was the same; except once, she carried on in her professional capacity regardless of all else throughout the rest of her life, and would certainly have continued to do so if she had had a family of ten to claim her attention instead of only one child at a time.

Her decision to write for Sam of course transformed the nature of their marital relationship and in due course had an equally fundamental effect on his business. From contributing three sets of articles monthly—for she added an extra feature called 'The Nursery' to the two she inherited—she went on to become editress of the *Englishwoman's Domestic Magazine* and *The Queen* and assisted in setting up a magazine for girls to partner the *Boy's Own Magazine*. In so doing, she ceased to occupy the traditional role of the dependent wife and turned her marriage into one of the most fruitful professional partnerships of the time. She was a fully fledged working wife in the modern sense in all respects but one— that she could not earn money of her own. That she should be entitled to almost certainly never entered her head; the fact that she represented an inestimable financial bargain never occurred to Sam either in crude terms, though he was extremely conscious of the extent and value of her work, and referred to her more than once, in a very humble spirit, as his 'master'.

Her first contributions appeared in April, the month after her twenty-first birthday. They were not dull, but brusque and didactic, as though she were challenging her readers to an argument; no doubt Sam, to counter her shyness, had told her to write firmly and authoritatively. She obviously put an immense amount of effort into them; they contain several of the epigrammatic phrases for which *Household Management* is famous and which, far from being spontaneous, were arrived at only after much polishing and paring down of words and are not to be found in any of her other journalistic work. Despite her off-putting tone, what she had to say was as sound and worthwhile as anything she wrote later (except that in the light of experience she changed her mind about certain culinary details). She commenced with a stern, intensely sincere homily on housekeeping, based on her own experiences over the past six months. Economy was her watchword: from the opening paragraph it seems clear that she was mistress of their private finances, if not already well acquainted with Sam's business affairs:

To Wives and Housekeepers

THE AFFECTATION OF FASHION

—It is the fashion now-a-days of many ladies to ignore their husbands' pecuniary affairs; they profess ignorance of money matters, and encourage themselves in the idea that *their* wishes at least must be gratified—with the rest they have nothing to do. Now the affectation of this is bad enough, but nothing can be worse than the actual practice—many a ruined house, many a bankruptcy and insolvency springs out of it—many a domestic circle is broken up, and the pride which caused the ruin is humbled to dust as a reward. . . .

The second paragraph began with one of her classic sayings:

SUCCESSFUL MARKETING

—*A daily supply is a daily waste;* the running to and fro from the street door to the chandler's shop; the purchase of an ounce of this thing, or a quarter of a pound of that is an error. Your grocery, candles, soap . . . should be obtained regularly in quantities from respectable traders; potatoes should come in a sack . . . apples by the bushel . . . and not only may you have many pleasant additions to your dinner table by adopting a system of wholesale purchase, but you will, upon the whole, have more and pay less; be free of the worry of sending out continually for small supplies, and have at hand a stock to meet emergencies.[3]

She presented the cookery column, which followed, in precisely the same manner as her predecessor. The original system of giving a selection of seasonal foods with recipes to correspond had long since degenerated into a random list of whatever recipes the contributor happened to have to hand, and she made no attempt at this stage to re-establish any kind of co-ordination; she simply gave half a dozen basic preparations, unfortunately accompanied by a string of over-emphatic comments, which were not necessary and wasted a great deal of her space. The following remarks about salads appear to have been inspired by her experiences in the south of France, and were of little relevance to her readers since salads were not, generally speaking, very popular in England and were certainly never served with garlic:

PUNGENT SALADS

—The praises of raw onions, raw garlic, and such strong-flavoured herbs are ill bestowed. Do they not make you sleep awfully sound—so sound that you do not wake till an hour after your usual time in the morning, and then you feel half stupid, your head aches, and the taste in your mouth is abominable. Should wholesome food produce such symptoms? Certainly not. . . .

The next recipe, which went into the book,[4] contained another nice phrase: 'HOW TO DRESS A DRIED HADDOCK.—The common method of treating this noble fish is to boil it, and that is to spoil it. . . .' In her last recipe, for 'A GOOD SPONGE-CAKE', she made the usual beginner's mistake of missing out the weight of one of the ingredients (particularly disastrous in a cake). To someone so methodical, this must have been especially exasperating. She corrected the omission in the next issue and never made a mistake in an article again, though there were a few *errata* in the first edition of the book—mostly printer's errors, it is true; however, it is reassuring to know that even she was not infallible.

'Things Worth Knowing' contained several bits of advice on cookery that she later rejected, such as mixing chicory with coffee and hints on 'The Art of Tea-Making'. By the time she came to write *Household Management*, her attitude to coffee had become as purist as Miss Acton's, and chicory was unmentionable: 'The coffee should always be purchased in the berry,—if possible, freshly roasted; and it should never be ground long before it is wanted in use.'[5] As for tea, she said disparagingly: 'There is very little art in making good tea.'[6] Other suggestions in this column were on such mundane subjects as cleaning boots, washing coloured clothes and economizing on coal. The feature she initiated, on the upbringing of children, where she had many years instead of only a few months of experience to draw upon, was much the longest of the three, taking up two and a half pages.

She was evidently extremely dissatisfied with her debut, for she was as prompt as possible in correcting her faults: by the very next month she had eradicated all traces of nervousness, and was writing smoothly, confidently, and professionally. Sam never doubted her competence, and advertised her forthcoming contributions in the same issue as her first articles, announcing triumphantly that in future the housekeeper's department of the magazine would be bigger and better than ever before—which represented something of a scoop, for the *EDM*, it must be remembered, was still at that time the only established woman's magazine with any pretensions to domesticity. He also inserted the first of a series of requests for recipes from readers: 'We are at all times thankful for tried and proved recipes, and shall be happy to receive them from our correspondents.'[7]

The enormous improvement in her May articles was achieved in spite of the fact that they were written a very short time after the birth of the baby. This, it seems, went off as straightforwardly as she had expected; but, no doubt because she had underestimated the demands of motherhood, she did not regain her usual health and strength as quickly as she should have done. Either normal (but at that time unrecognized) post-natal depression or anxiety about her work combined with the strain of round-the-clock feeding lowered her spirits and caused her to lose a little weight. There was obviously nothing much wrong with her, especially as she could well afford to shed a few pounds, but Sam, who had never seen her off colour before, was naturally concerned. The baby, meanwhile, who was named Samuel Orchart after his father, was reported to be doing well.

A friend of the Dorlings called Mrs English, whose husband was connected with the racing at Newmarket, had written to congratulate the Beetons on the birth of the baby. Isabella, understandably in the circumstances, had not got around to replying for some time. When she eventually did, in July, she mentioned that she was preparing to write a cookery book, possibly because she knew that Mrs English might be helpful; thus we know that at that time the book was already planned. In fact, the idea of it almost certainly originated from the time when she first agreed to write the cookery articles, as the immediate publication of the requests for recipes suggests (though does not prove, since she might have wanted the recipes merely for her column).

5*

Mrs English evidently knew nothing of Isabella's activities on the magazine and, of course, disapproved of the idea of her writing a book, on practical as well as other grounds. On the other hand, she was indeed knowledgeable about cookery, and when she mistakenly gained the impression that it was Sam rather than Isabella who was compiling it, she was almost embarrassingly ready with suggestions. Even to begin with, however, she was fairly forthcoming: having admonished Isabella for her tardiness in writing—'I thought you dead as Emma wrote to you by my wish 2 months since Relative to yourself and Baby but to which you never answered' (her grammar was not equal to her good sense)—she went on:

> I see difficulties in your way as regards publishing a book on cookery. Cookery is a science that is only learnt by long experience and years of study which of course you have not had. Therefore my advice would be to compile a book from receipts from a variety of the best books published on cookery and Heaven knows there is a great variety for you to choose from. One of our Best Woman Cooks who is now retired recently told me one of the best and most useful books is Simpson's Cookery. . . .[8] And is your intended book meant for the Larger or the Higher Classes or the Middle Class? The latter is one I should recommend you. . . .

Since her views tallied exactly with the Beetons' intentions, Isabella was greatly encouraged and showed the letter to Sam. It was because he wrote back to ask the name of the woman cook she had spoken of that she thankfully assumed that the book was his concern. Thereafter, names flowed thick and fast. This cook, who was called Mrs Munn, had been employed by an admiral, and Mrs English wrote to her forthwith, without further reference to the Beetons, telling her that Sam would call. She also supplied the name and address of the Duke of Rutland's cook, Mr Orpwood, and enclosed a recipe for 'portable soup' (the nineteenth-century equivalent to stock cubes) from Lord Wilton's cook, which was almost certainly the recipe to appear under that name in *Management*.'[9] 'You will find the stockpot is the great secret of the kitchen. Without it nothing can be done. With it everything can be done,' she declared, thus voicing the principles of all classical cooks—for stock was the foundation for sauces, and 'sauces in cookery are like the first rudiments of grammar'.[10]

But Mrs English was only one among numerous others who corresponded about the book and it would be easy to over-estimate her influence; in spite of her recommendation to write for the middle classes, she herself had not grasped the implications of this. All the cooks she referred to were or had been employed in great houses and cooked in a style which was impossible in ordinary middle-class homes. The book by Simpson was similarly quite unsuitable for Isabella's purposes, being by a former chef of the Marquis of Buckingham. For this reason, Sam did not bother to follow up any of her introductions, at which she was naturally indignant:

I am sorry you have not yet seen Mr. Orpwood. . . . As to Mrs. Munn, you can always see her, but have you not yet wrote to Her? You should have.

But as to Mr. Orpwood, if you intend seeing him—you will not have another opportunity for months to come, so see about it immediately. Please tell Bella I will write in a day or two.

She also urged him to come and stay with her in Suffolk, and warmly repeated the invitation to Isabella, complaining at the same time of his laziness.

I told Sam a fortnight ago to write or see Mr. Orpwood and Mrs. Munn, both cooks.

Respecting his cookery book I am sorry to find he has not done either for I fear when he wants them he will not find either of them at home. . . .

But if her contacts were no use, Isabella's desire to take further advantage of her knowledge was probably one of their chief motives for taking up her invitation—the other being Sam's anxiety about Isabella's health (perhaps he had faith in the restorative properties of Suffolk air, having once gone there himself to convalesce). Otherwise, it seems unlikely that they would have accepted; it was three years before they allowed themselves another holiday—partly because they could not afford it, but also because Sam could not tear himself away from

Bouverie Street. In the event, they set out almost immediately, accompanied by the baby, whom they had to take because at three months old he was still being fed by his mother.

Travelling with infants was not generally favoured by the Victorians because of the inconvenience and their almost obsessive fear of children catching cold; indeed, Isabella herself had written a warning paragraph on this subject only the previous month, in which she condemned 'the folly of that system of *hardening* the constitution which induces the parent . . . freely to expose it (the child) to the cold, cutting currents of an easterly wind.'[11] But it was not the east wind that was to blame for what happened. Probably there was no particular reason, but after a day or two at the Englishs', the baby was seized with an attack of what was declared to be croup.

This was a terrifying diagnosis. In the first place, croup was at that time a deadly affliction, 'by far the most formidable and fatal of all the diseases to which infancy and childhood are liable, and is purely an inflammatory affection . . . always sudden in its attack and rapid in its career, usually proving fatal within three days. . . .'[12] In the second place, the symptoms were particularly dreadful to watch, the patient suffering from difficulty in breathing and violent fits of uncontrollable coughing. The remedies advocated were scarcely less alarming, though one hopes such things were not attempted in the case of a three-month-old baby: very hot baths, ipecacuanha or other emetics, blistering, and (particularly disgusting) the application of leeches, which was a standard prescription in cases of inflammation. Whatever was done to relieve the child, it did not effect a cure, and Isabella, who had never been associated with an illness more serious than influenza in her life (unless, as seems very unlikely, she saw her father dying) was obliged to witness her offspring choking to death. It would have been more merciful to both if he had succumbed quickly, but he was clearly no weakling for he survived the prescribed period and did not die for several days more; Mr English, who was obliged to go away during the course of his illness, wrote: 'When I left . . . I really felt every hope and I may say almost certain of a speedy recovery. . . .'

The death of a small baby was a common enough occurrence in Victorian times, but it was nonetheless a very great shock. The blow was particularly hard for Sam and Isabella as it was their first child, and both of them had come from large, healthy families where the idea that any offspring would not live was never entertained. Isabella was more or less prostrated for a while and that month was the only time she ever failed to produce her contributions for the magazine. Sam, in the light of the strength of character he showed later, may be assumed to have shown more courage and fortitude than might have been foreseen. The event must have been intensely embarrassing as well as acutely distressing for Mrs English, but she was sufficiently practical to treat the situation fairly briskly, though she was evidently sympathetic too. Her friendship with her guests was in no way impaired: Sam went to stay with the Englishs again some seven years later, and slept in the room where the baby had died, which, as may be imagined, considerably affected him.

Predictably, the shock and distress of their baby's death had the effect of concentrating the Beetons' attention more earnestly than ever on work over the next couple of years, which were the most productive of their lives. They had every reason to suppose that within a short time another baby would be forthcoming and they submerged their feelings by plunging together into authorship for the first time. Their tasks were not dissimilar: Sam, in collaboration with a writer named John Sherer, began compiling what was to be the first of a series of works of reference, the *Dictionary of Universal Information*, an abbreviated historical and geographical encyclopedia; Isabella commenced her four-year marathon of writing and research for *Household Management*. In spite of her uncompromising attitude, it is quite likely that if her son had lived, it could not have been completed even in that time.

XIV

AUTHORSHIP

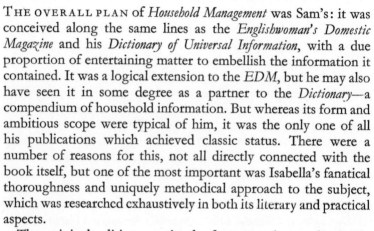

THE OVERALL PLAN of *Household Management* was Sam's: it was conceived along the same lines as the *Englishwoman's Domestic Magazine* and his *Dictionary of Universal Information*, with a due proportion of entertaining matter to embellish the information it contained. It was a logical extension to the *EDM*, but he may also have seen it in some degree as a partner to the *Dictionary*—a compendium of household information. But whereas its form and ambitious scope were typical of him, it was the only one of all his publications which achieved classic status. There were a number of reasons for this, not all directly connected with the book itself, but one of the most important was Isabella's fanatical thoroughness and uniquely methodical approach to the subject, which was researched exhaustively in both its literary and practical aspects.

The original edition consisted of over a thousand[1] closely packed pages, and covered pretty well every aspect of domestic knowledge a woman could require, from etiquette to legal advice. In addition, by way of entertainment, it contained vast quantities of miscellaneous information about food, which at first sight is so impressive that it seems incredible that it could all have been written by a girl of under twenty-five, especially when it is borne in mind that she started out in almost total ignorance of her subject and was equally inexperienced as an author. When her work is closely examined it becomes possible to see how she did it, but it remains an extraordinary feat—and one which she would have been too realistic to attempt if she had not been young and inexperienced; in the book, she said: 'I must frankly own, that if I had known beforehand that this book would have cost me the labour which it has, I should never have been courageous enough to attempt it.'[2] But to Sam Beeton's bride all things seemed possible—and after all, on the face of it, it was a no more formidable task than the compilation of his dictionary.

It took almost four years to complete, appearing as a finished volume early in the autumn of 1861, which was a remarkably short time in which to cover so much ground. Although the brunt of the research was carried out in the two-year hiatus between her babies, she must have worked at intense pressure for most of that time, putting in as long a working day one way and another as Sam. She was extremely efficient in her selection of material, and exceptionally shrewd in her use of it—which is one reason why the sources of her information have never been fully exposed. The miscellaneous gastronomic information proved to be her greatest challenge, the testing of recipes her greatest chore; the non-culinary parts of the book cost her less effort (and in many ways were more interesting) than the overwhelmingly longer and more famous cookery section.

She never laid any claim to originality, as did Acton and Soyer and other professional cookery writers; *Household Management* was not intended to be more than a collection of other people's ideas, and with her invariable scrupulous accuracy, she even rejected the title of 'author', calling herself merely 'editress'. She gathered her information, culinary and otherwise, from every source available, and gave a general acknowledgement for the recipe section, and for some (but not all) the other parts of the book, in the Preface:

> For the matter of the recipes, I am indebted, in some measure, to the correspondents of the 'Englishwoman's Domestic Magazine,' who have obligingly placed at my disposal their formulae for many preparations. A large private circle has also rendered me considerable service. A diligent study of the best modern writers on cookery was also necessary to the faithful fulfilment of my task. Friends in England, Scotland, Ireland, France, and Germany have also very materially aided me. . . .

In fact, a great many recipes came from books and relatively few from friends, so this was misleading, albeit unintentionally; it is impossible to be precise about exact numbers since almost all of the recipes were published anonymously and only a few, for reasons of courtesy, interest, or copyright, were specifically credited. All she said about the rest of the book was that three

chapters were contributed by 'gentlemen fully entitled to confidence; those on medical subjects by an experienced surgeon, and
the legal matter by a solicitor.' She made no mention of the
sources for all the rest of her material.

Though they were not invented by her, her recipes had
what was at that time the exceptional merit of having been
conscientiously tested. Apart from a few preparations guaranteed
by friends, she herself tried out everything she included, which
added enormously to the burden of her work; over the four years,
she must have experimented with at least one dish a day—more,
if allowance is made for the ones she rejected. She had no particular aptitude for cooking, nor—if her willingness to abandon it
is anything to go by—did she get any particular pleasure from it,
though she enjoyed the intellectual exercise of budgeting and
planning meals. As this implies, she had none of Soyer or Acton's
creative talent, and claimed to have invented only one dish out of
about fifteen hundred that she published—characteristically,
Useful Soup for Benevolent Purposes, the most economical
preparation in the book.[3]

The recipes acknowledged to friends included Prince of Wales
Soup,[4] a depressing concoction of turnips from 'a philanthropic
friend' to be distributed to the poor as a celebration of the Prince
of Wales's coming of age (this prompted her to add a patriotic
quotation from Sam's *Dictionary*); Soup à la Solferino,[5] which was
drunk by the troops at Solferino in 1859; Baroness Pudding, from
the Dorlings' neighbour, the Baroness de Tessier;[6] and Beefsteak
and Kidney Pudding from a lady in Sussex.[7] Five puddings
labelled 'German' presumably came from a German cookery book
sent by the Heidel sisters. Louisa wrote hastily in the middle of
the end-of-term confusion: 'My sister is sending with best wishes
a German cookery book for Isabella, in which she will find all
kinds of German dishes, much more precisely and better than my
sister could have given them.' There was nothing to distinguish
Mrs English's Portable Soup, nor a Newmarket recipe for a
pickle, which may have been another of her contributions.
Altogether, the number of recipes contributed privately was
probably not more than a couple of score—as was to be expected,
for in spite of Sam's Fleet Street friends, who were not likely to be
very useful, their circle of acquaintances was not large enough to
yield more.

The magazine readers, on the other hand, provided a fair proportion—though not so great as the publicity for the book implied. Sam continued to run the requests for recipes until the end of 1859: 'We shall be exceedingly obliged to any lady who will spare a few moments to write out for us some of her choicest recipes, and thus make the *Englishwoman's Domestic Magazine* a means whereby her knowledge and skill may be communicated to the world for the benefit of all.' According to the advertisements, the response was fantastic, and over two thousand were sent in. This suggests that they constituted the bulk of the book, but in fact Isabella did not include more than about a third of them, probably because she found when she came to try them out that the majority of them were unreliable, impractical, or repeated each other. The balance of her recipes, which amounted to about half, and nearly all her culinary ideas and principles came from other cookery books, as Mrs English had suggested.

'Heaven knows there is a great variety for you to choose from,' she had said—and indeed the proliferation of cookery books caused almost as much contemporary comment as it does today. There were literally hundreds Isabella could have wasted her time studying, of which at least a hundred had been published within the last fifty years.[8] The majority, however, like Simpson's, were meant for cooks in large households rather than for middle-class women, and were not of the slightest use to Isabella since they gave only vague, inadequate directions, and omitted the elementary details upon which the success of any dish depends—such as cooking times and the quantity of ingredients required. But there were in addition a handful of books in quite a different category, which were in their various ways excellent. These included Soyer's famous trilogy and the works of his less famous but scarcely less influential preceptor Ude. It was this class of book that Isabella meant when she referred to 'the best modern cookery books', although several of those she drew on, like Ude's, were by no means recent.

Two long-established titles she almost certainly referred to, simply because they were so popular, were *The Art of Cookery Made Plain and Easy* by Hannah Glasse (1747) and *A New System of Domestic Cookery* (1809) by Mrs Rundell (signed 'By a Lady'), both of which were in their twelfth edition by the time she started work. Their success was deserved, since both were intended for ordinary women running homes on a modest scale, and both were relatively practical, though they did not always give sufficiently precise instructions. 'Clean it carefully, boil it gently, and take it out of the water as soon as done,' was all Mrs Rundell had to say of cooking salmon, though she added as an afterthought, 'If underdone, it is very unwholesome.'[9] One or two of her soup and pudding recipes look as if they provided the basis for Isabella's equivalents,[10] and earlier editions of her work had a series of engravings showing the different cuts of meat, as well as a very sensible introductory chapter about servants and domestic management. These, however, were omitted from the 1852 version, the one Isabella was most likely to have seen. Upon the whole, except for a few recipes, it must be concluded that neither book served as more than a general example to her rather than as a direct source of ideas or material.

The oldest book she definitely made use of—though perhaps the most modern in spirit—was Dr William Kitchener's *The Cook's Oracle*, which first appeared in 1818 and was still being reissued in the 1880s. Kitchener was a doctor who could not practise professionally in England because he had qualified in Scotland, and had settled down in London to a life of writing, cooking, and entertaining his friends, who formed a Committee of Taste to pass judgement on his recipes. As a person, one can imagine that he was prissy, demanding, and dictatorial, but as a writer he was extremely witty, with a pungent, epigrammatic style, which was one of the reasons for the exceptional staying-power of his book. It was this above all, plus his dry, medical common sense, which especially appealed to Isabella. His underlying theory was that good health began with sensible eating: '—Those who say, 'Tis no matter what we eat or what we drink, —may as well say, 'Tis no matter whether we eat or drink';[11] and because '—*The energy of our* BRAINS *is sadly dependent on the behaviour of our* BOWELS',[12] he invented a laxative pill with the splendid name of the 'Peristaltic Persuader'.

When he began *The Cook's Oracle*, he was in a similar situation to Isabella, never having cooked before, and like her began by examining existing cookery books. He claimed to have gone through about 250 before coming to the conclusion that they were all exactly the same, as 'Like . . . as one Egg to another', composed with the aid of scissors and paste rather than pen and ink. His own work, in contrast, consisted entirely of the results of his own experiments (approved by the Committee), which yielded recipes as simple as those of Mrs Glasse and Mrs Rundell, but much easier to follow.

If *Household Management* had an ancestor, it was *The Cook's Oracle*. Isabella was preceded by Kitchener in very many essential respects: he was the first cookery writer ever to give accurate weights and measures; he included detailed marketing tables listing the seasonal prices of foodstuffs, most of which came direct from the tradesmen themselves; and he emphasized economy rather than elegance, taking as his motto: 'ORDER AND ECONOMY ARE THE BASIS OF COMFORT AND INDEPENDENCE'.[13] Also, his introduction included a few words of advice to guests, to whom he was particularly stringent about punctuality, and a chapter of 'Friendly Advice to Cooks and other Servants' (which was very much friendlier than anything she ever wrote). Later, he produced a separate book on housekeeping, *The Housekeeper's Oracle*,[14] the opening sentence of which might as well have been written by her: 'To understand the Economy of Household Affairs is essential to a woman's proper and pleasant performance of the duties of a Wife and Mother. . . .' Although she could not consistently imitate his style, his influence can be detected in her polished phrases, and perhaps also in her frequent use of quotation, for which he had an inordinate liking. It is perhaps surprising that she did not pay him the compliment of using more of his recipes; but she limited herself to very few,[15] presumably because his book was still one of the most popular on the market—and did not acknowledge any.

Soyer's friend Louis Ude, who until eclipsed in the public eye by his exuberant compatriot had been regarded as the leading exponent of French cooking in England, had been in the employ of no lesser personages than Louis XVI and the Duke of York before going on to become chef at Crockford's Club. His book, *The French Cook* (1828), was essential reading for anyone aspiring to culinary knowledge. Although, like Simpson's, it was intended for the guidance of chefs in large establishments, Isabella attributed five preparations to him, including a lengthy account of how to cure a ham and a two-and-a-half page essay on making turtle soup. Complicated as it was, it seems that she tried it since her version was only 'founded on' his instructions. It was almost

the only dish in the book for which she did not give the number
of servings or the exact cost, saying only, 'This is the most
expensive soup brought to table.'[16]

The book on which she drew most extensively for recipes,
however, was Eliza Acton's *Modern Cookery for Private Families*,
which came out in 1845. This in effect served as the culinary
backbone of *Management*; it seems that wherever the magazine
correspondents or other sources proved inadequate, Isabella
referred to it to fill out her chapters. This can be taken as proof of
her excellent judgement as it was the best book ever to have been
produced for ordinary households, and though from a twentieth-
century standpoint it appears that she treated its author very
shabbily, one has to remember that she was only doing (rather
more cleverly) what almost everyone else did at that time.

Eliza Acton was another who did not know how to cook when
she first embarked on her work, though as she spent her childhood
in France she probably started out with a better gastronomic
education than Kitchener or Isabella. Born in 1799, she was a
brewer's daughter, like Isabella's grandmother, and was sent
abroad when still only a girl for the sake of her health, where in
due course she fell in love with an army officer; marriage,
however, was not the outcome, and she returned to England to
pour forth her soul on paper and become a poet. Though not very
successful, she was extremely determined, and when eventually
she had had several of her poems published, she took a collection
of them to Longman's. Her interview there has been variously
reported, but the upshot of it was that her poems were refused
and she was sent away with the suggestion that she should write
a cookery book instead—an idea presumably offered as a sop
rather than as a serious proposition; Longman was doubtless
amazed when she returned years later with a masterpiece. Her
literary ability was not wasted, for one of the joys of her work was
that every recipe was beautifully described, with scrupulous
attention to the finer points of culinary detail. She also had a
gentle sense of humour, which emerged in names she gave some
of her puddings:[17] The Young Wife's Pudding, The Elegant
Economist's Pudding, The Poor Author's Pudding (a plain
bread-and-butter pudding), and The Publisher's Pudding (with
almonds, fruit, cream, and brandy). She never became famous in
the same sense as the chefs Ude and Soyer but her book was very

successful, running to three editions in its first year, and she was appointed cookery correspondent to *The Lady's Companion.* The only other cookery book she wrote was *The English Bread Book,* which came out in 1857, the year Isabella started work.

Although plagiarism was practically the rule, it greatly incensed Miss Acton, and she was already complaining bitterly in the 1855 edition, which was almost certainly the one Isabella used: 'At the risk of appearing extremely egotistical, I have appended "Author's Receipt" and "Author's Original Receipt" to many of the contents of the following pages . . . in consequence of the unscrupulous manner in which large portions of my volume have been appropriated. . . .'[18] She died in 1859 but she must have turned in her grave when *Management* appeared: Isabella had used her book for about a third of her soup recipes, a quarter of her fish dishes, over a score of her sauces, and many other preparations besides, and acknowledged the origin of only two: her methods of boning poultry and making bread. She re-wrote all the preparations she included to fit in with her own system of presentation, but in the case of Miss Acton's, presumably because of the fuss she had made and the scale on which she used her work (for she was not so careful about other people's), she also slightly altered them, adjusting the ingredients in a way which protected her from accusations of copying but did not perceptibly affect the finished dish.[19] Her method worked, insofar as that nobody made any comment at the time; recently, however, Elizabeth David has remarked, '. . . . it is difficult to find any standard cookery compendium of the latter part of the Victorian era—works such as Warne's series of *Model Cookery* books and Cassell's *Dictionaries of Cookery,* not to mention the Beeton volumes—which do not include a quantity of Miss Acton's recipes.'[20] At least Isabella's amendments have the merit of proving that she really did cook all the dishes, since there is no other way by which she could have altered them so subtly.

As Elizabeth David has also pointed out,[21] it appears that she also took advantage of Miss Acton's book in another important respect. The latter, in her endeavour to give 'directions so practical, clear, and simple as to be at once understood, and easily followed, by those who had no previous knowledge of the subject',[22] gave a summary of the ingredients and cooking times required at the end of some of her recipes; Isabella adapted this into a uniform system, and arranged all her recipes with the ingredients at the top and a list of other basic details at the bottom. It was this which made her directions the easiest to follow ever written.

Books by obscure women had an uphill road in any case, but one of the reasons why *Modern Cookery* (like *Household Management*) did not receive the attention it deserved was that unfortunately for Miss Acton, it was overshadowed by the works of two chefs of national reputation which came out the very next year. These were *Modern Cook* by Charles Elmé Francatelli, *maître d'hôtel* to Queen Victoria and Ude's successor at Crockfords, and the *Gastronomic Regenerator* by Alexis Soyer. Both were on the same pattern as Ude's, and aimed at professional chefs; but Soyer, aware of the existence of a wider cooking public, included a chapter at the end of his book called 'The Kitchen At Home', which contained nearly three hundred excellent, practical, every-day recipes. This was received so enthusiastically that parts of it were reprinted in *The Lady's Newspaper* the next year, and a little later Soyer followed it up with a whole book for the middle classes, *Modern Housewife*. It proved an instant best-seller, and was given an accolade by almost every newspaper in the land. 'All who have food to cook must buy the book'. . . . 'No extract can give an idea of a book which, from cover to cover, is so full of good things, none of them requiring labour to digest'. . . . 'We may truly state that a more instructive book could not be desired'. . . . 'The far-famed Soyer has achieved a fresh triumph.'[23] *The Times* waxed most lyrical of all, declaring that it comprised 'almost every style of composition known to mortal writer' (it was written in epistolary form, with a mixture of letters, lectures, remarks, and recipes). 'It is at once a grave essay in prose and a most felicitous poem; it deals with that undoubted reality, the human stomach, yet with a pen essentially romantic and imaginative. It is at once didactic and dietetic, dramatic and culinary. Here we are moved by a sentiment; there we are brought face to face with "pig's cheek". . . .'[24]

Such enthusiasm of course did not spring from the virtues of the book, which, though from a culinary point of view a very worthy little volume, could hardly compare in other respects with Miss Acton's; and even in terms of cooking one would not have expected it to go down as well as hers because of its French bias (even Soyer could not entirely dispel popular prejudice against foreign food; the Englishness of Eliza's book was one of its chief recommendations to Isabella). It was just that Soyer had an irresistible personality and a remarkable flair for publicity, and everything he did was a success: his re-designed kitchens at the Reform Club, where he was chef for a long period, became a place of pilgrimage for everyone concerned with cooking (a detailed description of them was published in the *Regenerator*, along with designs for domestic kitchens of various sizes); his soup kitchens, where he dispensed soup that he claimed cost only three farthings per quart to make, set a fashion which lasted for years; and some of his inventions, such as Soyer's Sauce and his portable Magic Stove, which was used as standard equipment by the Army, became legendary. With his floppy hat and flapping clothes, he was a kind of national cult, and while he lived no writer on cookery could hope to rival him. He wrote six books altogether, three of which were not strictly cookery books; his third book of recipes, *Soyer's Shilling Cookery for the Poor* (1854), because it was the cheapest, was the most successful of all and sold a quarter of a million copies. His other works were a sixpenny pamphlet, *Charitable Cookery or the Poor Man's Regenerator* (1847), *The Pantropheon* (1853), which was a history of food, and *Soyer's Culinary Campaign*, an account of his experiences when he went to cook for the troops in the Crimea, where he encountered Florence Nightingale. He died in 1859, whereupon Francatelli endeavoured to take over his role as culinary champion of the middle classes and the poor, with *The Cook's Guide* and *Plain Cookery for the Working Classes*, which both appeared in 1861; and whereas Soyer's flight of fancy was *The Pantropheon*, his was the *Royal English Confectionary Book*, published barely a year after the other two.

Isabella did not pilfer recipes from either Soyer or Francatelli. She read Soyer's books with close attention, and was perhaps encouraged by him to include a chapter on invalid cookery, which was dealt with (very well) near the beginning of *Modern Housewife*. This was however a standard idea; Mrs Rundell, for instance, had also written about 'Sick Cookery'. The idea of giving advice on planning kitchens, too, may have come from the *Regenerator*, though it was Count Rumford, who wrote at the end of the previous century, whom she mentioned in this context.

Isabella gave twelve of Soyer's recipes, but, because they were so well known, conscientiously acknowledged them all;[25] her chief use of his work lay elsewhere. Francatelli she ignored for the simple reason that those of his books which might have been relevant to her came too late, appearing in the same year as *Household Management*. Rather than being of assistance to her, he was her rival, and it was to her advantage that he lacked Soyer's common touch and was too supercilious to be able to write successfully for the lower classes.

These authors, along with the early contributor, or contributors, to the *EDM*, from whom she took about a dozen preparations, were her chief published sources of recipes and culinary principles; but they did not represent by any means all her research for the culinary section of the book. The many pages of varied gastronomic information it also contained involved her in a separate, if sometimes overlapping, programme. This part of her work, presumably envisaged initially as a way of giving her book some kind of entertainment value, soon evolved into something more, and instead of being merely a substitute for the journalistic patter which came so easily to Sam, became an integral part of her purpose. It was almost certainly to this aspect of her research that she was referring when she said that if she had known how much labour it would cost her, she would never have dared to begin. It was much the most demanding part of her project, and involved her in a labyrinth of myth, philosophy, and the specialized fields of natural history, biology, and science. Whether it was worthwhile was a separate question, but at least it gave her public something to read, which was part of her intention.

It was in this context that Soyer was most directly useful to her. *The Pantropheon* was a somewhat idiosyncratic compilation of myth and facts about the origins of food, mostly garnered from the Classics; in terms of scholarship, it was an extraordinary achievement but in spite of the usual good reviews, it had not, by the very nature of its contents, been nearly so successful as his other books and was therefore less likely to be recognized. She used it to supply some of the historical notes which were scattered amongst her recipes. It is impossible to mistake the origin of her entry about lemons; Soyer wrote: 'Lemons were only known to the Romans at a very late period. . . . A considerable number of anecdotes have been told of the anti-venomous properties of the lemon. Athenaeus speaks of two men who did not feel pain from the bites of dangerous serpents, because they had previously eaten of this fruit.'[26] She wrote: 'In the earlier ages of the world, the lemon does not appear to have been at all known, and the Romans only became acquainted with it at a very late period. . . . Many anecdotes have been related concerning the anti-venomous properties of the lemon; Athenaeus, a Latin writer, telling us that on one occasion, two men felt no effects from the bites of dangerous serpents, because they had previously eaten of this fruit.'[27] Similar examples were on parsley, leeks, lettuces, and lentils. Soyer must also take the credit for a long introductory passage entitled 'Fish as an article of human food'.

Another writer who provided a rich fund of varied gastronomic information was a French lawyer, the Chevalier Jean-Anthelme Brillat-Savarin, who published his famous gastronomic treatise *La Physiologie du Goût* in 1825. He was the most dedicated and brilliant member of a gourmet family who lived near Lyons, one of the most epicurean parts of France, and was obviously born to be the author of a masterpiece on food—though he was a man of varied talents. He rose in his profession to become a judge, and was a sufficiently accomplished violinist to be able to earn his living playing with an American orchestra. He wrote several other works, but none have survived except *La Physiologie*.

It was no part of his intention to produce a cookery book: 'When I came to consider the pleasures of the table in all their aspects, I soon perceived that something better than a mere cookery book might be made of such a subject . . . bearing so closely upon our health, our happiness, and even our work.'[28] He included a few choice recipes by the way (that there were not more led to the rumour that for all his gastronomic pretensions, he could not cook), but the bulk of his book was given over to a series of 'meditations' on the nature and importance of gastronomy, the history and philosophy of cooking, the functioning of the organs of taste and digestion, and the chemical composition of food. All this was thickly decorated with a sparkling stream of anecdote and reminiscence.

Isabella admired his work immensely, and made full use of the amusing and philosophical side of it, though, with scientific material of a more professional nature to hand, she picked her way warily through his more technical and abstruse theories. Nevertheless, his influence is perceptible in almost every chapter of the culinary section of *Management*. She quoted (with acknowledgement) his only three practical recipes, and a great number of his stories and aphorisms, which because his book was in French had the advantage of being new to the popular English public—and were translated by her to very good effect. Her chapter on 'Dinners and Dining', in particular, leaned very heavily on him, and ended:

> . . . a great gastronomist exclaims, 'Tell me what kind of food you eat, and I will tell you what kind of man you are.' The same writer has some sentences of the same kind, which are rather hyperbolical, but worth quoting:—'The pleasures of the table belong to all ages, to all conditions, to all countries, and to all eras; they mingle with all other pleasures and remain at last to console us for their departure. The discovery of a new dish confers more happiness upon humanity than the discovery of a new star.'[29]

Among the stories Isabella quoted was one about some huntsmen who put their steaks under their saddles and galloped on them rather than cooking them; another was about a beautiful girl, of whom Brillat-Savarin seems to have been more than ordinarily fond, who died of drinking vinegar (frequently taken as a slimming potion); a third was about the Prince of Soubise, whose cook used fifty hams to prepare a single dinner. One day, when the Prince, a well known gourmet, was giving a party, he asked to see the bill of fare:

> His chef came, presenting a list adorned with vignettes, and the first article of which, that met the Prince's eye, was 'fifty hams'. 'Bertrand,' said the Prince, 'I think you must be extravagant; Fifty hams! do you intend to feast my whole regiment?' 'No, Prince, there will be but one on the table, and the surplus I need for my Espagnole, blondes, garnitures, &c.' 'Bertrand, you are robbing me: this item will not do.' 'Monseigneur,' said the *artiste*, 'you do not appreciate me. Give me the order, and I will put those fifty hams in a crystal flask no

longer than my thumb.' The Prince smiled and the hams were passed.[30]

The more technical part of her miscellaneous information, including the kind of physiological theory for which she distrusted Savarin, was the one field of her research where Sam, or rather some of his employees, were able to help her; indeed, if they had not, it is hard to see how she could have included a lot of it, since short of going to the British Museum Reading Room (like the pioneering woman journalist Eliza Lynn Linton) she could not possibly have located the various handbooks and encyclopedias she needed; for besides talking about food and its constituents and effects, she set out to give historical and biological details of every plant and animal mentioned in her recipes. With the conspicuous omission of the *Origin of Species*, she worked from the most reliable and up-to-date sources available, which were presumably supplied by the naturalist on the *BOM* and others, probably including John Sherer, Sam's collaborator on the *Dictionary*. Some of the books she referred to were doubtless also used in the course of compiling the dictionary, and a few of her notes on food and other subjects came directly from it.

She made altogether over thirty references to scientific authors, among them Sir Humphrey Davy, Justus von Liebig (a famous German chemist, who was also cited by Eliza Acton), and Erasmus Darwin the grandfather of the author of the *Origin of Species*. The *Origin of Species* came out two years before *Management*, and was resolutely ignored by Isabella because, with its atheistic implications, it was too controversial for her purposes. But in spite of such an impressive list of names, most of her material, as with the recipes, came from a few key sources, from which she almost certainly quoted further references secondhand. For instance, it is most unlikely that she read Liebig's books on chemistry and agriculture herself;[31] she did not need to in order to quote him, since his work was referred to by numerous contemporary writers.

Her most important source of biological information was *A Cyclopedia of Agriculture*,[32] contributed to by 'Upwards of Fifty of the most Eminent Farmers, Land Agents and Scientific Men of the Day', edited by John C. Morton, who was also the editor of the *Agricultural Gazette*, and author of *Morton's New Farmer's*

Almanack and many other works. The *Cyclopedia*, which was published in parts in 1850 and as a book in 1855 by the Glasgow publishers Blackie & Son, was exactly right for her because it was written from a farmer's point of view, giving general information about all the varieties of animal reared for food and detailed accounts of their lives from birth to preparation for table. From here came all the sections in *Management* on the breeding, health, slaughtering, and carving of pigs, cows, and sheep, including some of the diagrams. She did not alter Morton's text more than she could help, merely paraphrasing it to avoid copyright problems and changing the order of the material. From a literary point of view there was no point in doing more, as Norton's version was admirably written; also, she may not always have felt able to, as some of the passages she saw fit to include were by no means easy. One such was this very long, almost incomprehensible, but unexpectedly accurate description of the digestive processes in animals, which appeared in her introduction to soups. It was an almost *verbatim* transcription from the *Cyclopedia*:

ANOTHER CIRCUMSTANCE GREATLY AFFECTING THE QUALITY OF MEAT is the animal's treatment before it is slaughtered. . . . It will be easy to understand this, when we reflect on those leading principles by which the life of an animal is supported and maintained. These are, the digestion of its food, and the assimilation of that food into its substance. Nature, in effecting this process, first reduces the food in the stomach to a state of pulp, under the name of chyme, which passes into the intestines, and is there divided into two principles, each distinct from the other. One, a milk-white fluid,—the nutritive portion,—is absorbed by innumerable vessels which open up the mucous membrane, or inner coat of the intestines. These vessels, or absorbents, discharge the fluid into a common duct, or road, along which it is conveyed to the large veins in the neighbourhood of the heart. Here it is mixed with the venous blood (which is black and impure) returning from every part of the body, and then it supplies the waste which is occasioned in the circulating stream by the arterial (or pure) blood having furnished matter for the substance of the animal. The blood of the animal having completed its course through all parts, and having had its waste recruited by the digested food, is now received into the heart, and by the action of that organ it is urged through the lungs, there to receive its purification from the air which the animal inhales. Again returning to the heart, it is forced through the arteries, and thence distributed, by innumerable ramifications, called capillaries, bestowing to every part of the animal, life and nutriment. The other principle—the innutritive portion— passes from the intestines, and is thus got rid of. It will now be readily understood how flesh is affected for bad, if an animal is slaughtered when the circulation of its blood has been increased by over-driving, ill-usage, or other causes of excitement, to such a degree of rapidity as to be too great for the capillaries to perform their functions, and causing the blood to be congealed in its minuter vessels. When this has been the case, the meat will be dark-coloured, and become rapidly putrid; so that self-interest and humanity alike dictate kind and gentle treatment of all animals destined to serve as food for man.[33]

Significantly, she made no reference to Morton in relation to the many passages she borrowed from him, and only gave him credit for one long extract on the curing of ham, which she quoted directly, observing: 'The following is from Morton's "Cyclopedia of Agriculture" and will be found fully worthy of the high character of that publication.'[34] Yet this single acknowledgement was probably more than he got from others who treated his matter in a similar way, perhaps not even bothering to change the wording. As in the similar case of Miss Acton, Isabella's conscientiousness in this respect acted as a completely adequate cover for many years, for the *Cyclopedia*, now long forgotten, was never associated with *Management* or its offshoots (the parts containing Morton's contributions were not retained in later editions).

Blackie & Son also published *A History of the Vegetable Kingdom* by William Rhind (1857), which Isabella must have used though she did not make any reference to it; she did, however, mention a work by John Hogg called the *Natural History of the Vegetable Kingdom*, of which no trace can now be found.[35] Her entries on pigeons, poultry, and rabbits, which were re-used in an expanded form by Sam in *Beeton's Book of Home Pets*, apparently came from a book by Bonington Mowbray which has likewise disappeared. Among other books she made use of were John Prideaux Selby's

Illustrations of British Ornithology,[36] Thomas Pennant's *British Zoology*,[37] and William Yarrell's *A History of British Fishes*.[38]

Compared to the problems of copyright, recipe testing and adapting, and scientific technicalities that were posed by the cooking section, the research for the rest of the book was relatively straightforward. There were two chapters by the doctor, which were simply the medical contributions from the *EDM* reprinted in continuous form; further medical material was provided by Florence Nightingale's *Notes on Nursing*, from which Isabella quoted freely. The legal advice might have been the work of Frederick Weaklin, the friend who had given Sam the Murray's guide to France. The beginning of the book, on the mistress of the house, was the easiest for her, since she was able to draw on her own upbringing, though she no doubt reinforced her knowledge with the handful of guides to etiquette that were then available, plus the introductions to one or two cookery books, such as Kitchener and (possibly) Mrs Rundell. At some time, though more likely as part of her general education than directly in connection with *Management*, she must surely have read a series of books on ladylike behaviour by Mrs Sarah Ellis, at any rate the one entitled *The Daughters of England, their Position in Society and Responsibilities*. All the books were arch-exponents of the doctrine of feminine subordination, and written in a particularly cloying, irritating tone, but they had relevance to her work because of their emphasis on the importance of domesticity and the ladylike virtues.

As well as books, several useful sets of magazine articles had appeared in recent years, including one in the *Family Friend* of 1850, signed 'M. R.', and another in *The Ladies' Treasury*, the competitor to the *EDM*, which had been founded by the firm of publishers called Ward and Lock. The chief function of this magazine was to teach its readers how to be genteel, to which end it carried lessons on French and German and instruction in drawing, as well as a cookery feature called 'Aunt Deborah's Receipt Book' and the etiquette articles. These were presented under the intimidating title 'Conduct and Carriage; or Rules to Guide a Young Person on points of Etiquette and Good Breeding in Her Intercourse with the World', and consisted of a rather unconvincing dialogue between an ambitious mother and her unnaturally docile daughter. As in *Management*, the importance of neatness, punctuality and good temper were stressed; hostesses were advised to avoid over-ambitious menus and try out new dishes on their families before serving them in company; and ladies who wished to be thought refined were advised against beer, onions (it was not thought necessary to mention garlic), cherries (because of the indelicacy of spitting out the stones), and cheese—one of Isabella's pet aversions.

The material for the chapters on servants was collected from acquaintances and readers of the magazine in the same way as the recipes, and apparently with rather more success; amateur formulae for boot polish and grate blacking were perhaps more reliable than those for cakes and puddings. Mrs English said in one of her letters, 'When you see Mr. Orpwood refer to him for rules and regulations of Belvoir Castle, no house in England was better regulated.' Isabella must have relied largely on information collected in this way, for apart from *The Housekeeper's Oracle*, which was not much more than an elaboration of *The Cook's Oracle* and not nearly as amusing, very few books had been written on housekeeping; on this topic, the ladies' magazines were more fruitful, for the ever-recurrent servant problem was a favourite theme in the correspondence columns, and occasionally erupted into articles, some of which were extremely revealing. *The Ladies' Companion* (the one to which Eliza Acton contributed) ran a practical guide for the mistress of the house called 'The Housekeeper's Room'; in 1858 the *EDM* itself ran an article entitled 'Sister Sally' on the difficulties of ignorant servant girls[39] (it was not written by Isabella, as might have been the case, but by someone with much greater understanding of the lower classes); and some years previously, the *New Monthly Belle Assemblée* had published an extraordinary series of letters purporting to come from the servants themselves, aptly entitled 'Voices From Below'. It is not impossible that the Beetons saw this because it came out at around the time Frederick Greenwood was working for the magazine. It furnished some memorable illustrations of the kind of disorganization that, among other things, Isabella's book was designed to prevent; part of a letter from a cook, whose lucidity, and literacy also, were well above average, ran as follows:

My mistress is what in perlite society is called wimsical; she makes me more arrands in one Hour than can be counted in two; and then if the meat is not Dun to a Turn, and the vagetables Biled to a T, the consequence is sich Disagreement as need not be *subscribed*, and aught not in a genteel Fammely to eggsist.

She never nose till a Quarter of an hour too late whether the meat is to be rost or biled, or what Pastawry she will have; consequence is, Master being fond of Puncuation, and always home to a minnit within six o'clock, I am frequently reprooved for keping back the Dinner, or sending it up Hunderdun. . . .

I am well awear that Servants are frequently trubblesome people; but surely, maddam, the same may be said (with all dew Difference) of employers. . . .

Maddam, it is not ill disposition but innconsideration which gives rise to all our littel trubbles; and if kind arted Laddies would only put themselves in a servant's plaise for a week, they wood soon manage us better.[40]

She was the kind of cook for whom Isabella's recipes were intended, whose range was limited to roasting and boiling, and whose mastery of grammar, however rudimentary, certainly far exceeded her knowledge of sauces.

Elizabeth Dorling—
Isabella's mother

A sketch of the Dorling family attributed to
Elizabeth Dorling

Sam Beeton

Isabella aged about 26

A fashion plate from the *Englishwoman's Domestic Magazine*

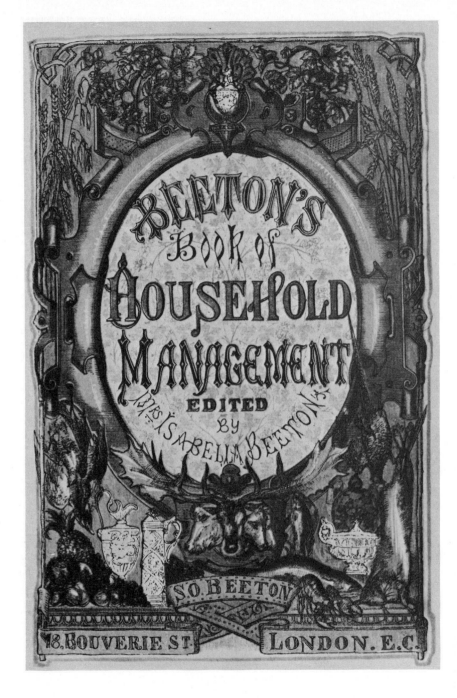

The original title page of *Household Management*

Mount Pleasant Greenhithe

In the garden—Isabella standing with baby Orchart

Mrs Browne and her son Meredith

XV

JOURNALISM

———— ◈ ————

In 1858,[1] the year after Isabella began her research, Lucy went to stay at Pinner and formed a very unfavourable opinion of Sam; and it is not difficult to see that from a child's point of view, his behaviour might well seem less than gracious, since he had gone to work before she came down in the mornings, and had frequently not returned by the time she went to bed. As breakfast was so early, it was sent up to her in her room; her daughter-in-law, Mrs Philip Smiles, says that she never forgot how she was given a vase with flowers freshly cut from the garden each morning—and indeed, to an inmate of the Grand Stand, the whole idea of breakfast in bed must have seemed the height of luxury. Then, during the day, Lucy found that instead of leading the leisured life she associated with being a wife, her sister spent her time at her desk and in the kitchen with the servants testing recipes. Nancy Spain tells the story of how one day a currant cake failed to rise, and Isabella exclaimed in exasperation, 'This won't do at all!'[2] (No doubt it was one of the innumerable unsatisfactory recipes sent in by the magazine readers.) The child was also duly shocked by the fact that the Beetons did not go to church on Sundays, and being too young to make the distinction between ritual and belief, took it for granted that Sam was an atheist. She told Bessie afterwards that so far as she could see, Isabella had a miserable time and she never altered this view, despite her own marital experiences—her husband Willy was at least as obsessive about work as Sam, and certainly less easy to live with.

However, in spite of the various unpleasant impressions she took away, it was almost certainly not as a result of this visit that she came to share the general family belief that her sister was prone to miscarriages, for she was only ten and not old enough to know about such things—besides which, Isabella had hardly had time to have any at this stage. This particular rumour must have been put about later, by whom it is impossible to say, just as it is impossible to say whether there was any truth in it; a similar rumour was always current about Elizabeth. Either way, after their first setback, Sam and Isabella were naturally concerned at the interval of over two years which elapsed before the arrival of their next baby—not a very long time on normal reckoning, but a little surprising after the immediate conception of the first. The delay may have had something to do with anxiety and tension, or Isabella's pre-occupation with her book, though medical opinion would not necessarily bear this out. As it happened, however, the timing was convenient, for when the child was born in the autumn of 1859, Isabella had broken the back of her work, which was sufficiently advanced for Sam to be able to announce the first instalment of the book at the end of the year. Thereafter, although it was still nearly two years before it was finished, it no longer monopolized her life.

Like the first, their second son was called Samuel Orchart, after his father—an unlucky name as things turned out, but in his case appropriate, since he seems to have been very like him; at any rate, he was an exceptionally attractive child and captivated everyone who saw him. Of all their babies, none was welcomed by his parents with such profound satisfaction and relief, for by the time their next offspring arrived their pleasure was somewhat overshadowed by their past experiences, and they never had time to enjoy the fourth.

The first publication of *Household Management* followed almost before Isabella had had time to recover from the birth. As with the *Dictionary of Universal Information*, it was brought out in parts before being offered as a volume, which was particularly advantageous because it was unusual, if not as yet unknown, for a cookery book to come out in this way, and the parts were therefore the cheapest sources of recipes on the market; it also ensured that the book was within the means of its most obvious purchasers, the readers of the *Englishwoman's Domestic Magazine*. Each part cost threepence and contained forty-eight pages, complete with illustrations—exactly the same value page for page as the magazine (which was twopence for thirty-two pages). The serial was planned to run for fifteen to eighteen months, depending on length, but as Isabella wrote more than had originally been anticipated, it continued until the volume itself appeared.

Sam promoted it with an enthusiasm such as never before; the first advertisements, which appeared in the Christmas number of the *EDM*, entirely transformed the magazine, for they were printed on a special four-page insert of startling yellow, headed in heavy type:

A NEW AND PRACTICAL WORK

Adapted for every family and one that will save
money every day and last a life-time.

He used a similar selling technique as for the magazines, offering an impressive list of prizes to all those who found subscribers. 'These lists of subscribers will be received . . . at any time during the progress of the book. . . . Each person's list may be kept open as long as desired. . . . The Publishers will send the prizes *immediately* to any person who prepays the subscription. . . .' The prizes were a ten-guinea gold watch for 250 subscribers, a five-guinea gold watch for 125, a silver one for seventy-five, a gold pencil case for fifty, a silver one (or a silk umbrella) for twenty-five, and 'A Beautiful Steel Engraving' for ten. A lengthy description of the book stressed particularly that everything had been personally tested by Mrs Beeton, and that she had covered a far wider range of information than had ever been attempted before.

Isabella was no doubt grateful for his efforts but she was nevertheless extremely nervous; she did not quite share Sam's faith in the power of gold watches and after two and a half years of writing articles she had had enough experience to know that however careful and conscientious she was, there would always be critical readers ready to fly for their pens. Furthermore, she was naturally still doubtful of her ability to write at length, even though she had realized at the outset (or been told by Sam) that the terse style of her articles would have to be expanded, and had done everything in her power to make her work readable— with conspicuous success, as we know. But to her at the time the only reassurance that could have any meaning was the decisive proof of whether the parts would sell. They did, of course. Readers were soon writing in with urgent requests for back parts and replacements; and the confidence this gave her was noticeable in her journalism thereafter, especially when she started writing about fashion a few months later.

This was the winter when Sam moved his offices to the Strand and planned his enlargements of the magazines. He discussed the possibilities for improving the *EDM* with Isabella, who from her own middle-class point of view had always regretted that the magazine lacked the glamour that a fashion feature would have given it. By this time, in fact, it already had one, since besides the Practical Dress Instructor, which scarcely counted as such, a contributor called Mademoiselle Roche had recently added a column of general fashion news along the same lines as those in the ladies' journals; without illustrations, however, it lacked effect, and it seems that it was Isabella, perhaps encouraged by Mlle Roche, who suggested the next stage—the addition of fashion plates. Sam, in his most optimistic mood since his marriage, took up the suggestion with enthusiasm and began making inquiries without delay.

He may have been told of the work of the most talented fashion-plate artist of the day by one of his engravers, a Mr Woods, who gave him a letter of introduction to a colleague in Paris; or he may already have been familiar with a French magazine, *Le Moniteur de la Mode*, in which this artist's work appeared—and, it must be said, once seen, it was irresistible. The maestro was Jules David, a retiring man whose signature was to become familiar to many in this country, but who remained personally unknown even to Sam and Isabella, who were soon among his most important customers. The fact that he worked in France would in previous years have put his designs financially out of reach of the Beetons, but as it happened a new trade agreement was made at just about this time,[3] which meant that importing plates, though still not cheap, was at least a viable proposition.

Le Moniteur de la Mode was an unusual publication. It was produced in Paris but it was intended for an international readership, and was distributed by agents in Spain and America as well as London; until Sam took over the agency, its London base was in Covent Garden. It had a high reputation in fashionable circles, at least in England, where Queen Victoria herself was one of its patrons. The text throughout was in both French and English, though there was very little of it since its sole *raison d'être* was fashion. Each issue contained four large, lustrous, gorgeously-coloured plates by Jules David with accompanying descriptions, and a short story thrown in as a filler. The only other item it contained was a full-sized paper pattern in the form of a sheet about five foot square folded into the magazine, with a dress pattern on one side and an embroidery pattern on the other; neither were cut, so that readers could either cut out one and use it in the ordinary way, or use both by devising some means of tracing the uncut design on to the material. Such patterns were not unusual in France, where they were offered by at least three other contemporary journals, but the idea had never been taken up in England. They were of course the logical development of the Dress Instructor, and needless to say, were no less irresistible to Sam than the plates.

The publisher of *Le Moniteur de la Mode* was a man named Adolphe Goubaud, whom Sam, after some correspondence, finally arranged to visit in Paris at the beginning of March. As it was planned to begin the new features in the May issue of the *EDM*, this, as Isabella admitted, was somewhat later than might have been desired. The delay was presumably made in order to give her time to wean the baby (who would then be six months old) before she went—she being not only included on the trip, but the most important person concerned; for by the time their ideas had progressed to this stage, she had been put in charge of the whole venture.

That this was so is evident from a diary she kept of their brief excursion—a small, neat, leather-bound volume with a slotting flap like a handbag to keep it shut. In it she noted everything they did during the six days they were away, describing their very uncomfortable seventeen-and-a-half hour journey, listing all their calls in connection with the new features, and making a list of what they spent. Very regrettably, but all too typically, she omitted almost everything not strictly factual, so that for the most part it ran more like an expense-account record than the sum of her impressions.

It makes very modest reading, for under her vigilant eye they were remarkably economical, cutting their extras to the minimum possible: they never spent more than two francs on dinner (though it must be said that for this modest sum they got four or five courses, often with wine included); scarcely anything on fares, since in spite of appalling weather, including snow, they walked almost everywhere; and nothing at all on entertainment. On their last evening, M. Goubaud, with whom by this time they were on very friendly terms, gave them tickets for the Théâtre des Varietés: '. . . he told us they were for Tuesday, so took our seats and just after the performance had commenced were very politely turned out and told our tickets were only available for Wednesday. Not worth paying for, so walked about the Boulevards. . . .'

Apart from Sunday, which they spent sight-seeing, this was literally the only occasion during the whole course of their visit when they were not occupied with business. Their first day was entirely taken up with calls. The first was to an English bookseller in the Palais Royal, Mr Fowler, whom Sam was planning to appoint as his agent. Mr Fowler's role was not only to dispatch the plates and patterns to England every month, but also to sell Beeton's publications in Paris; and with this in mind, Sam had brought a large box of books from England, which, typically enough, he had forgotten to register as imports, with the result that they were promptly confiscated until the appropriate documents had been signed and the fee of five francs paid (there had been another muddle at Boulogne over passports, when Isabella had been dumped in the nearest café while he went to see the consul). Their next visit was to another Englishman, a Mr Gowland, whose part in their transactions Isabella did not specify; their third to the key figure in the deal, M. Goubaud, at 92 Rue Richelieu; and a fourth to Mr Meyer, who had something to do with the patterns. During the following days they went to see all of them again, as well as a series of editors and others, and most of the rest of Isabella's time was occupied in Goubaud's offices and workrooms.

Three of their evenings were spent with Fowler, whom she liked—'found Mr Fowler a very agreeable man'—but this was all she had to say about him. Presumably his evenings were free because he was a bachelor, unlike Goubaud and the others. Gowland was an unpleasant, somewhat sinister character, about whom she remarked, unusually tellingly, 'Sam expected every moment to have a rap on the back of his head.' However, she liked his wife, in contrast to Meyer's, whom she described as 'a fat, dirty old woman'. Of the Goubauds she said nothing, which was a pity for they were to become the most valuable of all their business colleagues—as, over the years, the Beetons became theirs. Sam and Adolphe struck up a deep and permanent friendship; five years later, Sam described Goubaud as 'one of my best friends and the best of men', and fourteen years later he invited him to stay with him in London: '. . . he looks thin but is well and is doing gymnastic exercises every day for an hour and then jumps into a cold bath [evidently this was not an exclusively English habit]. His three little girls wanted to come to England with him. . . .'

To Isabella, Mme Goubaud was as important a link in the chain as her husband. Like her English counterpart, she played a major part in her husband's business; almost certainly, it was she who supplied the text for *Le Moniteur de la Mode*, and probably the translations as well, and in the course of a long career she wrote a number of books on fashion, dressmaking, embroidery, and knitting. As part of the Goubaud-Beeton deal, she received and fulfilled all the orders for patterns, and later on other items as well, which readers were instructed to address directly to her; by the end of the 'sixties the English side of her business was doing so well that a London office was set up either at or near the Goubauds' former agency in Covent Garden. In addition, she sent Isabella full descriptions of all the clothes illustrated, and a monthly newsletter covering the Paris fashions as a whole. This extremely efficient system continued for as long as the *EDM* existed, even through the siege of Paris, when the fashion news-letter had to be sent by balloon.

The only two people Isabella described with any degree of feeling were an insinuating, shabby, but cultivated doctor whom they met on the train on the way out, and an impressive old man with long white hair called Jules Tardieu, who told her he had been translating Tennyson, 'which he said he found very difficult'—this presumably struck a chord in her as a fellow-translator. The first man, Dr Levison, disgusted her by trying to pick up Sam. 'Before we had been seated on our journey to Folkeston ¼ of an hour he told me he had taken a great fancy to Sam; can't tolerate that sort of thing; he seemed endeavouring

to fasten himself.' Unfortunately for her, however, he was 'of a
very intelligent turn of mind', and kept up 'an incessant conversation about books etc.' all the way to Paris, which Sam, tickled
and no doubt flattered, could not resist encouraging, leaving
Isabella to stare disapprovingly at the flat, desolate countryside
out of the window.

Despite having spent three years continuously cooking and
writing about food, Isabella was not very forthcoming on the
subject. She displayed no curiosity about French cooking, and
the only comments she made about their dinners were 'nice',
'tolerably nice', and once, when they had dined with Fowler,
who obviously went to considerable trouble to entertain them
well, 'beautiful'. They were as conservative as possible in their
choice of menu, and had chicken every night, almost always
preceded by vegetable soup and *fricandeau* of veal, and followed
by Russian or apple Charlotte. If anyone stands as proof of the
maxim that a gourmet is born and not made, it is Isabella. As
always, they ate an enormous breakfast, invariably consisting of
steaks or chops, eggs, and potatoes; then they had a light
lunch and a very early dinner—in contrast to the French custom
of a large lunch and late dinner. But the French in Paris were
used to English eating habits, and the only disadvantage (if it was
one) was that when the Beetons dined in their hotel their meal was
served in the coffee room rather than the restaurant. Isabella did
not mention asking anyone for recipes, but some of those labelled
'French' in the book may well have come from the people they
met.

The thing which comes across most vividly from her brisk
pages was their energy and cheerfulness. They trudged round the
icy streets all day from interview to interview, greeting everyone
with the same eagerness and enthusiasm, and were out until late
every evening; and even then, despite being tired out, Sam went
for a run round the block every night 'to warm himself'. Isabella
kept up the diary on subsequent trips—to Ireland that summer
and to Paris and Germany several years later—and the outstanding
impression was always the same. Similarly, her enthusiasm for the
new project was unbounded, and her attention to every aspect of
it characteristically keen: she saw the fashion plates being coloured
by teams of girls (the usual system was for the pictures to be
passed from hand to hand, each person painting in one colour

only); criticized the patterns for 'b—work' (Berlin woolwork): 'did not like them much, but as there is so little time must content ourselves with them for the first month'; and, under Sam's supervision, wrote out the contract with M. Goubaud. On the last page of the diary was her costing of the patterns, from which she concluded, after adding up all the components—paper, gum, composition, editing, and engravings—that '12000 just pays'. This was very promising when considered in relation to the *EDM*'s circulation, which by this time was approaching sixty thousand. It was very natural that, with any young woman's excitement when confronted with beautiful clothes plus the near certainty of doing good business, her main interest thereafter was transferred from housekeeping to fashion. As with *Household Management*, however, she approached her task exceptionally shrewdly and never lost sight of the practical needs of her readers, who as well as not being able to afford dresses from Paris had never before set eyes on a full-sized paper sewing pattern.

This trip marked the beginning of the second phase of her professional career. For the first four years of her marriage she had worked as Sam's subordinate, writing the features he asked her to write in the way he suggested; her book too had been formed and master-minded by him. But with the introduction of the fashion features in May, her status changed. She became as potent a force in her own sphere (as well as influencing his) as he—and her sphere now encompassed the whole domestic side of the magazine, for she not only had charge of all the Paris pages but retained the editorship of her original columns. This transformation must have had its effect on every aspect of her life, including her marriage; until then, in spite of Sam's liberal ideas, she had not been able to shake off the notion of him as her superior, but now she effectively assumed an equal position in their partnership. She was twenty-four, and with her priorities established and her confidence as a journalist increasing, not to mention her experiences of birth and death, she had advanced very far from the girl he had married. She was not merely independent but forceful and assured, ready to make her own decisions and carry them out regardless.

As fashion editor, she no longer worked as a contributor from home but took her place in the new Strand offices. To the amazement and indignation of the other passengers, who were unaccustomed to the inhibiting presence of a lady at such an hour, she travelled to town with Sam on the commuters' train in the mornings, upright, immaculate, and purposeful. If she was still modest about her literary skill, she did not take long to discover that the job of administrator suited her abilities exactly; had she not felt sure of herself, she certainly would not have taken on additional and much heavier responsibilities the very next year. She was completely undeterred by the oddity of her position as a woman in the office (in Ireland that summer she was quite happy at finding herself the only woman in a restaurant: 'Dined at the Table d'Hote which was very crowded indeed, I was the only female there'). As in any such office, all Sam's regular staff were male; Mlle Roche and a woman artist he sometimes used, Marianne Dear, almost certainly worked as Isabella had formerly done, from outside. Had it not been for Sam's popularity, and the fact that she had met his senior employees before, her incursion might have caused something of a trauma; but apparently, partly perhaps because of her own firmness, she was assimilated without fuss.

The new features transformed the magazine almost out of recognition. The plates were not so impressive as those in *Le Moniteur de la Mode* because, although the size of the *EDM* was increased, it was still not big enough, as *Le Moniteur* was, to display David's work to maximum advantage; but the draughtsmanship was delicate, the colours bright, and the compositions gay and animated. Each picture showed two or three plump, rosy-cheeked, innocent-looking young ladies engaged in appropriate activities—hobnobbing in ballrooms and on terraces, strolling along wind-swept beaches waving tiny parasols, or caressing cherubic children. It is perhaps a tribute to their attractiveness that a great many of the plates have been cut from surviving copies of the magazine.

The text which accompanied them was written by Isabella; Mlle Roche, thus rendered superfluous, was swept abruptly into the background—but not out of sight, for it would seem that she continued to work for the Beetons: initials which were presumably hers appeared thereafter in both the *EDM* and *The Queen* —though not under articles on fashion. Isabella's fashion copy was the very model of cool professionalism: thanks to Mme Goubaud's newsletters, she wrote as though she lived in Paris, attending all the fashionable functions, making regular visits to the leading dressmakers (this was before the days of the great couturiers), and commenting on the smartest outfits to be seen in the streets—whereas in fact she only went to France once a year, in the late summer, when the new designs for the autumn could be seen. The ludicrous impracticality of the fashions, which at the time she wrote were becoming more and more fantastic as the crinoline grew ever huger, did not temper her delight in the least, perhaps because she herself never seemed to notice their inconvenience—though she did once or twice suggest that for aesthetic reasons it was time for the crinoline to go. Her first article began:

> We have just been inspecting the show-rooms of our first houses, and will describe two or three outdoor garments for the beginning of the fine season. In the first place, for the country and sea-side, we saw a *demi-saison* made of thin grey cloth, in the form of a jacket, with side-pieces. It has a narrow square collar bordered by diminutive fancy trimming; buttons in front as far as the waist. . . . [The accompanying fashion plate showed two ladies in fanciful bonnets with a much be-frilled and be-flounced little girl.] Bonnet of white crepe, with a bunch of feathers at one side. . . . On the right-hand side of the bonnet is a bunch of ostrich feathers, which should be so arranged as to fall a little over the front of the bonnet, and the tips fastened in the cap. . . . Dress of white muslin, with a double shawl of the same material. The dress has seven flounces, each one trimmed with small ruchings of green. . . .[4]

The second outfit was a sophisticated creation in black, white, and violet, the bonnet trimmed with violet poppies. The little girl wore a candy-striped pink and white frock with a wide straw hat.

She took immediately to Mme Goubaud's chic; it was not long before the change in her own appearance was remarked on, for her clothes were a constant topic of conversation among her sisters (who assumed that she had wardrobesful of the latest models, though in reality it would have been unlike her to have spent more on her appearance than most of her readers). She was nevertheless a very indifferent fashion journalist. The same incapacity for chatter that made *Household Management* the master-piece it was rendered it impossible for her to leaven the endless lists of sartorial details which confronted her. It was a necessity for a fashion writer to give detailed descriptions, since without mass production the clothes could not be bought, and readers needed sufficient information to be able to copy them; and this side of her function she fulfilled admirably. But as reading matter, her pages were hard going, and to the modern reader even seem confusing—in contrast to those of her successor on the magazine, whose journalistic touch was as light as Sam's.

For every outfit illustrated in the plates, a pattern was supplied. Isabella's expectations were more than justified, for these patterns turned out to be the most popular, and probably the most profit-able, of all Sam's innovations. She ran them as a separate service rather than incorporating them into the magazine, since although the price of the *EDM* was raised to sixpence, it was still impossible to issue them free, as in *Le Moniteur de la Mode* (which in England cost the considerable sum of 3s 6d). Moreover, as she promptly perceived, perhaps as a result of her experience with cookery, it would have been asking for trouble to sell them in the form of uncut sheets when none of her customers knew how to use them. They were therefore sold on request ready cut and tacked for 3s 6d, the same price as *Le Moniteur*. This was undeniably ex-pensive, but the extra labour of cutting and tacking increased the production costs—and almost any price would have seemed a bargain to her English readers, to whom the patterns represented a unique and wonderful offer, placing Parisian designs within their reach for the very first time.

In spite of Isabella's care, there were of course complaints which, although she took them for granted, completely routed Sam. One instance, which occurred a month or so after the service began, was when he opened a letter from a belligerent lady named Sophia Anderson, who was convinced that a jacket pattern had no armhole.

> Commotion in the office of the *Englishwoman*. . . . the Editor and his staff looking like so many monuments of despair. Recovering himself, however, our chief bravely put the bomb in his pocket (with other most kind and compensatory letters, be it gratefully said), and delivered it to the Editress. . . .

Undismayed, but evidently hurt at the ingratitude of Sophia and her friends, she calmly traced the pattern on to some whitey-brown paper: first pinned it together, and then tacked it, showing us triumphantly a little boy's jacket in paper, with armhole, sleeve, and cuff, as complete as possible. So when SOPHIA ANDERSON 'would like to know how it would be possible,' &c., she has only to write. . . .[5]

The eventual Paris deal included not only the coloured fashion plates, but also coloured needlework patterns. This was an extra Sam had not originally envisaged but the attraction had been obvious to Isabella, despite the fact that she 'did not like them much' (the Berlin woolwork design was one of them). But the popularity of needlework was such that they could scarcely fail; they continued to be a feature of the magazine for the rest of its existence, and if the number torn out is any indication, were even more popular than the plates.

Though the sections she edited directly were only a part of the magazine, her influence extended over the whole of it—as it was bound to do, though she and Sam may not have been aware of it. Some modification would have taken place in any case, since a sixpenny readership required something a little different from a twopenny one; for one thing, the women who bought it tended to be older and were therefore more likely to be married. Besides this, it was natural that the magazine's trend should follow the more mature outlook of its editor and (now) editress. But it was certainly partly due to her that, though it still retained some of its original flavour, it was no longer so unconventional: the critical articles that had once been one of its chief characteristics did not cease but over the next few years they were less in evidence, while drawing-room features such as poetry and book reviews were given more prominence. The book reviews were written with considerable sparkle by Sam (who had previously contributed them occasionally, but now included them every month). 'We have been making a little calculation and have discovered that since the publication of his last work, Mr. Trollope has been producing fiction at the rate of four chapters a week,'[6] was his rather dry comment on *Castle Richmond*, which came out that summer.

He also began his second correspondence feature, the 'Englishwoman's Conversazione', which from the very beginning was the life and soul of the magazine. The correspondence covered any subject, from slavery and education (which was still, as it always remained, one of Sam's main preoccupations) to the most trivial questions of dress and cosmetics. His feminist views were kept firmly in the background, but his delight in the foibles of the opposite sex was very much to the fore and the result was a rollicking hotch-potch of opinion, sentiment, fun, humour, and admonishment. The latter came sometimes from Isabella, who acted as his unofficial fashion and beauty consultant, and who, having no patience for the sillier obsessions of her sex, came up on occasion with some very deflating bits of advice. To 'EVA', for instance, who wanted to know how to make her cheeks look rosy, she said tartly, 'Water and friction—why should we not at once say, a good wash?'[7] But she was more sympathetic towards a reader who suffered from freckles, which were considered most unfortunate, and supplied three treatments, one of which she recommended as the latest remedy from Paris.

THE QUEEN

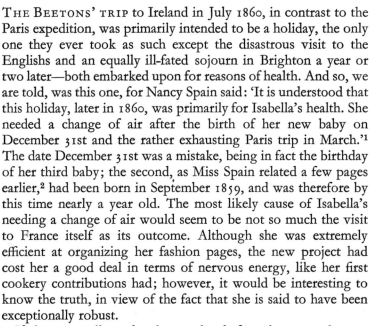

THE BEETONS' TRIP to Ireland in July 1860, in contrast to the
Paris expedition, was primarily intended to be a holiday, the only
one they ever took as such except the disastrous visit to the
Englishs and an equally ill-fated sojourn in Brighton a year or
two later—both embarked upon for reasons of health. And so, we
are told, was this one, for Nancy Spain said: 'It is understood that
this holiday, later in 1860, was primarily for Isabella's health. She
needed a change of air after the birth of her new baby on
December 31st and the rather exhausting Paris trip in March.'[1]
The date December 31st was a mistake, being in fact the birthday
of her third baby; the second, as Miss Spain related a few pages
earlier,[2] had been born in September 1859, and was therefore by
this time nearly a year old. The most likely cause of Isabella's
needing a change of air would seem to be not so much the visit
to France itself as its outcome. Although she was extremely
efficient at organizing her fashion pages, the new project had
cost her a good deal in terms of nervous energy, like her first
cookery contributions had; however, it would be interesting to
know the truth, in view of the fact that she is said to have been
exceptionally robust.

If she was really under the weather before she went, she was
very soon cured. This holiday, spent exploring the mountains of
Killarney, was perhaps the happiest time in her life—the wild,
dramatic scenery impressed and exhilarated her as nothing else
could have done. Every day she commented on it with renewed,
if scantily expressed, pleasure: 'Very much delighted. . . . Lovely
views of the surrounding country. . . . Sat for about ½ hour on the
edge of a rock overhanging the lake and admired the scenery.' For
her, the highlight of the holiday was when she and Sam climbed
Mangerton Mountain, the highest peak in south-west Ireland:

Started with pony about 9.30—Sam and I rode in turns. . . .
Very beautiful view from the punch bowl, but nothing to be
compared to that on top of the mountain. . . . From there the
view was superb of Kenmare Bay, Dingle Bay, Cork mountains. . . . Now we come to something far grander and more
majestic than anything we have yet seen . . . a series of rough,
rugged mountains with a dark stream at the bottom. From
some points it looked like a bottomless pit. Climbed down
again . . . arrived at the Hotel rather tired. Altogether the most
beautiful sight in Killarney.

Sam's appreciation of the countryside was scarcely less keen:

. . . the soft afternoon sun lying warm upon the hilltops, the
abundant foliage bordering the lake that lies sparkling below,
and the rippling of the water as the wind breathes gently over
its bosom.[3]

Holiday though it was, he made full journalistic use of it the
next year, when he wrote an extended description of Killarney in
an account of Queen Victoria's visit to Ireland in *The Queen*.
In spite of their delight in their surroundings, neither of them
abandoned their work, nor missed any opportunity of furthering
their projects. On the first wet morning (Friday the thirteenth)
they settled themselves into the ample chairs of the hotel lounge
to write their monthly copy for the *EDM*; Sam advised a shy
young man on the best way of proposing marriage, while Isabella,
appropriately, wrote about what to wear on holiday. 'As regards
travelling apparel, the most indispensable item is the HAT. . . .'[4]
This she decreed should be trimmed with enormous feathers—
preferably ostrich, though at a pinch pheasant would do; more
practically, she recommended dresses in dust colour, edged with
a darker shade of binding. Twelve days later, on 25 July (over a
year before they appeared), she sent off her instructions for the
coloured plates of *Management*. Probably, though again she did
not say so in her diary, she also picked up a few recipes: on the
way home, they stayed in Cork for five days and visited several
acquaintances—the Parrys, the Perriers, and Mr Murray—who
were presumably among the friends she referred to in the Preface,
and they spent several days in Bangor at an hotel very efficiently

run by a Miss Roberts, who might well have contributed something; otherwise, there was nobody in Wales they knew. It
rained almost continuously, and Isabella's chief interest was the
tubular bridge over the Menai Straits. 'Heard a train rattle
through, felt the vibration immensely; it entered the tube the
other side. . . . Examined the inside, were told about the expansion
and contraction of the iron; according to the state of the weather.'
From Bangor they went to Chester ('our impression of Chester
rather unfavourable—black, gloomy, and very dirty'), where the
diary ended for lack of space.

Isabella naturally took a particular interest in anything connected with her book. She made professional-sounding comments
about all their hotels: the Railway Hotel in Killarney was large
and comfortable, with 'good accommodation for ladies' and a
supply of guides and ponies for sightseers. 'The view not so good
as from the Hotels on the Lake but in every other respect much
better.' The Imperial in Cork she pronounced 'well managed'—
despite the fact that it was very full because of the Cork cattle
show, which she duly visited, and, thanks to her study of Morton,
found extremely interesting. She did not make a note of all their
menus, as she had in France, though she approved of the *table
d'hôte* dinners 'conducted quite in the French fashion'; she did,
however, list all the extras they consumed on a heavily crossed
out page at the back of the diary. They ordered beer and ginger
beer nearly every day, and sometimes a pint of sherry, but very
seldom wine. For breakfast they always had cold meat and boiled
eggs.

In spite of all this, perhaps simply because she was enjoying
herself so much, she never let business interfere with pleasure and
entered wholeheartedly into the spirit of the holiday—in contrast
to Sam, who fretted continually, plagued the local post offices for
parcels from London,—presumably containing books—devoured
the new issues of the *BOM* and the *EDM* with neurotic eagerness,
did the rounds of the booksellers in Dublin, and arranged their
leisurely return journey through Wales and the Midlands in order
to visit bookshops there as well. One way and another, he probably did better in terms of business out of this holiday than
from either of the ostensibly business trips they later made to
Europe.

From every other point of view, they seem to have been

absolutely at one throughout the entire three weeks they were away, and never left each other's side, except in Cork, where an amusing but very typical sequence took place. They set off together to see the prison on Spike Island, but discovered on landing, as they should have realized beforehand, that women were not allowed inside the prison. Sam, quite unconcerned, passed a long, interesting afternoon being shown round by two garrulous priests, while Isabella 'walked around the ramparts and enjoyed the view of the harbour, which was very full of shipping'. The next day she took her revenge by arranging to visit the Convent of the Isle (where men were not allowed) and spent a morning of unparalleled boredom: 'saw over it—the cells, the refectory, corridors &c.'. As it happened, she met one of the prison chaplains a day or two later, and had 'a long conversation' with him.

It was more than a year before the chief products of the Irish holiday came to light. Isabella's professional attention during that time was concentrated on fashion, and her interest at home was taken up by the development of her son, who was learning to walk and talk. Sam's most notable activity was the launching of *Beeton's Christmas Annual*, which continued, though latterly not in the same form, for the next sixteen years, and was probably the most profitable of all his publications. The idea was based on the annuals of the 'twenties and 'thirties, though his version was not much like them: they had been expensive volumes of miscellaneous trivia collected from—and bought by—the fashionable and famous, whereas his was a mixture of fairly humble Christmas entertainment for the family at the bargain price of a shilling— and it really was a bargain, with something for everyone: the first contained stories, a burlesque, an almanack, Chinese and Japanese puzzles, and 'Three hundred new tricks, Conundrums, Rebuses, Charades, Enigmas, Acrostics, Pictorial Proverbs, Hand-shadows, and Hieroglyphics.'

1861, however, was dominated by the appearance of his second women's journal, *The Queen*, which was launched after months of planning on 7 September. It was quite unlike the *EDM* in both format and intention: it was not a magazine, but a weekly newspaper, and aimed at a much better heeled, more sophisticated public. Although announced as a 'Ladies' Journal', its tone and wide-ranging subject matter were more akin to an ordinary review than to anything hitherto published specifically for women, and it was widely read by men as well. It is the only one of Sam's periodicals to survive to the present, and though it long ago ceased to be a newspaper and became an ordinary magazine, the original flavour is still perceptible.

It would have been impossible for Sam, already editing the *BOM* and the *EDM*, to give a third journal the same kind of continuous personal attention he had always devoted to the other two, particularly one of such a challenging nature; another editor was clearly required, and the obvious choice was Frederick Greenwood, who was accordingly appointed. It was Greenwood's big break, and he excelled himself, particularly during the first months; thereafter, the paper's quality dropped slightly, partly no doubt because neither editor nor proprietor had had previous experience of the pressures of weekly publication (which Isabella, with intuitive knowledge, assessed realistically from the outset), and also because between them they set a standard of liveliness and stringency which it would have been almost impossible to maintain over an extended period. The early issues, however, were superlative, with all the best qualities of the Conversazione and the *Gazette*; and their impact was enhanced by the novelty of the paper's large size, which was particularly advantageous in the matter of illustration, since it was possible to run really big pictures (the format may have been inspired by a similarly laid out but not similarly illustrated publication, the *Lady's Newspaper*).

Its function, apart from providing entertainment, was to supply a news sheet for every woman who wanted to keep herself alert and well informed and appear intelligent in society. The contents fell roughly under four headings, all pointing more or less in this direction: Society news; news of the arts; subjects of general interest, which besides giving the paper its wide appeal served as useful dinner-party conversation-starters; and women's features—at first only fashion and needlework, but later cookery and housekeeping as well.

There were several columns of Society news and gossip, but although the intention was to give the same sort of extensive, exclusive coverage as that for which the magazine is now known, they were extremely scanty in the early days, for the good reason that neither Sam nor Greenwood nor any of their friends had access to that sort of world. They were evidently well aware of this shortcoming, for by the next year there was a considerable improvement, but it was not until the paper fell into other hands that this side of its potential was fully developed. However, despite the lack of Society information, a good deal of space was given to the royal family, as the magazine's title promised; hence the long, profusely illustrated report of the Queen's Irish tour, and the gift which was offered with the first issue—an oval photograph of Victoria, which Sam claimed to be the first photographic portrait ever issued with a printed journal. It was taken from a photograph by Mayall, who was described in the *Athenaeum*, the leading London literary weekly, as 'supreme in portraits, and . . . unrivalled for breadth, manner, and finish. Either from the character of his sitters, or the taste of his composition, his portraits appear more dignified, self-possessed, and aristocratic than those of any other photographer.'[5] Apparently Victoria concurred with this opinion, since she sat for him several times, with pleasing results; the portrait used by Sam was extremely flattering, and did credit to all concerned. At the beginning of November, only a week or two before the onset of his fatal attack of typhoid, a companion portrait of Albert was issued.

It was almost certainly this emphasis on royalty which gave Isabella her otherwise inexplicable fascination for the Princess Royal, Crown Princess of Prussia, who formed the chief subject of her diary when she visited Berlin. In the second issue of *The Queen*, a large engraving of the Princess's children (which made them look almost unbelievably obnoxious) was accompanied by the following comments:

> BERLIN has many attractions, and is peculiarly interesting to Englishwomen, for it immediately calls up in their minds that mixture of loyal devotion and affectionate respect which, for many years, our beloved Sovereign and her family have completely possessed. Berlin is the home of our Princess Royal.
>
> The Princess's palace has a handsome exterior . . . everything has been done that was calculated to make the first daughter of England feel 'at home' in her new abode. . . . In truth, the Princess is *sehr gut*, so well beloved by everybody, say Berliners, Potsdamers, and all,—and the information is given with such evident satisfaction,—that there is no more doubt about her

permanent popularity than there is about the love owned by our own gracious Sovereign. . . .[6]

Isabella's observations echoed this: 'She is very much liked in Berlin, and seems quite to have won the people's hearts. . . . Every time she goes out in her carriage everybody takes off their hat and much more enthusiasm is displayed whenever she is seen in public than for any other member of the Prussian royal family.' And she dragged Sam round all three of the Princess's palaces, where everything was indeed 'quite in the English style', with plaid furnishings as at Balmoral, and 'beautiful needlework chairs given her by various English young ladies'.

The arts reviews were lengthy and informed, covering concerts, plays, exhibitions, and books in much the same way as their modern counterparts. The first issue contained a review of *The Last Travels of Ida Pfeiffer*, the famous Victorian woman traveller who did not, however, embark on her writing and travelling career until her husband was dead and her children grown up. In the next was a report of two very successful music festivals held at Birmingham and Hereford; and a few weeks later came a highly critical review of current publications, probably written by Greenwood himself, comparing the latest issues of the six leading journals of the day, from which the recently founded *Temple Bar* emerged most favourably.

The paper's unique, occasionally brilliant touch stemmed chiefly from the quality and originality of the general features. Every week brought something amusing, startling, or controversial: the first item of the first issue set out to shock with an article about the most elegant way to commit suicide, and in the second was a long report entitled 'Sweet Green' on the poisonous properties of a fashionable green dye, which was alleged to contain enough arsenic per ball dress to kill 15,000 people. Not all the articles were frivolous, however; among the regular features was a Mayhew-type series on the lives and hardships of the poor (possibly contributed by James Greenwood), beginning with a generously illustrated account of the homes of the Spitalfields silk weavers. There were many other socially conscious items besides, not forgetting the women's cause, which, though not pursued conspicuously, was by the very nature of the paper rather more in evidence than in the sixpenny version of the *EDM*.

Besides full-length articles, numerous miscellaneous tit-bits were scattered about, as, for example, a column called 'Notes and News', which was the adult equivalent of the *BOM*'s 'Facts, Fancies, and Phenomena'. Early entries included such curiosities as the following:

THE COMMISSIONERS FOR THE EXHIBITION OF 1862 have been asked for permission to exhibit 'specimens illustrative of the seven ages in the life of a flea.' . . .

ELEVEN OSTRICHES have been hatched at Marseilles, ten of which are alive and well. It is the first time the experiment has succeeded, though it has often been tried since the French occupation of Algeria. . . .

A TRADESMAN AT BODMIN courted a domestic servant during the temporary absence of a young lady to whom he was engaged to be married, but before the return of his fianceé he discarded the abigail. A few days ago he received a slice of bride-cake by post, which emitted a peculiar odour, and was found to contain enough phosphorus to kill four persons. The discarded servant-girl has been discovered to be the sender of the poisoned cake.[7]

The last item could as well have featured in 'The Black Book'— a crime report, which was unquestionably the cleverest idea in the whole paper. The crimes were at least as sensational—and in general rather more interesting—than might be the case now and made an extraordinary record of human eccentricity, malevolence, and despair; insofar as that they were written up absolutely straightforwardly, with no moralizing or dwelling on unsavoury details, they were presented responsibly, much as the cases were treated in the courts. A couple of brief examples (many items, especially the more horrific ones, tended to be extremely long) read thus:

At Westminster Police-court last week, a servant-girl charged her mistress, Mrs. Wright, wife of a corn-merchant in Clerkenwell, with having used threatening language to her. During the hearing the complainant was very impudent, and it came out that her master was in the habit of neglecting his wife and taking the servant to balls, concerts, &c., she being accustomed to wear her mistress's clothes. The girl said: 'I have been in danger for the past six months from the defendent, and so has her husband, poor fellow.' (A laugh.) The case was dismissed, amid loud hisses and tokens of disgust.[8]

A Mr. John Grayson Farquhar, of Grange-road, Smallheath, shot, on the evening of Thursday week, a girl of 20, named Elizabeth Brooks, who had been living under his roof as housekeeper, and had borne him a child, who is dead. Mr. Farquhar is supposed to have been drinking when he shot the poor creature; but he was not drunk. He knelt down beside her dead body, kissed her many times, and said, 'Oh, Bessie! Why did you tell me what you did? You knew I loved you.' He said, 'Policeman, I took her to town today to buy her a silk dress, and in my absence I found her talking to a young man;' adding that it had been his intention to marry her. To the last, the man seemed to feel severely the cruelty of what he had done. . . .[9]

The women's features were under Isabella's editorship, and at first consisted only of a page of needlework designs and a coloured fashion plate by Jules David, as in the *EDM*, except that the plate could not be bound into the newspaper and had to be issued as a separate supplement. Both features were written by her, and, making full allowance for the weekly nature of the work, she very wisely kept her copy to a minimum, relying for effect on David's skill and the large, handsome pictures and diagrams which illustrated the embroidery. She simply wrote a straightforward description of the clothes illustrated and a few sentences of comment on each needlework design, plus the directions, which she laid out like recipes, starting with an exact list of all the materials required. The opening number featured three designs, including that article so characteristic of the era, a d'oyley: 'Materials required to make one d'oyley: $3\frac{1}{4}$ yards of the best white linen tape, $\frac{3}{8}$ inch wide; $\frac{3}{4}$ yard white cotton fringe, $1\frac{1}{4}$ inch wide; 1 reel boar's head cotton, No. 20.' Nothing could have been briefer or more to the point than her remarks: 'Tapework will be found useful for many purposes besides that shown in our illustration, as every piece of which it is composed is made separately, and consequently can be enlarged to any size the worker may require. Another advantage is that all the materials used are well adapted for washing, and if the work be strongly made, it will last some considerable time.'[10]

But the public's insatiable appetite for needlework, which was a reflection of the number of idle hours they had to spend sitting in the drawing room, led almost immediately to the extension of one page to several. These were incorporated into the supplement, which only a month later had already swollen to four pages (by this time, similar supplements were also being issued with the *EDM*). The fashion text, too, was expanded, and presently included additional columns headed 'Dress' and 'Parisian Fashions'. The cookery articles were presented in epistolary form, which meant that they were considerably longer than Isabella's tightly written *EDM* articles (which ceased at about the time *The Queen* was launched), and went under the nostalgic title 'My Great-Aunt's Receipt Book'—a name suspiciously reminiscent of Aunt Deborah of *The Ladies' Treasury*. The household management feature, 'Household Economy and Domestic Science', was introduced at the beginning of 1863.

Of course, all this could not possibly have been written by Isabella; and in fact very little of it was, for she was by then in charge of a sizeable department, with at least two, and probably more, contributors; although the column on 'Dress' was at this time written by her, the French fashion piece was signed 'Eliane De Marsi' and some of the needlework was written up by a woman called 'H.B.L.'. She certainly had nothing to do with the cookery features, which were neither written with her authority nor contained her recipes. Even so, despite the assistance of staff and her own determination to keep the volume of her work within reasonable bounds, her responsibilities on *The Queen* were her principal professional preoccupation for the next two years, and doubtless would have continued to be so; but the strain of maintaining the paper eventually proved too much for Sam's resources, both financially and in terms of staff, and he sold it to the proprietors of *The Ladies' Newspaper*, further down the Strand at No 346, in July 1863. From his, and even more from Greenwood's point of view, this was a pity, but taking his business overall, it was unquestionably for the best, since if he had kept it, all his other publications would have deteriorated in the long run instead of becoming increasingly successful. *The Queen* was a brief and brilliant interlude in his life—and happily was carried on by its new owners in much the same manner as he had conceived it.

The new journal threw the publication of Isabella's book as a volume completely into the shade. As a result of the extra months required to finish publication of the monthly parts, it appeared almost simultaneously with the first issue of *The Queen*, and in the general excitement, Isabella herself probably did not take much note of the occasion. The readers of *The Queen*, on the other hand, had every reason to notice it, for long advertisements, paired with trailers for Sam's latest project, *Beeton's Book of Garden Management*, which was announced as 'an almost necessary pendant to the "Book of Household Management" just completed under Mrs. Beeton's editorship', proclaimed that it was now on sale and could be bought from 'all bookshops in town and country', price 7s 6d.

XVII

THE BOOK

ISABELLA'S AVOWED REASON for writing her book was given in the Preface:

> What moved me, in the first instance, to attempt a work like this, was the discomfort and suffering I had seen brought upon men and women by household mismanagement. I have always thought that there is no more fruitful source of family discontent than a housewife's badly-cooked dinners and untidy ways. Men are now so well served out of doors,—at their clubs, well-ordered taverns, and dining houses, that in order to compete with the attractions of these places, a mistress must be thoroughly conversant with the theory and practice of cookery, as well as perfectly conversant with all the other arts of making and keeping a comfortable home.

It was her inclusion of all the other arts which most obviously distinguished her work from that of her rivals, for in spite of the excellence of Soyer and Acton's books, neither they nor any other recent publication covered domestic management as a whole, whereas she dealt in the greatest detail with both housekeeping and the personal requirements of a lady; and the rapid enlargement of the middle classes and their exaggerated love of domesticity meant that by the middle of the century such instruction was sorely needed. There were countless women whose husbands, like Henry, had made good, who suddenly found themselves pitched into the position of ladies without any idea of how to live up to their new status; and, on the other hand, there was a veritable army of Boarding-school Misses, who were in the same position *vis-à-vis* housekeeping as Isabella when she got married.

The first chapter of the book was on the mistress of the household and was aimed primarily at the *nouveaux-riches* wives. The cookery section followed, and the last chapters instructed the reader how to run establishments of all sizes and to deal with almost every type of domestic problem conceivable, from doing the laundry to tending the sick. It is not easy to see quite why Isabella separated the mistress from her servants, unless it was that she feared that the latter section would be found dull. But in fact, largely because both the first and last sections were, of necessity, written from first-hand research and personal experience, they were from a literary point of view much the best.

The first chapter was the one to which she had given most thought, and, probably, a disproportionate amount of time. It displayed her common sense more advantageously than anything else she ever wrote, and gave the whole book, which might otherwise have seemed rather disjointed, its special character. It was in effect a concise but comprehensive essay on the art of being a lady—which by definition the mistress of the house was supposed to be.

In this chapter, Isabella displayed the same outstanding virtue as she did as a cookery writer. She covered every detail, did not leave even the most obvious points unsaid and began unhesitatingly with fundamentals. Her first injunction to the mistress was that she should get up early.

EARLY RISING IS ONE OF THE MOST ESSENTIAL QUALITIES which enter into good Household Management, as it is not only the parent of health, but of innumerable other advantages. Indeed, when a mistress is an early riser, it is almost certain that her house will be orderly and well-managed. On the contrary, if she remain in bed till a late hour, then the domestics, who, as we have before observed, invariably partake somewhat of their mistress's character, will surely become sluggards.[1]

And the second was that she should be clean: 'Cold or tepid baths should be employed every morning.'[2] The mistress was compared to the commander of an army; on her depended the tenor and efficiency of her entire household, and only if she herself set a good example could she expect good conduct and hard work from others. 'Her spirit will be seen through the whole establishment; and in just proportion as she performs her duties intelligently and thoroughly, so will her domestics follow in her path.'[3] This, as she was ready to admit, was a rather formidable prospect —but she was careful to stress that it was not as bad as it might appear at first sight, since it did not mean that the housewife had to give up any of her own pleasures and amusements (provided, of course, that they were 'proper', as Isabella obviously assumed they would be).

If the brighter side of a lady's life in the home required emphasis, it needed even more when it came to her conduct outside it, for social life, it seemed, was hedged about with limitations and frustrations in every direction. Nothing could have been more Victorian, nor more consistent with her own nature, than Isabella's inhibiting comments on friendship.

FRIENDSHIPS SHOULD NOT BE HASTILY FORMED, nor the heart given, to every new-comer. There are ladies who uniformly smile at, and approve everything and everybody, and who possess neither the courage to reprehend vice, nor the generous warmth to defend virtue. The friendship of such persons is without attachment, and their love without affection or even preference.[4]

Her discussion of the rules of etiquette sounded equally forbidding, but this was not entirely her fault, since, as others had found before her, it was a forbidding, and very complex, topic. The proliferation of formalities with which the more privileged classes surrounded themselves, and the degree of importance they attached to them, meant that Isabella had to go into every situation in considerable detail in order to give a practical guide. This was, perhaps, irritating to some of her more intellectual and sophisticated readers, but, as usual, she did not waste words and greatly simplified the subject by her orderly, logical approach. The customs connected with morning calls, for instance, which were often a source of confusion to the uninitiated, she managed to reduce to a perfectly reasonable set of rules clearly designed to protect the hostess from undue embarrassment or inconvenience. These calls (which, curiously enough, were made in the afternoon and not in the morning) were never supposed to last more than about twenty minutes, just long enough for a polite exchange of compliments but not so long as to inconvenience the called-upon. Since they were not staying long, visitors were not expected to take off their outdoor clothes (which, though Isabella did not say so, would have caused unnecessary trouble to the domestics); nor was it good manners to dress too elaborately (here she laid down the time-honoured maxim that it was better to be under-dressed than over-dressed). Perhaps most welcome of all to the gauche or inexperienced were her excellent, and surprisingly perceptive, remarks on the difficulties of leaving: 'When [other] visitors are announced, it is well to retire as soon as possible, taking care to let it appear that their arrival is not the cause. . . .'[5]

She was also perceptive when it came to the social aspect of giving dinner parties—to her, by far the most important element of such occasions. Her memories of Epsom still fresh, she regarded boredom as the worst affliction anyone could be asked to endure, and went to some lengths to explain how it could be avoided. The choice of amusing guests was obviously the first consideration, but that in itself was not necessarily enough; evidently, she had also observed the unfortunate consequences of throwing together too many people too fond of the sound of their own voices. 'Care should be taken by the hostess in the selection of the invited guests, that they should be suited to each other. Much also of the pleasure of a dinner-party will depend on the arrangement of the guests at table, so as to form a due admixture of talkers and listeners, the grave and the gay.'[6] At the same time, she was acutely conscious of the difficulty of getting the party going; pre-dinner cocktails had not yet been invented, but she would certainly have been among the first to welcome them.

THE HALF-HOUR BEFORE DINNER has always been considered as the great ordeal through which the mistress . . . will either pass with flying colours, or, lose many of her laurels. The anxiety to receive her guests,—her hope that all will be present in due time [lateness, she had already very firmly declared, was *not* fashionable],—her trust in the skill of her cook, and the attention of the domestics, all tend to make these few minutes a trying time. The mistress, however, must display no kind of agitation, but show her tact in suggesting light and cheerful subjects of conversation, which will be much aided by the introduction of any particular new book, curiosity of art, or article of vertu, which may pleasantly engage the attention of the company.[7]

Her remarks about family meals, and somewhat brief comments on table manners, over which she was not so explicit as usual (one of the few things she took for granted among her readers was that they would know how to use a knife and fork properly), also appear to have been prompted by her own experience. It was inconsiderate, if not exactly rude, she said, to ask for a second helping of the first course, because it kept everyone waiting for the second: 'a little revenge . . . taken by looking at the awkward consumer of a second portion'[8] was to her way of thinking well deserved. She was certainly thinking of her brothers and sisters when she recommended evening occupations for the young, and they were probably also at the back of her mind when she said that the presentation of meals for the family was as important as dinners for guests—which was later singled out in the one and only review she received as a particularly praiseworthy sentiment. An extended note about buying houses, on the other hand, probably came from an estate agent, though after the interest she had shown in the tubular bridge at Bangor, her technical-sounding remarks about types of soil, drainage, water supply, and ventilation come as no surprise.

The conclusion to this chapter was the most eloquent passage in the book, nicely calculated to win over every woman in England, and unquestionably written straight from the heart. Supporters of women's rights might well have held it against her, since it played upon the very sentiments which kept women in the home, but she did not see it in that light. All she was trying to do was to emphasize the point she had made in the Preface, which applied to all women in any situation—that domestic inefficiency made for suffering and discomfort.

She ought always to remember that she is the first and the last, the Alpha and the Omega in the government of her establishment; and that it is by her conduct that its whole internal policy is regulated. She is, therefore, a person of far more importance than she usually thinks she is. On her pattern her daughters model themselves; by her counsels they are directed; through her virtues all are honoured;—'her children rise up and call her blessed; her husband, also, and he praiseth her.' Therefore, let each mistress always remember her responsible position, never approving a mean action, nor speaking an unrefined word. Let her conduct be such that her inferiors may respect her, and such as an honourable and right-minded man may look for in his wife and the mother of his children. Let her think of the many compliments and the sincere homage that have been paid to her sex by the greatest philosophers and writers, both in ancient and modern times. Let her not forget that she has to show herself worthy of Campbell's compliment when he said,—

'The world was sad! the garden was a wild!
And man the hermit sigh'd, till *woman* smiled. . . .'

Cherishing, then, in her breast the respected utterances of the good and the great, let the mistress of every house rise to the responsibility of its management; so that, in doing her duty to all around her, she may receive the genuine reward of respect, love, and affection![9]

The only classes of servant discussed at the beginning of the book were the housekeeper, who was employed in large establishments as the mistress's substitute, and the cook, whose duties formed a necessary prelude to the cookery chapter. As part of her advice to the mistress, however, Isabella also gave general information about hiring and firing, giving and obtaining references, and rates of pay, the latter being illustrated with a couple of exceptionally interesting tables, which showed how much the various types of domestic could expect to earn and the number who could be employed at different income levels. In spite of the wide margins in the wages quoted, which were only slightly accounted for by the fact that some servants had to pay for their own beer, tea, and sugar (living in was taken for granted), the cheapness of all grades seems staggering, and was disproportionate even by the standards of the time. A housekeeper, the best paid, could be employed for £18–£45 a year, a cook for £12–£30, a housemaid £10–£20, and a scullery-maid, the lowest on the list, £4–£9. This was because in areas where there was no industry, domestic service was the only way for large numbers of women to earn their living; those who could work in factories almost invariably did so, for going into service had no more appeal than it has now—but it was better than starving (though in some households scarcely better: stories of starvation, overwork, and even the consequent deaths of servants were too numerous to be disbelieved). The one advantage of such low wages from the servants' point of view was that at least there were plenty of jobs, since every family with any claim to middle-class status could afford to employ someone: even a clerk earning £150 a year rated a maid, and £500 a year was enough to support a cook and two maids (from which it may be inferred that Sam's income when he married was a little more than this). Problems arose because servants, like big houses and fashionable clothes, were status symbols, and people tended to take on more than they could afford. Isabella's table was intended partly as a caution.

Logically, the section devoted to servants should have followed straight on from here, and in a way it is a pity it was stowed away at the back, for it was a remarkable achievement. Nothing approaching it had ever been attempted before; *The Housekeeper's Oracle* and other books with sections on servants gave no more than collective hints and advice, whereas Isabella discussed separately and at length the functions of no fewer than eighteen different kinds of domestic, ranging from the butler to the wet-nurse. It took her thirteen pages to set out the duties of the house-maid, eight for the lady's maid, and six for the footman. A well known example of her extreme thoroughness was her advice to the housemaid on bed-making:

> In bed-making, the fancy of the occupant should be con-sulted; some like beds sloping from the top towards the feet, swelling slightly in the middle [here, for once, it is impossible to see quite what she meant; it is virtually the only place in the book where her explanation was not absolutely clear]; others, perfectly flat; a good housemaid will accommodate each bed to the taste of the sleeper, taking care to shake, beat, and turn it well in the process. Some persons prefer sleeping on the mattress; in which case a feather bed is usually beneath. . . . Any feathers which escape . . . a tidy servant will put back through the seam of the tick; she will also be careful to sew up any stitch that gives way the moment it is discovered. The bed-clothes are laid on, beginning with an under blanket. . . . The

bolster is then beaten and shaken. . . . The pillows and other bedclothes follow, and the counterpane over all, which should fall in graceful folds, and at an equal distance from the ground all round. . . .[10]

Another instance of her exhaustive approach was the way in which she described not only the servants' chores and the exact manner in which they should be carried out, but how to make all the necessary polishes, cleaners, and other preparations: the lady's maid, for instance, was given recipes for shampoo, hair conditioner, hair restorer, shoe polish, and various stain removers—which serves also as a reminder of how many small as well as large tasks there were to be done in the home without ready-made products and other modern conveniences. In any household, the services of servants were a necessity to civilized life, not a luxury; among other factors which greatly increased the amount of domestic work were the large size of families, the use of coal as fuel, the fashion for amazing quantities of fussy furniture and ornament, and the great number of underclothes which needed laundering.

The lady's maid was lucky. Her duties were relatively light, consisting only of looking after her mistress's clothes, dressing her hair, and sewing; Isabella reckoned hairdressing to be the most important and even recommended the maid to take lessons. She advised her to use her spare time studying the fashion magazines 'so as to be able to aid her mistress's judgment', and learning how to alter and adapt clothes which were no longer fashionable into suitable outfits for the daughters of the family or others. 'The exigencies of fashion and luxury are such that all ladies, except those of the very highest rank, will consider themselves fortunate in having about them a thoughtful person, capable of diverting their finery to a useful purpose.'[11] Because of the intimate nature of her position, the maid was also expected to pay particular attention to her conduct, and behave always with 'Quiet, unobtrusive manners . . . and a delicate reserve' [12]when speaking of her employers.

Respect and discretion were of course required of all servants, whatever their jobs, but others for whom Isabella especially emphasized its importance were the valet—the masculine equivalent of the lady's maid—and the footman. One of the footman's

main duties was to wait at table, and this task, carried out professionally, called for a considerable degree of skill and intelligence, but above all, according to her, silence and self-effacement
—the ability to be seen and not heard. She was almost neurotic
in her dread of unseemly interruptions and distractions during
meals, having a particular aversion to squeaky boots, which she
described as 'an abomination',[13] and an even greater horror of
unsolicited comments. As an illustration of the embarrassment
this could create, she told a story about a Scotsman who forgot to
pour wine for one of his guests. His servant nudged him and said
very loudly, 'What ails you at her in the green gown?'[14] It was,
incidentally, in speaking of the footman, who was responsible for
looking after the family glasses and china, that she used the
famous phrase, 'a place for everything and everything in its
place';[15] she also used it in reference to the housekeeper but
presumably it was not her who invented it as on the first occasion
she put it in quotation marks.

   The sections on the various nurses, the two chapters by the
EDM doctor, and the recipes for invalids in the cookery part of
the book covered all contingencies connected with family health
likely to be encountered in a normal household. The advice to the
sick-nurse, who, as Isabella said, anyone might have to become
at a moment's notice, was based on Florence Nightingale's *Notes
on Nursing*. Miss Nightingale's fame was then at its height after her
heroic spell of nursing in the Crimea. The nurse's main requirements, 'which most women worthy of the name possess',[16] were
good temper, compassion, and sympathy. It appeared, however,
that there was little hope of finding such qualities in the other
types of nurse. The wet-nurse, who was employed to supply milk
in case of default of the mother, was presented as the greatest
villainess ever likely to set foot inside a respectable home. She
was supposed to restrict herself to simple, digestible foods, but
(not surprisingly in view of the insupportable dullness of Isabella's
suggested diet):

   . . . many nurses, rather than forego the enjoyment of a
   favourite dish, though morally certain of the effect it will have
   on the child, will, on the first opportunity, feed with avidity on
   fried meats, cabbage, cucumber, pickles, or other crude or
   injurious aliments, in defiance of all orders given, or confidence

reposed in their word, good sense, or humanity. And when the infant is afterwards racked with pain, and a night of disquiet alarms the mother, the doctor is sent for, and the nurse, covering her dereliction by a falsehood, the consequence of her gluttony is treated as a disease, and the poor infant is dosed for some days with medicines, that can do it but little if any good and, in all probability, materially retard its physical development. . . . In all such cases the infant should be spared the infliction of medicine, and, as a wholesome corrective to herself, and relief to her charge, a good sound dose administered to the nurse.[17]

Furthermore, mothers were warned to be on their guard lest the nurse should tranquillize the child with dangerous drugs such as Godfrey's cordial or syrup of poppies: 'The fact that scores of nurses keep secret bottles of these deadly syrups, for the purpose of stilling their charges, is notorious. . . .'[18]

The chapters by the doctor constituted a remarkably complete guide to home diagnosis and treatment. One chapter dealt with the rearing of babies and childhood diseases, and the other with emergencies, when what was done before the doctor arrived could spell the difference between life and death. The usefulness of the latter can only be appreciated when it is remembered that transport was no quicker than the horse, and professional help sometimes took a very long time to arrive. Taking into consideration the extremely reactionary attitude of the medical profession as a whole, the treatments prescribed were enlightened and up-to-date, and the doctor himself was not only experienced, as stated in the Preface, but exceptionally sensible—indeed, at times his professional detachment verged on cynicism, and one is glad to know that his jokes were not attributable to Isabella. For example, there was his crack about bleeding people:[19] this treatment, he said, should always be carried out with the patient standing up, in case he should faint. The cure for fainting was to lay him down flat on his back, but if he were lying down already, there could be no cure:

Should a person, under these circumstances, faint, what could be done to bring him round again? The great treatment of lowering the body to the flat position cannot be followed here.

It is in that position already, and cannot be placed lower than it at present is—except, as is most likely to be the case, under the ground.[20]

The lawyer's chapter was in itself boring, but its inclusion was a noteworthy innovation, which in this instance was as likely to have come from Isabella as Sam. As married women had no separate legal existence, it was not theoretically relevant to the majority of the book's readers; but Sam might have been anticipating the time when that situation would change, and Isabella had already said, in her first-ever article, that women ought to take an interest in such matters. Notwithstanding his feminine audience, the contributor could not break his habit of addressing the male sex only, and referred to men throughout (which was not, however, very noticeable, as he wrote in the usual dry, impersonal legal style). He dealt, fairly efficiently, with practical matters such as buying and leasing houses, making wills and IOUs, and the wife's situation in cases of the husband's cruelty or desertion (though he devoted rather less space to this than he might have done), and did not mention divorce at all, despite the recent Act.

This completed the non-culinary section of *Management*. Taken all in all, it was a triumph: it succeeded in giving women a complete guide to the ideals and usages of middle-class society in such a straightforward way that even the most stupid among them could not go far wrong. Its main fault was Isabella's unnecessarily peremptory tone; one feels that she could have made the mistress's life sound a rather less daunting prospect without sacrificing any of her authoritativeness, and, perhaps more important, shown greater understanding in her attitude to servants, whom she tended to look on as automatons rather than as individuals. On the other hand, it was in her favour that at least she avoided the sentimental tone of Mrs Ellis's books. In terms of content, the only subjects she might with advantage have developed further were elementary table manners, the upbringing of older children (which she scarcely touched on), and perhaps interior decoration and furnishing. Some of these were dealt with in later editions, along with other, more peripheral subjects, such as the care of dogs and other pets, and flower-arranging. These additions, however, in conjunction with a great many extra recipes, made the book impractically long and unwieldy; so far as she was concerned, it can fairly be said that no writer has ever crammed more into a mere 175 pages, which was all that the household chapters took up.

Five sixths of the book was devoted to the cookery section, which consisted of forty chapters of recipes and background information arranged alternately, each group of recipes being preceded by an introductory chapter about the type of food in question and the general principles to be observed in preparing it. Every kind of cookery suitable for an ordinary home was covered, from soup to wine-making. Isabella took the food in the order it was eaten at dinner, the most important meal, followed by dishes required at subsidiary meals, and ending with menus, or 'bills of fare'. Within this plan, she subdivided the main dinner courses into their basic ingredients, i.e. the kind of meat, poultry, game, and vegetables. This was tidier and much easier for reference than the usual arrangement, whereby all the dishes for each course were lumped together.

It was her system of writing recipes, apparently inspired by Eliza Acton's summaries, which was the most remarkable factor about this part of the book. Previous writers had given only the method of preparation; she appended a list with the months when the dish was seasonable, its cooking time, the number of people it served, and its average cost at the bottom of her instructions, and began every recipe by itemizing all the ingredients, with precise weights and measures, so that the cook could check that she had everything she needed in the correct quantities before proceeding. In this way, she eliminated any possibility of uncertainty and transformed domestic cookery from a skill which had to be learnt by experience into an accomplishment which could be practised with reasonable chances of success even by complete beginners. The importance of this can scarcely be over-estimated, and recipes have been written on this pattern ever since.

The most notable overall feature about the recipes themselves was that, contrary to general belief, all of them were basically simple. Isabella never for a moment allowed herself to forget that the people who would use them were untrained, barely educated cooks, and that to include preparations demanding any kind of specialist skill would be simply defeating her purpose. In this respect, her inexperience was the greatest asset she could have had, for she was able to use her own limitations as a measure; anything she herself could not manage she threw out. Thus she excluded the French dishes described in the *Regenerator* and *Modern Cook*, which called for several stages of preparation, extravagant sauces, and elaborate garnishes, and included the traditional English roasts and baked and boiled puddings, which required attention but no expertise (and which, on the evidence of her diary, she herself preferred). Virtually the only exacting recipe to be found in the whole of *Management* was Ude's turtle soup, which she included because of its special status as a festive dish. For the rest, though there was plenty of chopping and straining for the maid, there was nothing to tax anyone's ability. And this, rather than any gastronomic superiority, was the reason for the popularity of her recipes; some of them were pretty dull, but even the dullest dish properly made was better than foreign delicacies hopelessly bungled.

The third distinguishing factor about the cookery chapters was, predictably enough, her emphasis on economy. Right at the beginning of the book, directly after her comments on cleanliness, she said: 'Frugality and economy are home virtues, without which no household can prosper.'[21] She supported this in a variety of ways. Some of her recipes were about as cheap as was consistent with edibility—if soup made of stale crusts[22] or eggless and fatless suet pudding[23] can be so classified. Her family menus were plain in the extreme, and ingeniously devised to use up the previous day's left-overs. Miscellaneous hints on economy were scattered throughout the text wherever relevant; some, such as breaking an egg into a separate bowl to prevent a bad one from contaminating other ingredients, have become a traditional part of kitchen lore. Many are still as valid as ever, such as a note about buying meat: 'If the housekeeper is not very particular as to the precise joints to cook for dinner, there is oftentimes an opportunity for her to save as much money in her purchase of meat as will pay for the bread to eat with it. . . .'[24] This was because the best cuts of meat were always in demand, and butchers were often glad to dispose of the cheaper cuts for whatever they could get. Soyer also deplored the English housewife's tendency to buy expensive joints: 'Everybody has the bad habit of running only upon a few which are considered the best . . . ten of the prime are in daily use to one of the other, and principally for a want of the

knowledge of cookery. . . .'[25] Isabella's least worthy notion for
making the pennies stretch was her suggestion of serving children
suet pudding roasted under the joint before the actual meat, so
that they would eat less (a practice frequently resorted to in
boarding schools). Most of the food she recommended for
children was dreary, partly because of the need for economy in
large families, and partly because plain food was considered
morally and physically better for them. It is Isabella more than
anyone who deserves the blame for the tyranny of nursery rice
pudding.

Her most constructive idea for promoting economy, however,
was her policy of giving recipes for all kinds of ready-cooked
meat, poultry, and fish. The overriding popularity of roasts
meant that people's larders were constantly clogged with the
unattractive remains of joints, which for lack of other suggestions
were usually served cold just as they were, or (worse) re-heated
just as they were. This presented a problem which Acton, Soyer,
and Francatelli recognized but did not tackle systematically.
Isabella faced it squarely and gave scores of recipes under a special
heading, 'Cold Meat Cookery', which was also the title of one
of her most popular series of articles in the *EDM*. Since almost
none of these recipes appeared in other cookery books, it is to be
assumed that the magazine readers served her better in this
respect than most, and contributed the bulk of them. They were
not imaginative by present-day standards, but they were genuinely
economic, in that few called for much by way of extras, and to
contemporary readers they represented a major culinary break-
through.

But she did not allow herself to be too carried away by her
enthusiasm; she was very well aware that on occasion other
considerations were bound to prevail, and that luxury, or at least
the appearance of it, was of paramount importance to middle-
class hostesses anxious to impress. 'Economy and frugality must
never, however, be allowed to degenerate into parsimony and
meanness,'[26] she said as a hasty afterthought to her introductory
observations on economy. Her principle was that everything
should be the best of its kind: if stale crusts were what was
required, well and good, and if she specified stale ones, it was
because they served that particular purpose better than fresh ones;
but it would have been parsimonious to use second-best steak for

a beef-steak pie, or begrudge the quarter pint of brandy and sixteen eggs needed for 'An Unrivalled Plum Pudding'[27] (from experiments made with a number of her recipes, it would seem that the usual size of eggs was very small). It is for such recipes as these, and her guest menus, which will be discussed presently, that she has gained a very misleading reputation for extravagance.

Few cookery books maintain an even gastronomic standard throughout, and even *Household Management*, within the strict limitations Isabella set herself, varied from chapter to chapter. The soup, fish, and sauce chapters were among the best and most comprehensive in the book, and indeed for the plainer types of dishes have probably never been bettered. There were nearly 100 soups, almost 200 sauces, and 128 fish recipes. Isabella echoed Mrs English's belief in the importance of the stockpot in her chapter on soup-making: 'It is on good stock, or first broth and sauce, that excellence in cookery depends.'[28] She did not, however, stress it (as Soyer did) in relation to her sauce recipes, which, remembering that this was the heyday of extravagant and complicated sauces, were particularly distinguished for their simplicity. The fish chapters were notable for the number of eel, lobster, and oyster dishes—which were not an extravagance in those days as lobsters and oysters were relatively cheap: a dozen oysters cost about sevenpence.

Nowadays, the meat chapters strike one as unrealistic because of the large size of joints recommended, which is partly explained by the fact that they were expected to feed a family for several days (hence the excess of cold meat). The preponderance of roasts also makes them look dull.

Roast beef has long been a national dish in England. In most of our patriotic songs it is contrasted with fricasseed frogs, popularly supposed to be the exclusive diet of Frenchmen.

'O the roast beef of Old England,
And O the old English roast beef.'

This national chorus is appealed to whenever a song-writer wishes to account for the valour displayed by Englishmen at sea or on land.[29]

The other national passion, port, was reflected by the number of recipes calling for it where we should now use red wine; garlic was of course consistently omitted, except once, in a chutney. Even Soyer used it only on the sly. 'I often introduce onions, eschalots, or even a little garlic in some of my most delicate dishes, but so well blended with other flavours that I never have a single objection even by those who have a great dislike to it.'[30]

In contrast to the recipes for meat, the chapter on vegetables was unexpectedly imaginative, though perhaps not more so than Eliza Acton or Soyer's. According to the latter (again), most people in England ate nothing but plain boiled vegetables—surprisingly, under rather than over-cooked—and all three writers endeavoured to encourage more variety and care in their preparation. Isabella included a number of unusual ideas, such as carrots stewed in cream, broad beans with herbs, asparagus pudding, and cooked endive and celery salad. Although vegetables *per se* (as opposed to in soups or as garnishes) were eaten at family meals much as they are now, on grander occasions they were served only with the second of two meat courses, and, in contrast to present customs, in far less quantity and diversity than the meats; there would seldom be more than one dish of them to accompany as many as six meat dishes. This may have been partly due to snobbery, since except for truffles, and perhaps tomatoes, which had only recently come to be widely used, there was no kudos attached to them; also, they could only be preserved by means of drying, and the choice was therefore limited by the seasons. Besides this, many kinds were considered indigestible. The exact nature of their nutritive value was not understood; although their anti-scorbutic properties were well known, it was another half century before vitamins were discovered.

In an age of cans and packets, Mrs Beeton's puddings come as a revelation. There were of course numerous suet-based puddings, whose popularity, despite a decade of stiff competition from jellies, remained unchallenged; no dinner party was complete without at least one, and even on a picnic a cold plum pudding would be taken along so as not to disappoint devotees. But in addition she offered a mouth-watering welter of creams, ice creams, water ices, custards, fruit compôtes, Charlottes, pies, tarts, and numerous other pastries. The pastry recipes, which ranged from the richest, butteriest puff paste to the cheapest kind of dripping crust, were as

7*

infallible as any pastry recipe can be (here I speak from experience having tried them all).

The section on jams and preserves was also excellent, and extensive, as it had to be when there was no other way (except, again, by drying) of preserving fruit. The process of tinning was known, but not yet in general use. Also, the bought products were notoriously inferior; according to an almost libellous article in *The Times*,[31] confectioners were in the habit of using all their fruit for making jellies, and boiled up jam simply as a convenient way of getting rid of the pips and skin.

For the rest, the egg and cheese recipes were limited, clearly because Isabella was not interested; cheese she strongly disapproved of, as will be seen later, though presumably she did not actually dislike it since she and Sam had it several times when they went on picnics in Ireland. She permitted it a place on the lunch table, and occasionally recommended it for family dinners, but banished it firmly from all dinner parties, mercilessly leaving the gentlemen without the natural partner to their port. The chapter on drinks contained everything that could be made at home, from a version of instant coffee to punch—but neither here nor elsewhere was there so much as a sentence about wine, which Isabella, who was as ignorant as any woman on the subject, did not consider a lady's concern. This was a pity, for if she had broken through the traditional, illogical, and gastronomically very undesirable separation of food from drink, it might not have persisted so rigidly. The invalid food was distinguished chiefly for the sensible comments which preceded it:

> For invalids, never make a large quantity *of one thing*, as they seldom require much at a time; and it is desirable that variety be provided for them.
>
> Always have something in readiness; a little beef tea, nicely made and nicely skimmed, a few spoonfuls of jelly, &c. &c., that it may be administered as soon almost as the invalid wishes for it. If obliged to wait a long time, the patient loses the desire to eat, and often turns against the food when brought to him or her.
>
> In sending dishes or preparations up to invalids, let everything look as tempting as possible. . . .[32]

By far the most fascinating of all the recipe chapters was the last, 'Bills of Fare', which gave menus for all occasions throughout the year. For every month there was one dinner-party menu for eighteen, twelve, ten, and eight guests, and two or four menus for six people. There was also a fortnight's worth of family dinners—presumably on the assumption that for the second half of the month the mistress could begin serving the same dishes again. In addition, there were two menus for ball suppers, the larger being the one also recommended for weddings; one for a game dinner; another for a picnic; and suggestions for the other meals of the day.

The dinner-party menus are astounding for the immense amount of food considered necessary. Modern guests would be disgusted; Isabella herself was distressed by the superfluity. The fare for eighteen in May, to take a random example, was as follows. First course: asparagus soup, oxtail soup, salmon with lobster sauce, brill with shrimp sauce, fried sole, and fillets of mackerel. Entrées (light, usually elaborate dishes served as appetizers to the second course): lamb cutlets with cucumber, ragoût of veal, curried chicken, and lobster pudding. Second course: saddle of lamb, raised pie, braised ham, roast veal, roast chicken, and boiled capon (no vegetables were specified on this particular menu). Third course: goslings, ducklings, lobster salad, plovers' eggs (as delicacies, game and shellfish were served as part of the pudding course), College puddings, Nesselrode pudding, almond cheesecakes, tartlets, Italian cream, Charlotte à la Parisienne, and two sorts of jelly. Dessert: fruit, nuts, cakes, biscuits, ices, and various sorts of confectionery, including chocolates, which were still very much a luxury. The dessert was the time for the maximum display of magnificence, when all the choicest silver, china, and glass were brought out; fruit was arranged in huge, stemmed dishes called tazzas, which were often fantastically decorated with flowers, cherubs, nymphs, and scenes from Classical mythology—though the ones illustrated in the book, which were probably Isabella's own, were relatively plain. The dinner for twelve for that month consisted of proportionately fewer dishes, but was still excessive: two soups plus salmon and turbot; seven meat dishes; ducklings, goslings, and seven puddings; dessert as before.

However, gargantuan as these feasts may now seem, to

contemporaries they were if anything more moderate than might have been expected, for a large and sumptuous array of dishes at dinner parties was the invariable custom. Isabella, as can be imagined from her aversion to waste and extravagance, as well as from her impatience with the tedium such elaboration entailed, was placed in an embarrassing position: she could not afford to challenge the convention, but was hard pressed to rationalize her support of it. She compromised by recommending what she considered the socially acceptable minimum of food, and said, without much conviction:

> The variety of dishes which furnish forth a modern dinner table does not necessarily imply anything unwholesome, or anything capricious. Food that is not well relished cannot be well digested; and the appetite of the over-worked man of business, or statesman, or of any dwellers in towns, whose occupation is exciting and exhausting, is jaded, and requires stimulation.[33]

The complicated menus appear less confusing, though no less large, when considered in relation to the way they were served. Everything in each course was set out on the table at the same time, so that the diners had to choose whether to have the soup while it was hot, and put up with tepid fish, or eat the fish hot and forgo the soup. As the host was usually expected to do all the carving, everything in the second course was liable to be cold by the time it had been served; it was because the dexterity of the carvers made as much difference to the guests' enjoyment as the skill of the cook that Isabella gave detailed instructions, with diagrams, for the carving of all the meat and poultry she mentioned. Only the entrées, which were served alone, had a fair chance of being eaten in an appetizing state. This method of dining was called *service à la Française*; because of the opportunities it offered for making a splendid show, it was still almost universal at the time Isabella was writing, despite its obvious disadvantages. The guests were regaled with the sight of a groaning table at each successive course, and as nothing was divided before reaching the dining room, the cook's imagination in the matter of garnishes and ornamentation was allowed full play. At grand dinners their attempts could be spectacular indeed; for example, one of Soyer's most celebrated *pièces de résistance* was the *Gâteau Britannique à l'Amiral*, a cake in the shape of a ship with a chocolate-covered hull and spun sugar rigging.[34]

Later in the century, the French method was superseded by the much more convenient *service à la Russe*, when each separate dish, or set of alternatives, was served as a course on its own, having been previously cut up in the kitchen. This meant that the table looked bare throughout the meal until dessert; it was also expensive, because it called for more crockery, cutlery, and servants than the older method. For these reasons, despite the much greater comfort it afforded the diners, it was slow to be adopted in this country. Isabella was sufficiently forward-looking to include two *à la Russe* menus, and suggested decorating the table with the dessert for the duration of the meal, but she did not go into further details because she knew that for most of her readers it was not a practical proposition; and despite her rather optimistic remark that it was more economical in terms of food than service *à la Française*, the menus she gave were even more abundant, consisting of a procession of fifteen courses with between two and six alternatives in each.

After all this, the family dinners come as something of a shock. They were economic, unpretentious, not particularly copious, and consisted of the same type and number of dishes as we would eat today, except for the rather more generous servings of meat. Sometimes, but not always, they began with fish or soup, followed by one or two meat dishes, potatoes, and nearly every day in summer and three or four times a week in winter, a second vegetable. This was succeeded by suet or milk pudding or a pie, varied every now and again by a vegetable dish, macaroni, shellfish, fondue, or cheese. The Sunday roast was invariable (but there would not be more than one), and its reappearance on Monday or Tuesday, either cold with mashed potatoes or as a 'Cold Meat Cookery' dish, equally inevitable; for the most interesting thing about these menus was the mathematical exactitude with which Isabella manipulated them so as to avoid waste. The liquor from boiled meat always became soup, and even half-eaten puddings were re-served cut into slices and fried. The majority of the meals were not unattractive, though they were very fattening; every now and again, however, her urge for economy became distinctly depressing, as in these two meals for January and April respectively: pea soup made from the previous day's boiled beef, cold beef and mashed potatoes (no salad), and batter pudding;[35] and vegetable soup, toad-in-the-hole with remains of mutton, and rhubarb and custard.[36]

Among her final remarks in this chapter, the last on cookery in the book, her suggestions for the breakfasts of which she was so fond make a heartening parting shot; they were exactly as one might expect, right down to the flowers Lucy had so much appreciated:

Suffice it to say, that any cold meat the larder may furnish, should be nicely garnished, and be placed on the buffet. Collared and potted meats or fish, cold game or poultry, veal-and-ham pies, game-and-rumpsteak pies, are all suitable. . . .

The following list of hot dishes may perhaps assist our readers in knowing what to provide for the comfortable meal called breakfast. Broiled fish, such as mackerel, whiting, herrings, dried haddocks, &c.; mutton chops and rump-steaks, broiled sheep's kidneys, kidneys à la maître d'hôtel, sausages, plain rashers of bacon, bacon and poached eggs, ham and poached eggs, omelets, plain boiled eggs, oeufs-au-plat, poached eggs on toast, muffins, toast, marmalade, butter, &c. &c.

In the summer, and when they are obtainable, always have a vase of freshly-gathered flowers on the breakfast-table, and, when convenient, a nicely-arranged dish of fruit: when strawberries are in season, these are particularly refreshing; as also grapes, or even currants.[37]

From a journalistic point of view, it is virtually impossible to find fault with this part of the book; Isabella's realistic assessment of the average cook's ability, her accent on that most prized Victorian virtue, economy, the precision of her directions, and above all her innovatory system of writing recipes came near to genius. It is for cookery that she is remembered, and because of it that *Household Management* became famous. But although her work has been so influential, it must be remembered that its distinction was purely journalistic, not gastronomic. If her recipes *seemed* better than anyone else's, it was because they were easier to follow, and therefore stood a better chance of yielding good results. This is in no way to belittle the excellence or importance of what she did: it was incalculable, for in effect she formulated an independent school of middle-class British cookery, and in so doing improved enormously the general standard of cooking in this country. It was something no chef imbued with the principles of French *haute cuisine* could ever have done, and without Kitchener, one would have said that no man—as opposed to woman—could have achieved. But Isabella did not invent it; the person who deserves the most credit for that is Miss Acton.

The introductory chapters to the recipes, in conjunction with numerous notes, contained the miscellaneous information Isabella had collected so painstakingly. In the introduction to the first cookery chapter, she said:

IT HAS BEEN ASSERTED, that English cookery is, nationally speaking, far from the best in the world. More than this, we have been frequently told by brilliant foreign writers, half philosophers, half chefs [this was Brillat-Savarin], that we are the *worst* cooks on the face of the earth, and that the proverb which alludes to the divine origin of food, and the precisely opposite origin of its preparers, is peculiarly applicable to us islanders. . . . One great cause of many of the spoilt dishes and badly-cooked meats which are brought to our tables, arises, we think, and most will agree with us, from a non-acquaintance with 'common, everyday things.' Entertaining this view, we intend to preface the chapters of this work with a simple scientific *résumé* of all those causes and circumstances which relate to the food we have to prepare, and the theory and chemistry of the various culinary operations.[38]

The result of this aim was the addition of a substantial subsidiary section to the culinary part of the book amounting to a kind of gastronomic encyclopedia. For the most part, the introductions consisted of either a historical survey of the type of food in question, or a detailed study of the relevant animals and plants, followed by culinary principles and 'chemistry', the latter being mostly of the same sort as the extract from Morton's *Cyclopedia* quoted earlier.

The opening to the cookery section as a whole started off, without much originality perhaps, but with considerable style and vigour, with an account of the development of the art of cookery in the early phases of human history.

Through these various phases, *only to live* has been the great object of mankind; but, by-and-by, comforts are multiplied, and accumulating riches create new wants. The object, then is not only to *live*, but to live economically, agreeably, tastefully, and well. Accordingly, the art of cookery commences; and although the fruits of the earth, the fowls of the air, the beasts of the field, and the fish of the sea, are still the only food of mankind, yet these are so prepared, improved, and dressed by skill and ingenuity, that they are the means of immeasurably extending the boundaries of human enjoyments. . . .[39]

This discourse in the prelude was balanced by the chapter at the end, 'Dinners and Dining', which contained the most entertaining few pages in the book, partly because of Isabella's use of poetry—one of the few things about them that had not been inspired by Savarin.

Dining is the privilege of civilization. The rank which a people occupy in the grand scale may be measured by their way of taking their meals, as well as their way of treating their women. The nation which knows how to dine has learnt the leading lesson of progress. It implies both the will and the skill to reduce to order, and surround with idealisms and graces, the more material conditions of human existence; and wherever that will and that skill exist, life cannot be wholly ignoble.

Dinner, being the grand solid meal of the day, is a matter of considerable importance; and a well-served table is a striking index of human ingenuity and resource. 'Their table,' says Lord Byron, in describing a dinner-party given by Lord and Lady Amundeville at Norman Abbey,—

> 'Their table was a board to tempt even ghosts
>   To pass the Styx for more substantial feasts.
> I will not dwell upon ragoûts or roasts,
>   Albeit human history attests
> That happiness for man—the hungry sinner!—
>   Since Eve ate apples, much depends on dinner.'[40]

Byron was followed by Milton, Keats, and Tennyson. 'We gladly quote passages like these,' she observed, 'to show how eating and drinking may be surrounded with poetical associations, and how man, using his privilege to turn any and every repast into a "feast of reason," with a warm and plentiful "flow of soul," may really count it as not the least of his legitimate prides, that he is "a dining animal." '41

The other introductions were not so impressive. The chapters on fish and all the main-course dishes were preceded by long passages culled from encyclopedias, plus Soyer's history of the eating of fish and the story of the hams, which was used as the preamble to sauces. Among the subjects covered in other chapters were the origins of puddings, the introduction of tea- and coffee-drinking into England, and (more practically), the principles of sugar-boiling.

For the most part, the notes, many of which served as captions to the engravings, consisted of whatever information she had not used in the introductions. A great many continued her biological theme; after one of her eel recipes, for instance, she inserted a paragraph on their wandering habits:

This fish is known frequently to quit its native element, and set off on a wandering expedition in the night, or just about the close of day, over the meadows, in search of snails and other prey. It also, sometimes, betakes itself to isolated ponds, apparently for no other pleasure than that which may be supposed to be found in a change of habitation. . . .

'Thus the mail'd tortoise, and the wand'ring eel,
Off to the neighbouring beach will silent steal.'42

And after Potted Salmon: 'The salmon is said to have an aversion to anything red; hence, fishermen engaged in catching it do not wear jackets or caps that colour. . . .'43 Likewise, the poultry recipes were flanked by descriptions of the remarkably numerous breeds of ducks and hens, and the vegetables with details of the different varieties. The meat dishes were annotated with a more diverse selection of extras, some of which were included simply in order to provide amusement; perhaps it is unfair to quote this example, but it was fairly typical (it was obviously not intended to point a moral):

A VERY VEAL DINNER.—At a dinner given by Lord Polkemmet, a Scotch nobleman and judge, his guests saw, when the covers were removed, that the fare consisted of veal broth, a roasted fillet of veal, veal cutlets, a veal pie, a calf's head, and calf's-foot jelly. The judge, observing the surprise of his guests, volunteered an explanation.—'Ou, ay, it's a cauf; when we kill a beast, we just eat up ae side, and doun the tither.'[44]

Other notes were of a more scientific nature. Wherever the information was available, she gave chemical analyses of the various foods—and very odd some of them were; she also indicated their nutritive qualities and digestibility. A large number of vegetables, plums, sugar, and (depressingly) hot rolls and new bread, were branded as indigestible; as for cheese:

It is well known that some persons like cheese in a state of decay, and even 'alive'. There is no accounting for tastes; and it may be hard to show why mould, which is vegetation, should not be eaten as well as salad, or maggots as well as eels. But, generally speaking, decomposing bodies are not wholesome eating, and the line must be drawn somewhere.[45]

In a later note, she added, '. . . cheese, in its commonest shape, is fit only for sedentary people, as an after-dinner stimulant, and in very small quantity.'[46] Among the items she designated as especially easy to digest were apples, almonds, asparagus, and gooseberries, and also biscuits (as being less likely to cause flatulence than bread).

The engravings were one of the book's greatest attractions, for they were delicate, informative, and very plentiful; there was an illustration of every ingredient referred to, and most of the equipment, so that nearly all the pages were decorated with a picture of some kind. In addition, an amusing, sometimes elegant, headpiece marked the beginning of each chapter: puddings were represented by an immense spherical Christmas pudding like a football, flanked by pies and exquisitely fluted jellies; poultry by a flock of birds dominated by a regal (if inappropriate) peacock; pork by a magnificent, hairy sow surrounded by piglets. All the pictures were by Harrison Weir, and although, as has been said, certain diagrams were copied from elsewhere, a chance remark of

Isabella's suggests that at least some of the illustrations of live-stock were taken from life.[47] This conjures up a somehow faintly humorous, but not improbable, vision of Harrison Weir sitting with his sketch book in fields, farmyards, and game preserves (his friend Birket Foster was roaming the country at around this time making studies for his book *Pictures of the English Landscape*).

But the great novelty about the illustrations was the fact that there were coloured plates, an almost unheard-of bonus in a book priced at 7s 6d. Furthermore, the colour was not added by hand in the usual manner, but printed by a new process, which was doubtless why the preparations had taken so long. The frontispiece was a jolly harvest scene in summery hues, complete with duckpond and fat farmer, and the title page a design somewhat similar to that of the *BOM*, with fruit, corn, and livestock surrounding a plaque bearing the title in green and red hand-drawn lettering. Twelve further coloured plates spaced throughout the recipes showed a selection of the finished dishes: one bore a silver tureen of scalloped oysters, a lobster rearing its head from a sea of parsley, and a huge, whole dressed crab; another, a second Christmas pudding (this one crenellated), a beautifully scalloped apple Charlotte, a ring of apples in custard, an enormous vol-au-vent, and an elaborately decorated, faintly macabre game pie, the feet of its contents sticking up through the pastry. The meat dishes were too realistic to be exactly attractive, but in all the pictures the colours were bright and clear, and very sensitively chosen. Each page was surrounded by a narrow green and carmine border, which added considerably to the effect.

The pictures were of course the main reason for the book's inviting appearance, but other factors also contributed to its general attractiveness. The pages were generously spaced, with well defined headings, and the notes, which might otherwise have been confusing, clearly separated from the main body of the text by small type. Isabella's exceptionally efficient reference system should perhaps also be mentioned here: as in the 1855 edition of Miss Acton's book, the index was in the front (where it took up twenty-eight pages), so that readers could look up what they wanted and turn to it immediately; in addition, every recipe or paragraph of instruction was numbered; and, most useful of all, the recipes were in alphabetical order within each chapter, so that

as soon as the reader was familiar with the book, it became
unnecessary to refer to the index at all. Few books written since
have been so convenient to the user.

Apart from the pictures they accompanied, however, and the
welcome effect they had of breaking up the page, it is hard to feel
that the majority of the notes, and still more the dense, lengthy
introductions, really added a great deal that was worthwhile to
the book—at any rate when considered in relation to the amount
of effort entailed. Doubtless the extra matter was not unwelcome
to many under-occupied mistresses; but although Isabella's theory
of the usefulness of knowing something about the nature of
foodstuffs was a pleasant idea, very little, if indeed anything, of
what she had to say was actually any help to the cook, though the
scientific information could have been invaluable if it had been
more complete and correct. For the rest, she might have done
better to leave out the wit and philosophizing and rely on the
very considerable power of her own style and mind. The very fact
that her book continued to sell with increasing momentum over
the years with all her extras exorcized seems to prove, if not that
they had been a waste of time, at least that they were far from
necessary. Of course, later editors excluded them partly for
practical reasons, for they very soon became dated, and the
expense of amending and adding to them would have been
prohibitive; besides which, changing life-styles meant that brevity
rather than compendiousness came into favour. But, as neither of
the Beetons could have foreseen when she began, the practical
parts of her work were more than strong enough to stand up
without them.

By this time, Isabella had learnt to expect a fairly lively response
from the magazine readers, but it seems that she was nevertheless
taken by surprise at the amount of correspondence she received in
the months following *Household Management*'s publication, and
even more at the enthusiasm expressed, especially for the 'Cold
Meat Cookery' dishes and other economic recipes; these were so
popular that she prepared a separate volume of them, the *Englishwoman's Cookery Book*, which went on sale in 1863.

Of all the letters she received, however, the one which probably
gave her most satisfaction was a tribute from an elderly lady called
Harriet Martineau, an emancipated journalist and writer who had

made herself a unique career as a political economist. Domestic economy was not her subject, but the Beetons had perhaps sent her a copy because she was a friend of Florence Nightingale and had reviewed *Notes on Nursing* when it came out. She was noted for plain speaking, and did not offer Isabella unmixed praise; but as her only criticisms stemmed from her known personal peculiarities, her letter can be regarded as very high commendation indeed.

In my feeble condition, [she wrote, in March 1862,] I feel it to be allowable in a general way to acknowledge this sort of gift by the hand of my niece, before reading them, but your book tempted me to wait, and finally write myself. It has given me a great deal of pleasure; and my niece, who relieves me of housekeeping, declares the book to be very valuable indeed in the cookery parts. To us it seems new to state the cost of the dishes, and in the last degree useful. In the course of time we shall have gone over a great deal of your ground with great thankfulness to you. The specifications of the servants are excellent too. The parts we like least are the instructions on Manners, and in Medical Matters. Being Homeopaths, we think the latter very dangerous, while being aware that that part is from a professional hand.

I just say this for honesty's sake, and because I know from my own experience that one is glad to hear what people think, when a second edition of one's book may afford an opportunity for reconsideration—whether one remains finally of the same opinion or not.

In nineteen-twentieths of the book, I think we may delight and rejoice; and I heartily wish you the joy of it.

Like Miss Nightingale, Miss Martineau lived as an invalid, having been told years previously that she was about to die; her homeopathic beliefs, however, dated from long before, when a previous bout of illness had apparently been cured by mesmerism, whereupon she had written a series of letters to the *Athenaeum* describing her miraculous cure in what was considered an indelicate degree of detail; thereafter, her views on medicine had become common knowledge. Similarly, Isabella was almost certainly aware of this formidable lady's notorious contempt for superfluous civilities, and was probably not surprised at her disapproval of the chapter on the mistress.

It was nearly a year before *Household Management* was reviewed in the national press. The Beetons were still at this stage unknown in the literary world at large, for Sam did not advertise outside his own publications, and his low prices and readership of women and children had kept them from the public eye (by the next year this situation had changed, but even then Isabella's book was excluded from the general limelight). More surprising than the lack of public notice, therefore, was the fact that there was a review at all. Possibly there never would have been had it not been for Francatelli's third book, which inspired the critic with such disgust that instead of giving it an article to itself, as he would have done in normal circumstances, he wrote about several other cookery books as well by way of contrast.

Like Miss Martineau's letters, the review appeared in the most prestigious place possible, the *Athenaeum*. The first half of it was taken up with comfortable general reflections, almost all of which originated from Isabella:

> Domestic cookery books have of late boldly encountered the difficulty of dealing with 'that poor creature,' cold mutton. Set dinner-parties are less thought of than the comfort of the family. The idea has been set forth and cherished that the husband and children are entitled to as much consideration as occasional guests, and that the table ought to be set out as carefully and neatly every day as on special occasions. There is a self-respect in such a fact that goes deeper than the clean table-cloths and dinner-napkins. . . . Cookery is not merely 'the art of providing dainty bits to fatten out the ribs,' as the scornful old proverb has it: it is the art of turning every morsel to the best use; it is the exercise of skill, thought, ingenuity, to make every morsel of food yield the utmost nourishment and pleasure of which it is capable. To do this or to legislate for the doing of it, does not depend on the amount of money spent; the same qualities of character are demanded whether the housekeeping be on a large or a small scale. A woman who is not essentially kind-hearted cannot be a comfortable housekeeper; a woman who has not judgement, firmness, forethought and general good sense cannot manage her house prudently or comfortably, no

matter what amount of money she may have at her command; a woman who has not an eye for detecting and remedying disorderliness and carelessness cannot keep her home fresh and pleasant, no matter how much money she may spend on furniture and upholstery. It is not money, but management, that is the great requisite. . . .

After this, it was rather hard that only one short paragraph was devoted specifically to Isabella's work; but the little that was said was as favourable as it could have been. The reviewer, having commented briefly on the scope of the book and the large number of illustrations, went on to quote the conclusions of an actual, and apparently very competent, cook: '. . . I consider it an excellent work; it is full of useful information about everything, which is quite delightful, and I should say anyone ought to learn to cook from it who never tried before. I don't hold to *all* the recipes; I like some of my own ways of dressing things better; but I *do* say it is an excellent work.'

This was followed by a very entertaining column on Francatelli's book, in which the writer, now warmed to his subject, really let himself go.

M. Francatelli is throughout much astonished at his own humility in addressing people who have to dangle their mutton on a string when it has to be roasted, for want of a 'meat-jack.' He is also profoundly ignorant of the manners, customs, and prejudices of the class he addresses. . . . These men would be more likely to fling the 'economical pot-liquor soup,' described in recipe No. 3, in their wives' faces than to eat it with thankfulness. The boiled beef, cabbage and dumplings recommended for 'a Sunday dinner' would most likely provoke a domestic beating, and the very children would turn up their dirty little noses at 'Broth made from Bones for Soup.'

The review ended with a few sentences on three relatively negligible publications: a shilling handbook of recipes from Cassell, a book about puddings, and *Passages in the Life of a Young Housekeeper*, *related by Herself*, which particularly appealed to the journalist because it had the personal, sympathetic touch Isabella lacked: '. . . the book is genuine and amusing, and young house-keepers will greatly sympathize with many of the difficulties and experiences; there are useful hints on how to govern their servants, and the peculiar difficulties which beset timid young wives are here related in a pleasant and spirited manner. . . .'[48]

On the evidence of the *Athenaeum* and Miss Martineau, it would seem that *Management*'s overall practicality was not lost on contemporaries. Its most popular attributes were the ease with which the recipes could be used and the stress laid on economy (as was also evidenced by the swift appearance of the *Englishwoman's Cookery Book*). Neither Harriet Martineau nor the reviewer were really in a position to appreciate its snob value, nor, apart from the former's approbation of the idea of giving the cost of each dish, did they remark on Isabella's innovatory system of setting out recipes. It was inevitable that some aspects of a work into which so much thought had been put should take a little time to prove themselves; but its immediate attractions were sufficiently obvious to sell sixty thousand copies in the first year, which put it at once into the best-seller class.

Thereafter it continued to sell steadily; in less than two years Sam was starting publication of a revised edition, in parts as before; in 1865 a second abridged version of the recipes, the *Dictionary of Cookery*, appeared; and in 1868, by which time the sales stood at over 125,000, a third full-length version was launched in twelve parts, the first being presented to subscribers free; this was issued as a volume two years later. Three more new, complete editions had come out by the end of the century, plus four of the *Englishwoman's Cookery Book*, and numerous other abridgements; to date, there have been ten separate revised editions of the whole book, nearly one per decade, and about twenty-six different abridgements.

This everlasting success has of course not been due to Isabella's work alone; later editions, which were extensively re-written and tended to grow fatter and fatter as more information was added, bore increasingly less resemblance to the original, so that after thirty or forty years only the idea rather than the execution of the work can be said to have been hers. Had it not been for Sam and her subsequent publishers' remarkable assiduity in keeping it in print and up to date, it would certainly eventually have died or lain dormant like Soyer or Miss Acton's books. Her publishers' task, even without her extra information, was mammoth—but fruitful, for by the beginning of this century they could truly claim that there was scarcely a self-respecting kitchen in this country without one. In considering the reasons for the book's extraordinary longevity, these endeavours, which are perhaps unique in the history of publishing, must not be forgotten; indeed, it is probably true to say that no other work in the English language has been the subject of so much effort and expenditure.

In the long run, therefore, its success was attributable to a combination of factors. It was the first book to deal with all aspects of housekeeping at a time when such a work had become particularly relevant; it was also the first to give exact, formalized directions; it was exceptionally cleverly and conscientiously compiled; it was attractively produced and cheap, with the enormous advantage of repeated part publication; and it was expertly handled over the years. It is difficult to assess the relative importance of all these circumstances, which varied as its career progressed, but overall the first and last were probably the crucial ones.

XVIII

RECOGNITION

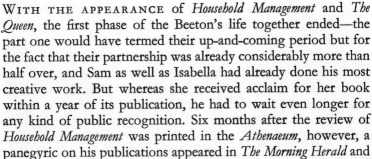

WITH THE APPEARANCE of *Household Management* and *The Queen*, the first phase of the Beeton's life together ended—the part one would have termed their up-and-coming period but for the fact that their partnership was already considerably more than half over, and Sam as well as Isabella had already done his most creative work. But whereas she received acclaim for her book within a year of its publication, he had to wait even longer for any kind of public recognition. Six months after the review of *Household Management* was printed in the *Athenaeum*, however, a panegyric on his publications appeared in *The Morning Herald* and *The Standard*, which had the effect of raising him from comparative obscurity into the circle of recognized, respected London publishers. Such acknowledgement meant a great deal to him, perhaps more than most; but it did not come before he and Isabella had suffered a second, even more wounding, personal loss.

If he had published more books earlier in his career, he would not have remained unknown in literary circles for so long; apart from *Uncle Tom's Cabin* and Readable Books, however, he had devoted almost all his attention in his first ten years in business to the magazines, and had brought out no books except *Household Management*, a volume of history called *Beeton's Historian*, and his *Dictionary of Universal Information*, which was not complete until 1862. But in the wake of these three, he had planned several further major works which in due course would have established him as a serious publisher even without the newspaper article. As soon as the first dictionary was finished, he began a second, which was much longer and more ambitious than the first, dealing with science, the arts, and literature; and three other reference books were by this time nearing completion, the *Book of Garden*

Management, which had been announced with the finished volume of *Household Management*, a *Dictionary of Universal Biography*, and the *Illuminated Family Bible*. All were initially published in parts, and all but the last on the same principles as Isabella's book, setting out to pack in as much information as possible (readably presented) for as low a price as possible.

The exception, the *Family Bible*, was the only expensive publication Sam ever undertook, his avowed theory being that it was the one work on which people might be expected to want to spend a substantial sum—for him, an unexpectedly naïve (or cynical) idea. No expense was spared and he produced it as beautifully as possible, decorating it with illuminated headings and borders and cartoons of Biblical subjects from the designs of established artists. The price of the finished volume was upwards of three guineas, which alone would have been enough to inhibit sales; but in addition, in contrast to the very good reception the other books eventually received, it did not get a good press, for although the cartoons and its general appearance were duly admired, the commentaries accompanying the text were severely criticized. 'The editor, a man of much learning, has displayed little taste or judgement in the accumulation of materials. No *system* of selection appears. Hence they are a medley of good and bad—the latter, unfortunately, prevailing.'[1] It was also unfortunate that Cassell brought out an illustrated Bible at about the same time, which, though not of comparable quality, was only half the price.

During 1862 he also began a series for boys, the 'Boy's Own Library', which was issued in sixpenny monthly instalments complete with both black and white and coloured illustrations. As the three titles published by the time the review of Beeton's output appeared in the *Standard* were serials which had already appeared in the *BOM*, they did not perhaps merit particular separate attention but the journalist was especially loud in their praise, partly because of the high standard of production. The first two works were by James Greenwood and a writer named William Dalton; the third, which was still in progress, was also by James Greenwood, and was applauded as 'a most interesting work . . . which is not only enthralling but is instructive in a very high degree, and is got up in a style that it is impossible to praise too highly. The monthly coloured frontispieces are veritable works of art.' Two further series in full swing at this time were

'Home Pets' and 'Home Games', on which the critic, who was evidently for the most part unfamiliar with these subjects, ventured only to remark, 'We can speak in very high terms indeed of the parts on billiards and chess.'[2] Also worthy of mention, though it was not commented on at the time because it did not come out until some months later, was a guide to journalism containing the (then) invaluable bonus of a dictionary of Latin quotations.

What had first attracted the journalist's attention, however, was the new, enlarged version of the *BOM* and its companion paper, the *Boy's Penny Magazine*, which was launched simultaneously—a worthy project doomed to failure, like the Bible, in spite of all Sam's efforts; after the earlier unsuccessful attempt to establish a penny publication for boys, Sam probably had no serious expectation of making it pay, but hoped to be able to carry it on his other profits. Remembering his particular interest in his works for boys, we may assume that he had been deeply engrossed in these two projects for some months past.

His preoccupation with them, and to a lesser extent with his other books, no doubt caused him to be more than usually forgetful about other aspects of his life at around this time, which in the ordinary way would have made no particular difference to anything; but it so happened that this was the autumn when the lease of the house at Pinner ran out, and he should have been considering what to do about it. Like any other young couple at this stage of their career, he and Isabella now wanted to buy their own house rather than continuing to rent—but this meant finding one, which as Isabella had blithely observed in *Household Management*, was not easy. Although she was certainly more concerned about the problem than Sam, her commitments on *The Queen* left her with no more time for house-hunting than he had. They were further hampered by the fact that their funds were very limited, as the modest, certainly far from expensive farmhouse they did eventually settle for shows.

When the time came to quit the house at Pinner, therefore, they had nowhere to go, and rather than taking lodgings or staying in an hotel, which were their only alternatives, they moved into the offices in the Strand. This was intended as no more than a temporary measure, since the offices already housed the staffs of three magazines, and were not large enough to accommodate the

Beetons and their entourage of nanny and servants in any sort of comfort. The house had a kitchen and other necessities, or they could not have gone there at all; nor, almost certainly, would they have stayed as long as they did if it had not been for the consequences of a holiday they took at Christmas, itself no doubt prompted chiefly by the discomfort in which they were living.

Soon after they moved in, Isabella's attempts to find a house were further delayed by an additional task she took upon herself— that of organizing a mammoth charity campaign. Eighteen months of civil war in America had completely disrupted the exports of cotton from the Confederate states on which the Lancashire cotton towns depended, and whole communities of workers were faced with destitution. The situation was widely reported in the press, and the Beetons responded by launching an urgent appeal in the *EDM* for contributions of money and clothing of all sorts: '. . . old cloaks or mantles, old rugs and wrappers, old carpets, old blankets, counterpanes, old hoods for babies, old shawls, old stockings, old caps for boys, old boots, old shoes; but above all, *woollen garments of every description*. . . . Let the gift be ever so small from anyone, it may be that it will sustain a sinking father, warm a shivering mother, or feed a famished child.'[3] Donors were directed to address their parcels to Isabella, and for months afterwards she was bombarded by a miscellaneous assortment of jumble, which had to be inspected, packed, and forwarded to the distressed areas.

Meanwhile, as always, London in the November fog had brought on Sam's cough, which was an additional reason for their decision to go away for Christmas. Apparently Isabella's family maintained that her son's health was also suffering, but a letter from her brother suggests that this was an assumption made after the event. It seems more likely that they took the child with them not because he was unwell but simply because it was Christmas and they wanted to have him with them, especially as at three he was just about old enough to enjoy the celebrations. Their choice fell on Brighton, where Isabella had holidayed as a child, and which she once described as 'an earthly Paradise'. It had a reputation as a breeding ground for fever, the result of overcrowding in the summer months, but Isabella may, very reasonably, have felt that there could be no risk in the winter.

The first days of their stay passed uneventfully; no doubt they enjoyed themselves in their usual manner, going for brisk walks along the sea front, Sam warmly wrapped in his old muffler, Isabella enveloped in a voluminous cloak. But a day or two after Christmas the infant fell ill, with a rash and high temperature, which was diagnosed as scarlet fever. For any child, delicate or not, there was nothing (except croup) which could have been more ominous; in its virulent form, scarlet fever was until recently a serious illness, and in the nineteenth century was looked on as comparable to diphtheria, with nearly as high a fatality rate. And fatal it proved to be. For the second time in her life, Isabella was obliged to watch her only child expire, this time in the festive atmosphere of a fashionable hotel on New Year's Eve.

Fortunately for everyone's peace of mind, the highly infectious nature of the disease was not known; nevertheless, with all the comings and goings and constant interruptions, being in a public place was the very last thing the Beetons could have wished at such a time. Their first reaction after recovering from the initial shock was to escape from their unsympathetic surroundings as soon as possible, and go home, but Sam's stepmother, now Mrs Wyatt, begged them to spend a few days with her before returning to the Strand. 'If you will come, do . . . at any rate till Monday. It will be too much to go home alone. Come to us. Mr Wyatt feels much for you both, and on Sunday we can be so quiet. . . .' Whether they went, we do not know; but one of Eliza's kindnesses was to make arrangements for the burial, which took place at Norwood cemetery.

Among other letters they received was the one from Isabella's brother John, now an independent and exceptionally good-looking young man. 'I was very sorry indeed to hear of your sad loss. I am sure you and Sam must have been greatly affected by the event. . . . I had heard that Sam's health was the cause of your visit to Brighton—but had not the slightest idea the boy's was the cause, as I quite understood that he was as well in London as he used to be in the country.' No communication from the Mayson sisters or any of the Dorlings survive, but according to Nancy Spain they took the same view of the case as John, and censured the parents for exposing their offspring to the City atmosphere. '. . . there were some adverse comments about it in Epsom, especially after the second tragedy.'[4]

And undoubtedly the fact that it was the second time added greatly to the strain of the situation. It had been easy for everyone to dismiss the first occasion as bad luck, but even someone as reasonable as Isabella must have found it difficult to accept another bereavement in a rational spirit. Apart from this, the loss of a child of three was a very different matter from that of a baby barely three months old, whose presence they had scarcely had time to get used to. It is hardly to be wondered at if Isabella, after seven years of marriage and the births of only two children, now both dead, gave up hope of having a family. . . . And yet, perhaps, once she had got over her immediate misery, such very hopelessness, in causing her to be more relaxed about the whole matter, did her good; at any rate, if there was any reason for the sudden increase in her fertility thereafter, this explanation seems as likely as any.

But that was some months in the future; meanwhile, January 1863, when she was homeless and childless, and had not even her book to turn to, was surely the grimmest time in her life. She and Sam went doggedly back to work, conspicuous in their black clothes. A very creditable consignment of clothing reached Lancashire, and no doubt the life of many another infant was saved, which possibly afforded her a little bleak comfort, and Sam had the publication of the boys' papers to take up his attention. And then at the end of the month came the article, nicely timed to lift them out of their doldrums.

It appeared in *The Morning Herald* on Monday 26 January, and was later reprinted in *The Standard*. It was spontaneous, if rather wordy—the reviewer had obviously only just come across the Beeton publications and had written them up in the first flush of excited enthusiasm.

The astonishing circulation of some of the periodicals and serials published by Mr. S. O. Beeton might seem to render a commendatory notice of them supererogatory, but as it is their exceeding merit that gains for them public esteem so that merit demands the avowal of our very decided approval. Great as is the circulation of one and all of these publications, there is no reason why it should not be greater still; and if by thus bringing them to the notice of our readers we should increase their circulation, we shall consider that we not less benefit our readers than do an act of justice to a publisher who in enterprise and judgement is one of the first in the kingdom. . . . Offering, then, first place to the ladies, we have before us the *English-woman's Domestic Magazine*, a wonderful publication in size, matter, and above all in price. . . . Then there are the periodicals for boys—one, *The Boy's Own Magazine*, at sixpence a perfect marvel for the money, and admirably adapted to what are called growing youths; and *The Boy's Penny Magazine*, which we confess to liking even better than its bigger and dearer brother. . . .

And so on, for nearly a column, in the course of which all Sam's works were praised with almost equal warmth, with the notable exception of Isabella's two principal concerns, *Household Management* and *The Queen*—an omission presumably due simply to the fact that the writer was unaware of their existence. It is hard to tell whether his remarks about the circulations of the magazines were made ingenuously or not; just possibly, he may have been trying to say not only that they deserved to be larger, but that it looked as if they needed to be.

Such a tribute could not fail to act as a tonic; what perhaps pleased Sam most of all was the remark in the conclusion: 'Mr. Beeton is, we conceive, doing a great work in our national education . . .'—which so closely corresponded to his most cherished ambitions. Nor was this all, for further laudatory notices followed; besides the repeat in *The Standard*, he was puffed in the *Penny Illustrated Paper*, which declared that he must have 'a higher motive than mere money-making',[5] and in the *Illustrated Times*, *The Literary Times*, and the *Weekly Dispatch*. The provincial papers, once they had recovered from the shock of the early *EDM*, had always generously supported him and now came out in eulogies.

After this, the progress of S. O. Beeton could be charted with accuracy from the pages of the *Athenaeum*, where he was soon regularly buying advertising space, along with all the other major London firms. His books for adults were reviewed as they appeared—both there and in *The Times*. Neither paper, however, condescended to notice his works for children, which, following his own inclinations and the lead given by *The Morning Herald*, he pushed as hard as he could over the next couple of years and

publicized vigorously. The next Christmas he took a whole page
to advertise his boys' books, which showed that he had put out
at least half a dozen new titles in the course of the year; and that
year's Christmas annual was also angled chiefly towards children,
its principal theme being ghost stories.[6]

XIX

COUNTRY LIFE

W HEN THEY HAD got over their depression after the death of
the child, Sam and Isabella did finally get around to buying a
house. It was at Greenhithe, about twenty miles down the Thames
from the City; the area was probably recommended to them by
one of their editors, John Tillotson, who lived in the neighbourhood. He was the 'man of much learning' who had been chiefly
responsible for the Bible, and was known to the readers as the
'Odd Boy' of the *BOM*; but above all, despite being a cripple, he
had the reputation for being the soul of cheerfulness, and there
was certainly no one who could have been a greater asset to Sam
during the weeks of torture following Isabella's death. When he
too died, a few weeks after her, Beeton wrote him an absurdly
sentimental but touching epitaph, which showed how deep his
regard for him had been:

> The lilac and laburnum trees which he so loved now droop
> their pendant branches unseen by him, in the sweet spring air;
> and the twittering birds are unable now to call him forth who
> was always joyous to hear their songs as they sang their solos
> in the nighttime. . . . The close friendship which has subsisted
> for the past ten years between himself and the sorrowful
> writer of these lines has never been interrupted—how gladly I
> say it!—by a single rough, hard word. Our cottages were only
> separated by a chalk-pit and a field, and one never saw him but
> to gladden under the bright influence of his beautiful mind;
> one never parted from him without feeling that it was a
> privilege to have listened to the good thoughts that had been
> spoken by the pleasant voice. Whether in the ordinary affairs
> of the business of literature, or in the privacy of home life, all

who knew him owned his accomplishments and were brought
within the power of his sympathetic heart.[1]

Greenhithe is now the site of a gigantic cement works, and it is
difficult to imagine how anyone could have chosen to live there,
but at the time it was a small village set amid undulating hills
which, like Pinner, had the advantage of being on the railway but
still fairly undeveloped. The Beeton's purchase was a low,
rambling farmhouse on a hill with a view towards the flat expanse
of country which has become a major industrial area, with the
Dagenham motor works only a few miles up the river. The house
was not large, and in terms of accommodation was smaller than
Chandos Villas, but, in contrast to the brash, newly-built villa, it
had a certain mellow charm. There were thick creepers covering
the walls and an old thatched summerhouse facing an arcaded
terrace, which Isabella hung with baskets of trailing flowers. As
before, the main attraction was the garden, which extended over
a couple of acres and by the time she had finished with it was
extremely pretty, with long terraces, a croquet lawn, and a
formal garden laid out with box hedges. To one side towered a
pair of magnificent oaks, and on the other was a field; this encouraged Sam to buy a horse, the mare Gerty, to whom he
became extremely attached, refusing to part with her even
when the house was sold. A decade later, when he was living in a
nearby cottage, he said, 'Gerty in her loose box in the poultry
yard enjoys herself very much; we let her into the field to eat the
grass, and she is as gentle as a lamb.' In Isabella's day there was
also a donkey to keep the mare company.

They moved into Mount Pleasant, as the house was called
(they seldom used the name, and referred to it simply as 'Greenhithe') in the spring, probably April, of 1863, and so began a
most pleasant and peaceful eighteen months. At about this time
Isabella found, no doubt to her intense surprise, that she was
pregnant again; as ever, she did not allow it to make any difference to her normal activities, and carried on with her work
and social life as usual.

If she had any fears about this third pregnancy, they were
dissipated by the robust appearance of the baby, who, ironically,
was born a year to the very day after the death of his brother,
and was called Orchart. Her happiness is obvious from a set of

snapshots taken the following summer, in which she looked radiant, and noticeably slimmer than when she was younger. At this stage, her fourth pregnancy (which must have come as something rather more than a surprise, since it began only four months after Orchart's birth), was not in evidence, and she herself may not yet have known of it. The photographs were taken on the occasion of a visit from some of her brothers and sisters—Henry Mayson, who was acting as escort, Bessie, Esther, Lucy, Frank (or possibly Alfred), and Isabella's youngest brother Horace, aged two. It was obviously a happy family gathering: Bessie and Esther dandled Orchart, Isabella nursed Horace, whom she had hardly seen, Lucy played croquet, and Henry Mayson chatted with Sam.

Besides their new house and family and their very real delight in their more countrified surroundings, the Beetons for the first time enjoyed relative prosperity—substantially boosted by the sale of *The Queen* in mid summer. They allowed themselves a number of small pleasures that hitherto they, or at any rate she, had not considered permissible. Gerty, the horse, was one and a certain amount of entertainment, as well as entertaining, were others. They had always been in the habit of having friends to dinner, but one gathers from a story about them in J. W. Robertson Scott's book—so far as can be found, the only one ever recorded about them by someone outside their immediate family circle—that they entertained in some style at Greenhithe. Mr Scott relates that one evening at a party given by Frederick Greenwood, they were introduced to Greenwood's young niece, Maria, who still remembered the meeting as a very old lady. Sam had perhaps not been at his most entertaining that night, since her only comment about him was that he seemed 'a very nice gentleman', but she recalled Isabella much more clearly, describing her as 'very lively and chatty and something of a practical joker'; she then went on to tell of how, at another party, some of Isabella's friends complained that their husbands had been grumbling because they could not cook as well as her, 'so at the next gathering at the house of Mrs. Beeton, she dished up a shocking meal in order to teach men not to criticize their wives.'[2]

Sam also accompanied Isabella on both her annual visits to Paris. The first year they extended their trip and spent a week in Germany. From Paris they went to Berlin as Sam had business

there, presumably connected with his boys' books—he had
already published stories and a serial by the German writer
Frederick Gerstäcker—and then they continued on to Dresden
and Leipzig for a short holiday. In contrast to Isabella's pre-
occupation on their earlier excursions, she did not mention
money once, and since they were not so worried about spending
it they went out to the opera or theatre nearly every night. But
for her, outdoor pleasures were still the best part of the holiday,
and her favourite day was when they climbed the Basten, a
mountain on the Elbe.

> The pleasantest day we have spent in Germany. Weather
> excessively warm . . . crossed the Elbe in a ferry to Weblen.
> There we commenced the ascent to the Basten. Huge over-
> hanging and perpendicular rocks. Good walking. The view of
> the Elbe and surrounding country one of the most lovely
> pictures imaginable. . . .

They were down again in time for dinner, which in Prussia
was eaten in the middle of the afternoon (on their first day in
Berlin she had said, rather disconsolately, 'Prussians [usually]
dine between 2 and 3, being seldom later'); after their meal,
therefore, they had time to ascend a second mountain to visit the
fortress of Königstein, where one of the things that most
interested her was a well over 600 feet deep, which she was told
had taken forty years to dig; with typical exactitude, she added:
'Water thrown from the top [takes] 17 seconds reaching the
bottom of the well.'

Their second visit to Paris was of little interest: Sam discussed
the plates of yet another magazine with Goubaud and made some
notes for a report on the Grand Prix (a horse race run at Long-
champs) which they attended on both occasions. It is obvious
from her familiarity with the British horses who were running
that she had kept up a fairly regular attendance at the Derby since
her marriage; she was also somewhat patronizing about the state
of the French course, which she recorded was too hard, and
covered with weeds.

Back at the Strand, she continued her work in relative tranquillity until the latter part of 1864; she now had only her *EDM*
contributions to worry about, and while Sam was concentrating

on his boys' publications, no fresh responsibilities came her way. On their return from Paris that year, however, she faced an exceptionally busy autumn, partly because she was compiling her second abridgement of *Management*, the *Dictionary of Cookery*, but chiefly because Sam was planning his fourth children's magazine, this time for girls, as a partner to the *BOM*—or rather, as the equivalent to the *Boy's Penny Magazine*, since it was brought out as a penny weekly. The *Young Englishwoman*, as it was called, was no less innovatory than the *BOM*, in that it was the first publication of its kind on the market—and unlike the boys' papers, remained without rivals for a surprisingly long time; the next specifically girls' periodical was the *Girl's Own Paper*, which came out sixteen years later. But despite the unchallenged position it held for so long, it has been ignored by most writers on children's literature in much the same way as the *BOM*, part of the reason perhaps being that as girls were treated as young women from an early age, it was not conspicuously different in content from an adult women's magazine.

Its nature was considerably influenced by Isabella, who, as usual, had charge of the fashion and needlework pages, and was consulted by Sam about its overall plan and character; this is demonstrated by a letter he sent her in October from New-market, where he was staying with the Englishs. The letter also suggests that there was some controversy in the office over the whole idea, possibly stemming from the extreme caution parents were wont to exercise over young girls' reading.

I have asked Sidney to get Young to write *his* notions on paper of what the Young E'woman should be, irrespective of mine, and if Y is there tomorrow, as I think he will be, ask Sidney to let you see him, and you can tell him what *you* think. Of course you will know, as the French say, how to tell him this without expressing any opinion abt. the wisdom of the step. Because that is toute autre question.

Send the description of the 8 pages you have already got up for the Young Englishwoman as soon as pos' with the clichés to Cox and Wyman and ask C.W. to let Poulter do the making up. This done, the next thing is the sheet of Dble Demy with 2 sets of diagrams and Needlework patterns, given us, that is to say, the Suppt. for the Young E'woman for 2 weeks. . . .

Goodbye, my girl, 'sweet kisses on thy fair-formed brow I'd give, but can't just now.'

Receive, I pray you my good master, the assurance of my highest consideration, the intimation of my most considerable respect, and the expression of the warmest love from him who is, and ever shall be, paper without end, A man (qui est réussi) S.O.B.

Largely as a result of Isabella's advice, which was doubtless backed up by Young and probably others besides, the *Young Englishwoman* was a very prudently conceived publication. It was as gay and informative as any of the other magazines, and certainly not prudish, but it was entirely innocent of any advanced notions, and concentrated almost exclusively on domestic topics; for this reason, apart from the actual fact of its existence, it was the least interesting of the Beeton periodicals. As well as fashion and needlework, it carried fiction, poetry, music, and a junior version of the Conversazione, 'Our Drawing Room'; the supplement Sam referred to was along the same lines as the dressmaking and embroidery supplements issued with *The Queen* and the *EDM*. Because of its innocuous character, and because by this time the name Beeton carried considerable selling power, it was an immediate success: it was enlarged several times during the next few years, and by the 'seventies was as fat and glossy as the *EDM*, which it outlived, under another name, by many years.

The first issue appeared at Christmas, when Isabella had only six weeks to go before the birth of her fourth baby. For the Beetons, it was an exceptionally prosperous and promising season, not just because of the new magazine and the imminent prospect of a second child, but in every sense. Their overall professional success seemed established; the celebrations for Orchart's first birthday must have done much to wipe out the memory of the other anniversary which fell upon that date; and their relationship with each other was as devoted as ever: Sam's letter shows that eight years had not in the least undermined the strength of his early affection, and his acknowledgement of her business capabilities was complete. With all these favourable circumstances, they had every reason to celebrate the gayest Christmas they had ever had. Isabella was certainly feeling light-hearted; the New Year fashions in the *EDM* were unusually frivolous and extravagant, showing two of the dottiest party dresses ever featured in the magazine. One was trimmed with yard upon yard of lace several feet deep, the other was ornamented with blue and pink love-birds and had a bird-festooned headdress to match—not at all to her normal taste, but that month she described them with unrestrained glee. Sam's Conversazione too was exceedingly cheerful, even allowing for his seasonal obligations to readers. 'The gay season promises well,' he prattled. 'New Christmas books over the table; new Christmas games tax the ingenuity of the curious; new Christmas pieces and Christmas entertainments invite us to enjoyment; to say nothing of the Christmas parties which are in store for us when the genuine Christmas season is over and the polite world begins to be festive.'[3]

XX

THE DEATH OF ISABELLA

ISABELLA'S CUSTOMARY, MORE restrained instincts had reasserted themselves by the time she came to write her copy for February, which was about brides—this, she was careful to explain to her English readers, was a very popular time of year for weddings in France and other Catholic countries because of the approach of Lent. Though she did not usually produce her articles until the month in question, the birth of the baby evidently prompted her to complete this one a few days in advance; had she not written it ahead of time, she would never have written it at all. When she went into labour, on 29 January, a Sunday, we are told that she was occupied in correcting the proofs of the *Dictionary of Cookery*.[1] The baby was duly born, so far as is known without complications.

By the next day she was running a temperature, and the doctor confirmed puerperal fever—the infection of the birth passage. Until the introduction of antiseptics, this was the chief danger of childbearing; by this time Semmelweiss had already published a paper indicating the need for antiseptic precautions, in which he recommended that doctors should wash their hands in chloride of lime before delivering babies. His findings were greeted by the medical profession with disbelief, however, and doctors were extremely indignant at the suggestion that it was they themselves who were the disseminators of the disease because of their unclean hands; as far as they were concerned, the cause of puerperal fever was still a mystery.

Only about a quarter of its victims died from it, however, and for the first few days of Isabella's illness Sam doubtless clung to the hope that, because she had always been strong and was still only twenty-eight years old, she would be among the majority who recovered. According to Bessie (who apparently gained her

8*

information from the Beetons' maid) he would not leave Isabella alone, despite the doctor's instructions that she should be kept quiet. 'Sam was told not to worry her anymore,' she is reported as saying. 'He went into her room and told her all his latest troubles—something to do with banking—and she turned her face to the wall.'[2]

It seems that the terror of losing her brought Sam to the brink of delirium. It is easy to understand how, after the optimism of the first few days, his hope turned to panic as she grew worse and he found it impossible to keep away from her; in a desperate attempt to find some reassurance, some sign of recovery, he visited her and talked about anything he could think of to stimulate a response.

Her strong constitution could not pull her through, however: in fact, her prior condition was more or less irrelevant as her chances of survival depended upon the type and virulence of the bacteria which had infected her. Evidently they were of a potent strain, for she died a week later.

There were various practical arrangements to be made after the funeral and her burial at Norwood cemetery. The most urgent problem was to find a wet nurse for the baby—who was named Mayson in memory of his mother—and in this respect at least Sam had a stroke of luck. A woman who lived only a few minutes away from Mount Pleasant had just given birth to a daughter and Sam was able to hand young Mayson over to her, thus avoiding the necessity of engaging one of the notorious professional nurses. Henry Mayson Dorling (Isabella's eldest stepbrother) was the only member of the Dorling family to do anything positive to help Sam, and with the kindness and sensitivity for which he has always been remembered by his friends, volunteered to look after the one-year-old Orchart while the stricken household recovered itself. His children thus provided for, Sam, though he admitted that at times he was as if paralysed, did not languish uselessly at Greenhithe, but returned to the office to face the problems created by Isabella's absence almost immediately.

This we know from a letter he wrote thirteen days later to one of her relatives in Cumberland, William Stagg. It was one of two documents which give some indication of his state of mind at this time, and the thing that comes across most forcefully from both of them, apart from his almost unendurable suffering, was his high morale and truly admirable courage. In the letter, which was written on stationery so thickly banded with black that the writing, in contrast to the message it conveyed, looked pale and feeble, he said:

> To tell you all:—my agony is excessive, but I have hours of calm and quiet which refresh me and enable me to meet the dreadful grief that well nigh overpowers me, and renders me unable to move or stir. But I hope to conquer at last, and will strive, with all the courage I have and can receive by appeals to her good spirit, and to the All-Ruler, to live a good life, honest and pure, to hold the love and respect of good men, and not to lose my own self-respect. In doing this, and in trying to bring up my two little ones, I shall obtain, I think, some comfort. . . .
>
> All have been to me very good, here and in London, and one strain only can be heard of respect and love for her memory.

He expressed his feelings at greater length in an obituary to Isabella in the *Dictionary of Cookery*. It was the most effective piece of prose he ever wrote, with none of his usual rambling imagery or flowery embroidery.

USQUE AD FINEM

Her Hand has lost its cunning—the firm true hand that wrote these formulae and penned the information contained in this little book. Cold in the silent tomb lie the once nimble, useful fingers—now nerveless, unable for anything, and ne'er to do work more in this world. Exquisite palate, unerring judgement, sound common sense, refined tastes—all these had this dear lady who has gone 'ere her youth had scarcely come. But four times seven years were all she passed in this world; and since the day she became wedded wife—now nearly nine years passed—her greatest, chiefest aims were to provide for the comfort and pleasure of those she loved and had around her, and to employ her best faculties for the use of her sisters, Englishwomen generally. Her surpassing affection and devotion led her to find happiness in aiding with all her heart and soul, the Husband whom she richly blessed and honoured with her abounding love.

Her Works speak for themselves; and although taken from this world in the very height of her health and strength, and in the early days of womanhood, she felt that satisfaction—so great to all who strive with good intent and warm will—of knowing herself regarded with respect and gratitude.

Her labours are ended here; in purer atmosphere she dwells; and maybe in the land beyond the skies, she has a nobler work to accomplish. Her plans for the future cannot be wholly carried out; her husband knew them all, and will diligently devote himself to their execution, as far as may be. The remembrance of her wishes—always for the private and public welfare—and the companionship of her two little boys—too young to know the virtues of their good mother—this memory, this presence, will nerve the Father, left alone, to continue to do his duty; in which he will follow the example of his wife, for her duty no woman has ever better accomplished than the late

ISABELLA MARY BEETON

The announcement of her death appeared in *The Times* three days later, on 8 February. There were no notices in any of the three periodicals which she had helped to build up, and over which she had ruled so potently, albeit anonymously, nor was her absence discernible in any other obvious way to her readers, the only immediate difference being the warmer, more personal style of the fashion reporting in the *EDM*. It is unlikely that many people noticed a mysterious, irrelevant paragraph in the March *Conversazione*:

Do you remember Longfellow on the 'Twilight Hour?'—

> 'Come read me some old poem,
> Some simple and heartfelt lay,
> That shall soothe this restless feeling,
> And banish the thoughts of day. . . .'

Pleasant memories or chastening regret, joyous anticipation of good or calm resolution to encounter evil, are good things. We are not all bone and muscle—not only animated machines— there is something better than gold or silver; the soul must have her aspirations and the heart its emotions. . . .[3]

And that, apart from a brief acknowledgement in the *Athenaeum* on the occasion of Sam's death, was the end of Isabella Beeton so far as the contemporary public was concerned. She was not an easy person to get to know in life, and no one but her husband really knew her; and she was unknown to the world at her death. No one could possibly have foreseen that her name would be revived and that in due course Sam, and even Soyer, would be eclipsed by her fame. Except for the deaths of her babies, her life was a triumphant progress, and, had they but known it, a unique example to her public of a woman who succeeded in a man's world without sacrificing any of the femininity they so highly prized—on the contrary, her success, paradoxically, was a consequence of it, for her career was her husband's creation; had it not been for him, the legendary Mrs Beeton would never have been.

Sam's grief was in no way blunted by the passage of time. Six years after Isabella's death, when the facts concerning puerperal fever were established but not yet widely known, he addressed an earnest, indignant, highly emotionally charged warning to his readers:

The practice of the hospitals sanctions the performance of surgical operations upon living subjects by gentlemen who are also engaged from day to day, and even five minutes previously, in dissection upon dead bodies. The combination of the two offices in the person of one man implies a degree of professional enthusiasm on his part which is in itself admirable. Engaged in the grim necessities of dissection performed upon half-putrid flesh, he is summoned at a moment's notice to the operating theatre, where, in the presence of a company of observers who cannot admire sufficiently the accuracy and rapidity with which he plies his terrible instruments, he manipulates, as he proceeds, the freshly-cut wounds of the unhappy patients. Such exhibitions tend to impress observers with the beneficence of such institutions, and they may well feel proud of the minute attention and ample comfort which surround the more fortunate of the sufferers. . . . But if such cases are followed up, if you would pour out oil and wine to hasten convalescence, and seek the individual patients for the purpose, you will discover how large a proportion of those who bore the operations with courage and without apparent harm, are carried off into the grave, not because the amputation hurt them so much, but because of the infection from the dissecting-room, conveyed into their open wounds by the hands of the too-enthusiastic practitioner. The disease they die of is known as hospital gangrene; and it is the very same thing in another form which is called 'puerperal fever', the cause of most of the deaths which are falsely attributed to childbearing. When you see that your family doctor has been engaged upon a *post-mortem* examination, and has given evidence thereon to a jury, who have been dumb with astonishment at his profound acquirements, and before a coroner who has complimented him; then, if a 'little stranger' is immediately expected in your house, avoid that indiscreet doctor as if he were a pestilence, as indeed he is for the time being.[4]

In view of Sam's relationship with Isabella's family, it was only to be expected that a few uncharitable remarks should have been made about her death. Bessie had already accused him of making Isabella worse by disturbing her during her last illness; but it must be remembered that Isabella was in a high fever and would have been more or less impervious to external events of any sort, so Sam's ramblings would have had no effect on her condition.

But it was particularly cruel that the Dorling family should have said, as they did, that her confinement had been carelessly handled: 'The actual confinement was not all it should have been. Doctor and midwife apparently neglected the elementary precautions of cleanliness that are now taken for granted.'[5] As the only precautions that would have saved her were medically unacceptable at the time, such a thing could only have been suggested years after the event, when the facts he wrote of had become common knowledge. Ironically, if Sam had been really negligent and not bothered to call the doctor at all, or if the doctor had been so tardy in coming that there was nothing left for him to do when he arrived, all would have been well. It was not carelessness, but conscientiousness, which killed her.

To Sam, and to their sons, the consequences of her death were even greater than could have been foreseen. It is possible that if she had lived, he might have avoided the calamity of the following year, so that his business would have continued to flourish and have passed in turn to his sons; like many publishing houses founded at around that time, it might still have been in existence now. He certainly would not have given rein to his convictions to the extent of sacrificing, in the eyes of many good men, the reputation he was so anxious to maintain. He had twelve years yet to live; and though in that time he did nothing which contravened his own principles, some of his activities laid him open to a great deal of criticism and misunderstanding.

＊

PART FOUR

'. . . A Life of Torture . . .'

＊

XXI

THE CRASH

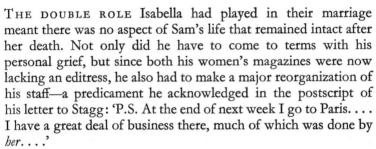

THE DOUBLE ROLE Isabella had played in their marriage meant there was no aspect of Sam's life that remained intact after her death. Not only did he have to come to terms with his personal grief, but since both his women's magazines were now lacking an editress, he also had to make a major reorganization of his staff—a predicament he acknowledged in the postscript of his letter to Stagg: 'P.S. At the end of next week I go to Paris. . . . I have a great deal of business there, much of which was done by *her.* . . .'

In trying to regain some kind of equilibrium, he was fortunate in that he had an exceptionally large circle of friends, colleagues and relatives who were deeply and genuinely attached to him, and in whom he was able to find very real consolation—a boon which Isabella, through no fault of her own, would not have had in anything like the same degree if the situation had been reversed. 'All have been very good to me here and in London,' he had written. Those to whom he referred included his neighbours at Greenhithe, a varied assortment of writers and journalists, and his employees, including Tillotson; also of note was a young man named Christopher Weldon, the future founder of the enormously successful *Weldon's Journal.* In addition were the large clan of Beeton relatives, who numbered not only Eliza and her children, but a generous endowment of aunts and uncles and, of course, his cousins.

He was also extraordinarily lucky in being able to find a fashion writer for the *EDM* who was not only a first-class journalist, but who, in a short while, was also able to replace Isabella in her capabilities as mother and housekeeper, though never as wife. Not far from Mount Pleasant in Greenhithe lived a lively, progressively-minded young couple called Browne, with whom Sam and Isabella had been on friendly terms for some time. Charlie Browne was a big, handsome man with a vigorous sense of humour, who at that time had a clerical job at the Westminster Fire Office (he threw it up a few years later to join the Swiss Ambulance Brigade during the siege of Paris); his wife Matilda, or Myra, as she was usually called, was a vivacious, sympathetic woman, attractive rather than beautiful, who, like Sam, was an enthusiastic believer in the importance of a proper education for women—no doubt because she had been given an unusually good education at one of the few English girls' schools where academic subjects were taken seriously. She had already demonstrated her interest in the Beetons' magazines by writing for them occasionally; furthermore, as Sam must have known, Charlie's job was not well paid, and the Brownes, who certainly had no private income, had always been rather hard up. In the circumstances, and the more because female journalists were still difficult to find, nothing could have been more obvious than for Sam to invite Myra Browne to work for him permanently. She became fashion editor of the *EDM* and began, somewhat tentatively, in the March issue: 'Imagination is already fancying new fashions for spring, and our fair readers expect from us the most explicit statement on the subject; as yet, it is not easy to predict what changes may be adopted.'[1]

This solved Sam's most pressing problem, but there was another, for which no such immediate solution could be found. By the greatest ill luck, it was just at this time that his old friend Frederick Greenwood, who had been with him continuously since he first set up in business thirteen years before, was invited by George Smith to take up the editorship of the new *Gazette*. Presumably Greenwood had been keeping an eye open for some such opportunity throughout the two and a half years since the sale of *The Queen*, but even if he had still been its editor, it is unlikely that he would have resisted such an offer, which promised a far wider scope for his mature abilities and interests than any of the publications owned by Beeton (though he never lost his interest in children, which had been fostered for so long by the *BOM*). He was by this time thirty-five, and had already developed the impressive personality which made him a memorable, if sometimes blunt, editor of what was to become a daily rivalling *The Times* in authority and respectability. Unlike *The Queen*, the

Gazette did not get off to a very good start, and the first few months were a strain on all concerned. Greenwood, grappling with the pace of daily publication and trying to put over the idea of an evening (as opposed to morning) paper to a conservative public—for the *Gazette* was the first-ever London evening newspaper—was totally engrossed, and with the best will in the world could not give Sam in his distress the attention he would have done at any other time. Sam therefore found himself abruptly cut off from both those who had been closest to him almost simultaneously, and at the same time lost his two principal professional colleagues; and while, as with Isabella, he was able to replace Greenwood in his journalistic function without too much difficulty, just as there were several on his staff and elsewhere who succeeded him as friends, he never again had someone of his—or Isabella's—stature to help him in the direction of his firm.

Having sorted out his staffing difficulties as best he could, he carried on business with even more energy than formerly, no doubt trying, intentionally or subconsciously, to numb his feelings by means of a neurotic burst of work, as he and Isabella had done together on past occasions. Over the next eighteen months, more boys' books appeared, including a handbook on chemistry, several collections of songs, and a two-volume *Book of Games*; he also brought out *The Nasby Papers*, signed 'P. V. Nasby', which he probably wrote himself. Obviously, he was making every possible effort to live up to the resolutions he had made at Isabella's death, and would have continued in the same vigorous, unexceptionable manner for the rest of his days had it not been for one further stroke of astonishing bad luck, which changed his life in the material sense as completely as his bereavement had changed its quality.

He deposited money with the leading City discount house, Overend and Gurney, the largest independent financial organization in the country, whose reputation was virtually synonymous with respectability. According to *The Times*, '. . . OVEREND and GURNEY were a household word. The "corner house" was one of the landmarks of the City. Private bankers resorted to the firm with their spare capital. . . . The company was practically the banker of the merchants';[2] and the *Banker's Magazine* put it rather nicely by observing that the directors' names were uttered

with 'that curious solemnity, almost under the breath'[3] that
suggested that they were almost too elevated to be spoken of at
all. But in August 1865, when Sam had been a widower for six
months, they turned themselves from a private firm into a
limited company, or, as *The Times* censoriously put it some
months later, from a discount business to a finance business. As
such, they were obliged to operate on competitive terms with
other finance businesses, which led them to offer improbably high
interest rates. An informed minority were as suspicious of the
change as events soon proved that they had every reason to be
(it had in fact been made by the distressed directors as a desperate
last resort); but because of the firm's enormous prestige most
people did not recognize it as a warning signal and looked on it
as a welcome vindication of limited companies, which over the
past few years had given rise to much discussion and disapproval.

At what point Sam began to have dealings with the house is
not clear. Miss Spain, who incorrectly referred to it as a bank,
states that he had borrowed from it extensively in 1862 or 1863,[4]
but although it is conceivable that he raised money at that time
to help towards the house and the general expansion of his
business which was then taking place, he cannot have done so
from them, since loans were not a part of the business of any
discount house. Conversely, it seems very likely that he took his
profits from the sale of *The Queen* there, but it is impossible to say
for certain whether he was already among the firm's customers
when the change took place. All that is clear is that by the
spring of 1866 nearly all his assets were tied up with it. One
cannot help adding that if he had still been influenced by
Isabella's instinctive prudence, he would probably, against the
general consensus of opinion, have steered clear of it in its new
form.

At first Overend, Gurney, and Co. Ltd appeared to do well—
which made the calamity that followed all the more dramatic.
On 11 May 1866, after only eight months of existence, the new
company closed its doors with liabilities amounting to ten
million pounds. The panic that ensued was remembered as one
of the landmarks of the century, and although the consequences
were not as dire as was expected, it was widely thought at the
time that the Bank of England's intervention would be needed

to tide the country over the crisis. In fact, the directors of the company had themselves applied to the Bank, but the Governors, it was said, 'felt that they could not help one "financing" business without being prepared to help all. . . . Perhaps they also felt that they ought not to bolster up an unsound business.'⁵

In spite of the inevitable moralizing, there was at first some degree of sympathy for the fallen directors, who had in recent months suffered a quite remarkable run of bad luck: in January there had been the failure of a firm of railway contractors called Overend, Watson, & Co., whose similarity of name proved most unfortunate (though they had in fact no connection with the finance business); in February came unsavoury revelations about the Joint Stock Company, to the detriment of finance companies in general; in April, a Spanish company backed by the firm collapsed, and were presently found guilty of various frauds; and then there was the fear of war between Austria and Germany. But charitable feelings did not last, and the directors were eventually (a very long time later) committed for trial. Punch celebrated the occasion with a particularly corny rhyme, which ended:

> In no issue a cheer, but a groan and a cry
> For the soil'd name of England, that once stood so high—
> Stood so high, has so fallen, through gold's abject lust,
> That they who would seek it must look in the dust.⁶

From the outset there was of course very great commiseration for the countless number of firms and individuals who had been ruined, and *Punch*'s rhyme was accompanied by a telling cartoon of a gaunt, aged shareholder sobbing on his wife's shoulder over the caption, 'Yes, they are committed for trial, but we, my child, to *Hard Labour for Life!*' So it was for very many; and for very many more, like Sam, the converse was true—their businesses were gone, and the fruits of a life's hard labour were lost. Sam's affairs had been such that as a result of the crash he found himself in debt.

This time, no letters remain to tell of his reactions, though according to Myra Browne,⁷ he displayed the courage and resignation that could have been predicted of him. The extent of his debts is uncertain: according to Mr Montgomery Hyde, who was a close friend of his younger son, he had been 'overtrading',⁸ but if all his capital had been invested with Overend, Gurney, his position could have been accounted for merely by advance supplies of necessities such as paper; either way, the sum involved can be assumed to have been substantial but not excessive. It was too heavy for his own family to be able to meet, but probably not beyond Henry Dorling's resources. In the general atmosphere of clemency towards the crash victims, it did not perhaps seem entirely vain to hope that in spite of everything, Dorling might do something for him, if only for the sake of his grandsons—and if the sum involved was moderate; but, whether for personal, financial, or other reasons (among which could have been a reluctance to publicize his wealth), he did not. It was surely Sam's bitterness at this final repudiation that was his main inspiration for the offensive passage in *The Derby Carnival*—a sixpenny paper devoted entirely to comment and information about the Derby. In a piece called 'Notes on the Paddock', he said:

> There appears to be some idea in the public mind that there is some occult difficulty about getting into this charming enclosure. . . . Half a sovereign is the difficulty—that is all. Indeed, you may take it for a certainty that for money at Epsom all things are possible. The Clerk of the Course has studied too closely for one and twenty years the art of filling his pockets from every available source, and is too fond of the red gold, not to have made everything that he had any control over quite easy to purchase. Ready, ay, ready to sell anybody or anything, that's the family motto.[9]

The arrangement he came to over the settlement of his affairs was with the firm of Ward, Lock, and Tyler, the publishers of *The Ladies' Treasury*—who, on hearing of his situation, offered to take over his business wholesale, and to retain him to run it as a salaried editor. The idea of being someone else's employee after a life-time of independence cannot have been very agreeable, especially as Ward, Lock, and Tyler had always been a prudent, rather conservative firm with the very opposite approach to business from his own, but as his only alternative was the bankruptcy court, which would have added irretrievable disgrace to what was otherwise not dishonourable misfortune, he accepted.

The contract eventually drawn up between them allowed him

a salary of £400 a year plus a sixth of the profits from his own publications, to rise annually to a quarter. A house in the City was entailed to provide for the education of his sons—a thoughtful provision that Ward and Lock no doubt conceded willingly enough, both being themselves the fathers of young families. The most restrictive part of the settlement was the stipulation that Sam should not undertake any form of work independently of the firm, which from the partners' point of view was a prudent safeguard, and suggests that they had some foreknowledge of their new employee's potential. According to Mr Montgomery Hyde, however, it was not this, but Sam's share of the profits which proved a slight bone of contention. Originally, Sam asked for a third of the profits from his side of the business, but the others considered this too high. 'I'm not much of a bargainer, although you think I am,' Sam protested. 'I only want to be "settled" and my future dependent on the moneys I aid in making....'[10]

It is difficult to estimate the generosity or otherwise of the agreement without having the figures for Sam's debts. Ward, Lock, and Tyler gained a great many profitable publications, including three magazines, the Christmas annual, and of course *Household Management*; and it must be said that in relation to the amount of business he brought, Beeton's basic salary was very low—though quite enough to live on respectably, as Ward and Lock knew from personal experience, having permitted themselves only half that amount when they first started out together. But even if the contract was fairly calculated in the light of the immediate circumstances, it was short-sighted as a permanent arrangement, for it offered Sam no hope of ever regaining his position; and in destroying every prospect for the future, served to weaken still further the reduced interest he naturally felt for publications that were no longer his. He remained with his employers eight years, and although during that time he never ceased to work to the limit of his capacity, and beyond—for his health grew steadily worse—it might have been predicted that in the absence of his former consuming motivation, part of his attention would be distracted elsewhere.

As the eight years he spent with Ward, Lock, and Tyler represented almost all the rest of Sam's working life, it seems worthwhile to say a little about them. Ebenezer Ward and George

Lock had set up in business a couple of years after Beeton with a thousand pounds provided by Lock's father; Lock was then twenty-two and Ward considerably older. In abilities they were well matched: Ward was the literary and intellectual partner and Lock a natural businessman. They set out to build up their position in the safest way which offered itself, which was to produce cheap reprints of standard works, mostly of an informative nature. To begin with, they had offices in Fleet Street, not far from Clarke and Beeton's original premises, and moved to Warwick House in Paternoster Row, in the City, shortly after Sam had established himself in the Strand. By this time they were doing very well, and the year before Sam joined them (when Tyler became a third partner), the firm was worth nearly nineteen thousand pounds.[11] Their list, too, had become rather more enterprising, and included Ida Pfeiffer's travel books and a fair amount of fiction, in particular the immensely popular novels of Miss Braddon and stories by the fat, flamboyant George Augustus Sala, who was the founder of *Temple Bar*, the periodical which had been given top rating in *The Queen*. It seems that Sam got to know Sala pretty well—at any rate, he featured him, along with at least one other friend, in several of the radical writings which were the eventual cause of his leaving the firm.

The Ladies' Treasury, the *EDM*'s rival, was Ward and Lock's most adventurous enterprise during their first few years, and, as has already been observed, it was edited to be as conventional as possible. The partners did not follow it up with further magazines, but, presumably in much the same way as Sam had been inspired with the idea of *Household Management*, they were induced to put out books on women's subjects, and by 1860 were advertising such titles as *The Wife's Own Book of Cookery* at 3s 6d, *The Practical Housewife* at 2s 6d, and *How to Make a Home, and Feed a Family* at 2s. Though they had no equivalent to Beeton's publications for children, it can thus be seen that the acquisition of his list was a logical extension of an already existing side of their business; and since Beeton had been their most formidable rival in this field, there was certainly nothing quixotic in their offer to him. It was a sharp stroke of business, and they did extremely well out of it—though they could hardly have foreseen just how well, since at this stage no one could have predicted *Household Management*'s future success.

Nor could they have anticipated the problems Sam brought them, though they were evidently aware of some of the difficulties of his position and did their best to minimize them by going out of their way to be tolerant and considerate. 'It is only fair to record that Ward, Lock, and Tyler treated him with considerable kindness and understanding . . .' says Edward Liveing, the author of a centenary history of the firm.¹² Perhaps for this, as well as obvious practical reasons, no alterations were made to any of his publications; all his staff were given the option of staying on with him and Christopher Weldon and Myra Browne retained their original positions under the new management. In day-to-day terms, therefore, the transfer to Warwick House involved the Beeton team in little more than a change of address, which Sam was able to explain away in the following terms: 'In consequence of MR. S. O. BEETON's premises being required by the New Courts of Law, he has arranged with MESSRS. WARD, LOCK, AND TYLER, of Warwick House, Paternoster Row, for the future publication of all his magazines and other works.'¹³

However deep and bitter his feelings over the loss of his business—and their strength can be imagined—they were as nothing in comparison to those over the loss of his wife; and compared to either of these, the relatively trivial inconveniences he suffered in his private life as a result of the crash were as nothing. Nevertheless, his stipulated income was less than he had ever had to live on before, or at least since the years before his marriage, and with his lack of interest in such matters, he would probably never have succeeded in coming to terms with it in the practical sense had it not been for Myra Browne. During the eighteen months she had been working for him however, she had developed a very great liking and admiration for him, which in view of their many similarities and shared ideals might have been foreseen; and even without such natural empathy, it would have been utterly against Myra's nature not to have been touched by his predicament: his poor health was beginning to be evident in his worn appearance, he had suffered great personal and professional misfortunes and, above all, he had two motherless children. Accordingly, she persuaded her husband to sell their cottage and go to live with him at Mount Pleasant, presumably arguing that the saving effected by running a single establishment would enable the three of them together to keep up the larger house. In this, however, she was mistaken, and a year or two later they were obliged to sell Mount Pleasant as well, and moved into a cottage by the Thames where all of them—herself, her husband, Sam, and the two boys (who were known as Dorch and Dace) lived extremely comfortably and amicably for the next seven years. They were not so poor that they could not afford the usual complement of servants, and had a cook, several maids (one of whom was very pretty), and a man to help in the garden, which, though not large, was productive: 'Gooseberries, cherries, as well as strawberries we have plenty of; and there are plenty of apples and pears. . . .' The balance of their ménage remained harmoniously stable; Sam lived for the rest of his life with his memories of Isabella, and Myra, whatever may have been her deeper feelings, always remained devoted to Charlie, referring to him as 'the kindest of men' and once or twice quoting his humorous remarks for the benefit of her readers; she missed him acutely while he was in France, and continued to be happily married for many years after Sam's death.

For her, however, the crash brought not only Sam but also the unqualified blessing of his sons. She had always wanted children, but had so far failed to have any and welcomed the two boys with profound delight and gratitude; soon after she had taken charge of them, she wrote:

> The dark hour, so piteously complained of by my readers, is, in many families, the happiest hour of the day:
>
>> 'Between the dark and the daylight,
>> When the night is beginning to lower,
>> Comes a pause in the day's occupation
>> That is known as the children's hour.'
>
> But, before the children came to bless my home, what is now known as the 'children's hour' was then the 'dark hour' or 'blind man's holiday', to me. Very long and very dark it used to be. . . .[14]

As for the boys, if she gained from their presence, they did so even more from hers; they were far too young to remember Isabella, and automatically looked on her as their own mother from the first, remaining to all intents and purposes unaware of the difference until they were much older. But they did not continue to be her only children, for as so often happens to childless women in similar circumstances, she presently gave birth to a child of her own, a remarkably good-looking boy called Meredith.

Over the next few years, her columns were scattered with incidental remarks and reminiscences about the boys, which, if they sound a little sentimental now, show that she was as lively and indulgent a mother as any child could wish, and that they had an exceptionally normal, happy, and healthy upbringing. During one of her children's hours when the boys were still very small she pretended to be an elephant, then a carriage, a train, a bicycle, a pudding, and a Christmas tree in rapid succession; then she told them stories; then she listened in turn to their stories; then 'at last these gentlemen who rule me decided on cleaning "somepit", and in desperation I sent them on a raid to the kitchen, whence they returned in triumph with a plate-cloth, pursued by the housemaid, who values plate-cloths highly. . . .'[15] When he was six, Mayson sent her a Valentine in a lace envelope: 'O the excitement, the fun, of buying and addressing Valentines! The delight of seeing a rosy cherub of six, full of the importance of his task, write, with anxious face and trembling hand, an address on a lace envelope. . . .'[16]

When they were a little older, they were sent to a preparatory school, and then to Marlborough. Myra described an idyllic summer holiday spent by the sea in Devon not far from the boys' prep school:

> The pleasant days glide on in this enchanting spot, varied by walks and pleasant drives; by raids on rocks, returning laden with stories of sea-anemone and wondrous seaweeds; by marvellous legends of perils of the deep . . . by visits to dairies and superintending of 'scalding' cream, and tasting the same with early strawberries; by feats in swimming on the part of the heroic boys and their father . . . by 'lessons in Latin' given by papa to the boys, and by the youngest boy to mamma, who is asked at all times and in all places to decline various words 'with cases'. Lost in rapture at the beauty of the earth, and sky, and sea, lying bewildered in a dream of beauty on the lovely

sward of Watcombe, or going over the beauteous Bay of Babbicombe, one is recalled to earth by a dear but peremptory voice in one's ear, 'Decline mensa, a table' . . . The last day of the boys' holiday is a memorable one—a delightful day, varied by attempts on the part of my youngest to be so *ill* as to be unable to go to school—a violent headache which lasted ten seconds, shocking sickness which abruptly left him at the sight of apricot jam and cream, and a mysterious sore *froat*, 'lower down than you can see', and in the night creeping in to cuddle mother and say, 'I am too little to go to school, I *am*'— which opinion entirely coincides with mother's. All this was vain, and in the morning the little fellow preserved a sorrowful and dignified silence, broken only once as a last appeal to his relentless parents—'I shan't never send *my* boys to school— I shall have a man-governess at home'—at which his unfeeling father laughed till the tears came. *Ayde me!* partings are sad, if only for a term. . . .'[17]

But once there, both the Beetons enjoyed school, Mayson more than his brother—if his forgetfulness about writing home was anything to go by. Sam constantly upbraided him for his laziness in this respect in his letters, which otherwise were filled with details about their various pets and their gardens (each boy had his own); as can be imagined, with his sense of humour and long experience of boys, he was no less the ideal father than Myra was mother.

I have been expecting to see your 'hand-write', as they say in Scotland, for many days. Mamma has written you and sent you things since her return; and I wrote you both in one letter just before we left. Let me know how you are, and what is the last new thing. I have just read a new book, intending to publish it next year for boys, 'Captain Kyd, The Wizard of the Sea'—a wonderful catalogue of adventures. . . . The canary that Mamma bought for Miss Beale died of the 'pip', whilst we were away in Paris—he was getting a beautiful bird; and I miss him very much. Mamma tells me that those little red-wax billed birds of hers are beginning to sing, and sound like a little musical box. I must ask Aunt Carrie to buy another canary. . . .

And again:

Old Moreau [a mule] gets quieter every day; and Rough, noisier; he barks at every one of us as we come in, but doesn't take notice of strangers—he is a curious old fellow! His mother has had another litter, and one of the pups, less than half Rough's size, is exactly like him. Goodbye. Dace did not write last Sunday; give him a hint to do it, when you write. . . .

Myra also protested:

My darling Dorch,
    Thank you for your kind letter. I am sorry I did not put enough stamps in and enclose 12. Yesterday the 29th was my birthday and I had your letter exactly on the day and was very glad indeed to have it. It is a pity you break up later, for we are all longing to see you. . . . Much love to Dace and yourself. Tell him he ought to write every Sunday as you do. I have told him that several times and I hope this is the last time I shall have to write about it.

To the culprit, she wrote rather desperately, 'Papa sends you some books; have you rec.d the box of chocolate I sent you by Mr. Townsend—I sent it in a parcel to Mrs. Treadwin and some books for M.r Townsend and have heard nothing from anyone.'
    In their different ways, both the boys were bright; Mayson was the one to inherit the literary talent, while Orchart, who of the two seems to have been the more like his mother, was good at mathematics and came top of the class. Sam was anxious for him to broaden his interests: 'English is your weak point, because you do not read books enough; and I do sincerely wish you may get a greater taste for seeing what all the greatest men in the world have said and written.' After leaving Marlborough, Orchart joined the army, which he made his career, and Mayson went up to Oxford and became a journalist. He spent some years as a Special Correspondent for the *Daily Mail* under Lord Northcliffe, and received a knighthood for his work in the Ministry of Munitions during the First World War. He died in 1947, the same year as Orchart, leaving three daughters, two of whom are still alive today.

MRS ENGLISHWOMAN

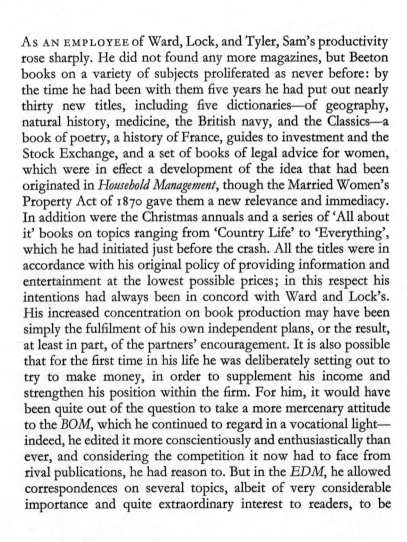

As an employee of Ward, Lock, and Tyler, Sam's productivity rose sharply. He did not found any more magazines, but Beeton books on a variety of subjects proliferated as never before: by the time he had been with them five years he had put out nearly thirty new titles, including five dictionaries—of geography, natural history, medicine, the British navy, and the Classics—a book of poetry, a history of France, guides to investment and the Stock Exchange, and a set of books of legal advice for women, which were in effect a development of the idea that had been originated in *Household Management*, though the Married Women's Property Act of 1870 gave them a new relevance and immediacy. In addition were the Christmas annuals and a series of 'All about it' books on topics ranging from 'Country Life' to 'Everything', which he had initiated just before the crash. All the titles were in accordance with his original policy of providing information and entertainment at the lowest possible prices; in this respect his intentions had always been in concord with Ward and Lock's. His increased concentration on book production may have been simply the fulfilment of his own independent plans, or the result, at least in part, of the partners' encouragement. It is also possible that for the first time in his life he was deliberately setting out to try to make money, in order to supplement his income and strengthen his position within the firm. For him, it would have been quite out of the question to take a more mercenary attitude to the *BOM*, which he continued to regard in a vocational light— indeed, he edited it more conscientiously and enthusiastically than ever, and considering the competition it now had to face from rival publications, he had reason to. But in the *EDM*, he allowed correspondences on several topics, albeit of very considerable importance and quite extraordinary interest to readers, to be pursued in a manner that was definitely prejudicial to the magazine's long-term interests.

Meanwhile, as editress, Myra soon became as influential in her own way as Isabella had been. Her light, intimate, sometimes sentimental style was ideally suited to the women's journalism of the time, and her columns vied with Sam's as the magazine's centre of attraction. As well as her monthly fashion reports, she wrote a feature called 'Spinnings in Town' signed 'The Silkworm' (a neat parallel to the Beeton beehive), plus a number of papers on the subjects she and Sam were now determined to plug, such as women's rights and women's education. When Isabella had begun her career fifteen years before it had been impossible to write freely on such subjects but by the end of the 'sixties the climate of social change had advanced so far that the 'Woman Question' had become one of the major issues of the day, and to speak out in favour of independence was to do no more than align the magazine on the side of progress.

Spinnings in Town was simply a rather rambling shopping guide, sprinkled with snippets of fashion advice and any other social or domestic news which happened to come to her notice. One month, for instance, she reported on a firm of photographers who claimed to have perfected a technique of portraiture which guaranteed that everyone, no matter how old or ugly, would come out looking flawlessly beautiful (there was no Trade Descriptions Act in those days); another time the column was entirely given over to a description of her trial of one of the earliest washing machines, which consisted simply of a tub with a rotary beater attached to a hand-operated crankshaft; on other occasions, she wrote about a knitting machine, waterproofed fabrics, and a whole catalogue of the other new inventions and conveniences that were fast becoming available. Whenever the opportunity presented itself, she encouraged women to earn their own living, and suggested various employments besides the usual governessing—hairdressing and nursing, for example; she also recommended employment agencies and life insurance, made possible for women for the first time by the Act of 1870. She herself took out a policy with the Metropolitan Life Assurance Society, and was delighted at the ease and courtesy with which the formalities were conducted, the only drawback, she said gaily, being the necessity of declaring one's age: 'Age admitted!

9

Awful words! when more than thirty summers have passed over a woman's head, leaving the inevitable winters that follow them to touch dark hair with snowy flecks. . . .'[1]

In 1869 she came up against the *Saturday Review*, which published what was probably the wittiest condemnation of the 'New Woman' of the century, the famous 'Girl of the Period' series of articles by the cruel, brilliant Eliza Lynn Linton—'that wonderful feminine pen in the *Saturday Review* employed to make fun of virtue, and laugh at morality, and tickle the minds of men and women into a state that shall no longer know right from wrong. . . .'[2] Miss Linton's mocking attitude infuriated her, and stung her to several moderately forceful protestations against the *Saturday Review*'s reactionary stance, and she was already embittered by the fact that earlier in the year the same writer had exercised her skill at Sam's expense; when she herself was accused of taking unfair advantage of her position as The Silkworm, she exploded into what was for her an unusually vehement retort, which is worth quoting just to show that she could hit as hard as anyone when she wanted.

Unwilling as I am to intrude personal matters upon my readers, I feel I owe to them as well as to myself some reply to an attack made upon the Silkworm in a late number of the *Saturday Review*, and therefore I will visit that Review along with other establishments, and will 'spin' about it. Let us enter the 'shop' in Southampton-street, let us examine the wares, let us note the quality and quantity of the 'articles' for sale. In the first place, let us look at the political articles, the dry goods I call them, finding them often very dry indeed; then we will enter another department, and look at the satins and moirés— very handsome, very rich with quaint sayings, with clever wit, and with profound knowledge. The 'heavy' articles are almost invariably well written; we will not linger over these, but hasten, not to the 'cutting out,' but to the 'cutting up' department. Here the work of many years, the deep labour, and study, and thought of men of genius suffer the incessant fire of the untiring critics, the 'blatant, indolent reviewers.' Like the 'small poets' who 'each kept on his hat' before the great Cardinal Richelieu while reviewing his poems, these critics ruthlessly 'cut up' the work of half a life-time—that is, unless the

'Jupiter' has nodded his gracious head in its favour a day or two before. 'If we are not critical, we are nothing,' and the *nil admirare* principle, if not carried too far, is commendable— in a reviewer; but to praise anything or anybody would be the ruin of a shop wholly devoted to selling lemon-juice and vinegar; and indeed, the Silkworm herself would be sorry to find, on opening *her* vinegar-jar, honey or 'milk of human kindness' mixed therein. It is very amusing to read the criticisms of the new novels, and indeed the stories are often told so cleverly as to prevent any wish to read the books. But the department which I have reserved to the last is the most interesting to Englishwomen, for there they are constantly discussed. Whenever a couple of columns are required to be 'filled up,' or when the editor is tired of toadying the ecclesiasticism of his proprietor, then the services of the 'bilious contributor' are called in, and the Englishwoman, whether as 'Girl of the Period,' 'Frisky Matron,' or 'Man's Disenchanter,' is torn to pieces, cut up, dissected. Nor is this all; horrible suggestions, tricks that would disgrace an Aspasia, are attributed to our young girls, to our English wives and mothers. If men think lightly of women, if subjects are discussed before our sex that were considered unfit for the ears of our mothers, if women are less respected than in former days, it is to this *Magasin des Mauvaises Idées* that we are indebted. . . .[3]

She did not write as sharply as this in her articles on 'Women's Rights' (signed 'By a Woman', but unmistakably written by her); indeed, these papers were distinguished more for their mildness of tone than for their aggressiveness, which with this particular topic was a far more effective approach than the militancy of many other feminist writers. Nowhere did she sacrifice her own femininity, nor did she exhort her readers to, for besides the fact that nothing could have been further from her ideal, she knew very well that human nature does not change.

That water will always rise to the level of its source is a fact that took ages to find out. The trouble men might have been spared if they had known it before! . . . The trouble men have been to lately to explain that if we take the barriers away, water will run uphill; that if we allow women to be doctors or lawyers they will all strike, and refuse to be mothers or wives![4]

She saw the two crucial issues of education and the right to work, not as alternatives to motherhood and marriage, but as the means of enhancing and enriching them, and of making existence worthwhile for those who could not have them—who, as she said, were by no means a negligible few, but a sizeable minority of nearly two million. The question of education was particularly stressed in all her articles, and naturally enough, the best article, because it was the most informed and to the point, was the one she devoted entirely to it. In this, she drew on a report by a member of the Committee of Council on Education, a Mr Fitch, whose conclusions corresponded very closely to those voiced by Sam nearly twenty years earlier: that girls' schools neither educated girls in the broader sense nor equipped them for marriage by teaching them domestic skills. All they received were insubstantial trimmings—in Myra's simile, mental nourishment of tarts and sweetmeats rather than bread and meat. In other words, the Boarding-school Miss was as useless as ever, which, as Fitch emphasized, was of course ultimately the fault of the parents.

But, as the magazine readers were by this time very fully aware, parents had considerably more than uselessness to answer for. While Myra was worrying about their daughters' intellectual development, Sam, in the Conversazione, had been drawn into controversies on other aspects of their education, in which parental crassness and cruelty reached the most horrifying extremes—and seemed scarcely less outrageous to contemporaries than to us. One of the most horrifying things about these discussions, however, was the fascination they exercised over readers and editor alike; as time went by they got completely out of hand, and assumed a lurid significance which unfortunately somewhat obscured their fundamental importance, so that for once the *Saturday Review* was not unjustified in doing a little of the 'cutting up' that Sam, once a certain point had been reached, should have done for himself.

The first was on the subject of tight-lacing. As far back as March 1867, when Sam had been with Ward, Lock, and Tyler only seven months, a letter arrived from Edinburgh from the distressed mother of a teenage girl to complain of the tight-lacing to which her daughter had been forced to submit at a fashionable boarding school near London. Having left her there for four years while she was abroad, she sent for her as soon as she returned, and was appalled at the transformation that had been wrought in her absence.

I expected to see a fresh, rosy girl of seventeen come bounding to welcome me. What, then was my surprise to see a tall, pale young lady glide slowly in with measured gait and languidly embrace me? When she had removed her mantle I understood at once what had been mainly instrumental in metamorphosing my merry romping girl to a pale fashionable belle. Her waist had, during the four years she had been at school, been reduced to such absurdly small dimensions that I could easily have clasped it with my two hands. 'How can you be so foolish,' I exclaimed, 'as to sacrifice your health for the sake of a fashionable figure?' 'Please don't blame *me*, mama,' she replied; 'I assure you I would not voluntarily have submitted to the torture I have suffered for all the admiration in the world.' She then told me how the most merciless system of tight-lacing was the rule of the establishment, and how she and her forty or fifty fellow-pupils had been daily imprisoned in vices of whalebone drawn tight by the muscular arms of sturdy waiting-maids, till the fashionable standard of tenuity was attained. The torture at first was, she declared, often intolerable; but all entreaties were vain, as no relaxation of the cruel laces was allowed during the day under any pretext except decided illness. 'But why did you not complain to me at first?' I inquired. 'As soon as I found to what a system of torture I was condemned,' she replied, 'I wrote a long letter to you describing my sufferings, and praying you to take me away, but the lady principal made it a rule to revise all letters sent or received by the pupils, and when she saw mine she not only refused to let it pass but punished me severely for rebelling against the discipline of the school.' . . . On attempting to discontinue the tight-lacing, however, my daughter found that she had been so weakened by the severe pressure of the last four years that her muscles were powerless to support her, and she has therefore been obliged to lace as tightly as ever, or nearly so. She says, however, that she does not suffer much

inconvenience now, or indeed after the first two years, so
wonderful is the power of Nature to accommodate herself to
the circumstances. The mischief is done; her muscles have
been, so to speak, murdered, and she must submit for life to be
encased in a stiff panoply of whalebone and steel. . . .

The irate mother immediately went to confront the headmistress, who blandly informed her that the majority of parents
were entirely satisfied with her system, the enforcement of which,
she added, required 'unremitting perseverance and strictness':

Finding that I could not touch the heart of this female
inquisitor, who was so blinded by fashion, I determined to
write to you and inform your readers that if they do not wish
their daughters tortured into wasp-waisted invalids, they may
avoid sending them to schools where the corset-screw is an
institution of the establishment.[5]

Except for the lady's ability to write effectively, there seems no
reason to doubt the genuineness of her letter, for, as emerged in
the ensuing correspondence, tight-lacing was the accepted practice in very many girls' boarding schools, being regarded in
much the same light as other feminine accomplishments—indeed,
to ensure that their daughters would have fashionable figures
was all too often parents' chief motive for sending them to
school. But the mother's polished narrative immediately aroused
the suspicion of another lucid letter-writer, a cynical young
woman signing herself 'STAY-LACE', who, though missing
the point so far as school-girls were concerned, opened the
debate to the wider issue of tight-lacing in general.

In reply to the invitation from the lady from Edinburgh to a
discussion on the popular system amongst our sex of compression of the waist, when requisite to attain elegance of
figure, I beg to say that I am inclined, from the tone of her
letter, to consider her an advocate of the system she at first
sight appears to condemn. This conviction of mine may arise
from my own partiality to the practice of tight-lacing, but the
manner in which she puts the question almost inclines me to
believe that she is, as a corset-maker, financially interested in

the general adoption of the *corset-screw*. Her account of the whole affair seems so artificial, so made up for a purpose, so to speak, that I, for one, am inclined to totally discredit it. A waist 'easily clasped with two hands.' Ye powers, what perfection! how delightful! . . . Then again, how charmingly she insinuates that if we will only persevere, only submit to a short probationary period of torture, the hated compression (but desired attenuation) will have become a second nature to us, that not only will it not inconvenience us, but possibly we shall be obliged for comfort's sake to continue the practice. Now, madam, as a part of the present whole of modern dress, every one must admit that a slender waist is a great acquisition, and from my own experience and the experience of several young lady friends similarly addicted to guide me, I beg to pronounce the so-called evils of tight-lacing to be a mere bugbear, and so much cant. Every woman has the remedy in her own hands. If she feels the practice to be an injury to her, she can but discontinue it at any time. To me the sensation of being tightly laced in a pair of elegant, well-made, tightly-fitting corsets is superb, and I have never felt any evil to arise therefrom. I rejoice in quite a collection of these much-abused objects, in silk, satin, and contil of every style and colour, and never feel prouder or happier, so far as matters of the toilette are concerned, than when I survey in myself the fascinating undulations of outline that art in this respect affords to nature.[6]

STAY-LACE's suggestive phrases and uncompromising attitude released a tidal wave of pent-up feeling, and replies expressing every possible shade of opinion on corsets and their consequences surged into Warwick House month by month, the impetus increasing as the year wore on, until by the following November nearly thirty letters had been published. Some were earnest and sensible, some vain and silly, some shocked, some cynical, some merely curious, and there were a few with a decidedly narcissistic or erotic edge, though most of the lascivious ones did not appear until later; all but the most mischievous, however, had the missionary flavour with which the writers' present-day descendants might discuss slimming, with waist measurements being flaunted instead of weight, and different kinds of corset replacing different systems of diet. The original victim wrote to corroborate what her mother had said, which was supported by a similar tale from another girl, except that she claimed to have suffered no ill effect whatever, despite implausibly successful results: 'I was placed at the age of fifteen at a fashionable school in London, and there it was the custom for the waists of the pupils to be reduced one inch per month until they were what the lady principal considered small enough. When I left school at seventeen my waist measured only thirteen inches. . . .''

An Edinburgh headmistress who believed in tight-lacing at least as firmly as the first observed that her countrywoman had only herself to blame for what had happened to her daughter, since if she had not wanted her to have her figure trained 'in what everyone knows is the fashionable style',[8] she should not have sent her to a fashionable school. A number of men were swift to seize the opportunity of confirming the attraction of tiny waists, including 'A YOUNG BARONET' and several who admitted to being corset-wearers themselves, to the intense disgust of many readers (most of the male addicts, however, sounded pretty old, and it must be remembered that corsets for men had been the fashion early in the century). Even a doctor, anxious to establish that not all members of his profession were old-fashioned reactionaries, wrote in to give qualified support to the system.

One of the leaders of the argument on the other side was a forceful lady called 'BRISBANE', who was herself a doctor's daughter. She declared that she had been put off lacing for life after seeing a picture of a woman's liver literally cut in two after years of constriction:

> If girls knew the harm they do themselves by tight-lacing, surely they would desist. They may not feel the effects *now*, but wait till they have arrived at a maturer age. How many mothers have around them a family of poor, puny children, some of them perhaps crippled or deformed, and for which they have only themselves to blame, for having given way to the folly, to call it by no worse name, of tight-lacing.[9]

Her opinion was supported by the overwhelming majority of doctors, whose condemnation of the practice was reiterated not only in the course of correspondence, but in other newspapers and periodicals. For instance, the medical magazine *The Lancet* was quoted as commenting, 'The mischief produced by such a practice can scarcely be over-estimated';[10] and a truly horrible report had been published a few years before in Ward and Lock's own *The Ladies' Treasury*, in which a scandalized doctor told of a girl who had been padlocked day and night into stays so tight that she could scarcely sleep or eat, her only release being her once-weekly bath.

The lungs have been compressed till there is no breathing room, the heart has become diseased, and altogether she is a deplorable object so far as the interior of her frame is concerned; outwardly, this is not seen, but she is maimed for life. Should she live, which I doubt, she will be an invalid wife, and no children will ever call her mother. . . .[11]

In November, having given the subject its head for nine months, Sam pronounced the correspondence closed. Thus far it had unquestionably served a useful, indeed very necessary purpose, for the facts it exposed, despite intermittent medical protest, were not sufficiently known. The ridiculously small waists claimed by many of the correspondents were obviously exaggerations, albeit unintentional, the measurements given having probably been taken from the alleged size of the corset when new. Doris Langley Moore, the costume historian and collector, says that the smallest waists in her collection of dresses of the period are twenty-one inches, and that the average for a fashionable young woman was twenty-four[12]—not much smaller than today, except that several of those inches were accounted for by underclothes and the bulky corsets themselves. In spite of this, perhaps because it was the fashion for women to be plump and full-figured except round the waist, the practice was widespread, and undoubtedly responsible for many of the illnesses attributed to it, as well as lesser complaints such as acne, bad circulation, and other unbecoming ailments.

But Sam's declaration that the correspondence was at an end, though made in all good faith, served in effect only as a punctuation mark; for a couple of months there was a stop, and then the flow began again, this time with greater vehemence and a much

9*

stronger tinge of perversion than previously. This was because, at the same time as closing the subject, he announced the preparation of a book called *The Corset and the Crinoline*, by 'W.B.L.', which was a history of the two items of dress in question, and included a selection of the letters so far received. Naturally enough, the announcement roused a new burst of enthusiasm, besides some facetious comments in the press, and Sam, his overriding instinct as a publisher overcoming his judgement as an editor, simply could not bring himself to maintain his prohibition. 'This irrepressible subject *will* make itself heard, and some of the letters received have been too interesting to discard, unprinted,'[13] he exclaimed. And in the face of the pressure from readers, one can scarcely blame him; the very first of the new spate, for instance, began:

DEAR MRS. ENGLISHWOMAN, I beg—I pray—that you will not close your delightful Conversazione to the Tight-Lacing question: it is an absorbing one; hundreds, thousands, of your lady readers are deeply interested in this matter, and the subscribers to your excellent Magazine are increasing daily, to my own knowledge, by reason of this interesting Controversy; pray wait a little, and you will see how the tight-lacers and their gentlemen admirers will rally round the banner that has been unfurled. . . .[14]

The letter which followed this was one of the most stinging condemnations of lacing in the whole correspondence, its impact springing from the fact that instead of appealing to common sense, like BRISBANE and most of the other anti-lacers, it attacked the practice on its own aesthetic, sexual, and social grounds. It came from 'AN ENGLISH GENTLEMAN':

May I be allowed to say a very few words upon this subject . . .? *Imprimis*, then, I believe that this supreme folly is perpetrated by women solely for the admiration of one another. I never yet met with a man who admired a small waist. Personally, I cannot conceive that to be an elegant figure which approximates to that of the wasp, an insect I could never yet bring myself to think handsome. Moreover, to reproduce an oft-reiterated argument, the Venus de Medici is universally admitted to be the standard model of a perfect female figure; and this is as far removed from the hour-glass shape admired by some few silly women as it is possible to imagine. In the next place, this idiotic mania for cutting themselves in half is almost entirely a middle-class weakness, rarely extending beyond the daughters of professional men, if even so high. Ladies (and by ladies I mean women of birth and position who are actually in society) have for a long time, I am most thankful to say, risen superior to an act of silliness which did, I fear, in years gone by, originate with a very few of them. If you want to see tight stays now-a-days you must seek for them, not in the best English houses, but in the back-parlours behind shops, in 'genteel' boarding-schools, or behind the bars of railway refreshment-rooms. The 'maids' of whom some of your fair correspondents speak as employed to lace them up tightly are, I firmly believe, 'maids-of-all-work'. If the person signing himself A YOUNG BARONET, who wrote to you some time since, be really what his signature indicates, he will, I am sure, corroborate me in the assertion that he does not know one girl in a hundred in his own rank of life possessing such a figure as he professes to admire, and that he must go out of his own set entirely to find it. . . .[15]

By this time another correspondence, of a similar nature but more sinister and of lasting rather than merely period import, was about to get under way. Nearly a year before, a particularly disagreeable communication had been sent to Sam advocating the whipping of female prisoners, in which the writer (this time from Glasgow) supported her argument with the statement that girls were whipped by mothers and governesses in a spirit of 'the tenderest love'. Sam commented in utter disgust:

We can only say that we totally disagree with our correspondent. Degrading and indecent punishments never do good, and in nearly all circumstances do harm when applied to boys or men. Their application to girls or women is revolting. It is not a little startling that our correspondent should look upon a punishment which she would inflict on the vilest criminals in jail, as a proof of tender love when applied to a comparatively innocent girl at home.[16]

But, startling as it may have seemed to him then, it presently became all too clear that a large proportion of Victorian parents and teachers disagreed with him, regarding the chastisement of girls as a normal and necessary means of discipline. Some months later, whether or not as a result of the letter from Glasgow it is hard to say, several parents wrote recommending the birching of children.

Many naughty children are only to be startled into better conduct by sudden corporal punishment. . . . Be sure it is severe, and in the old-fashioned style; a good birch of twigs hurts more and injures less than the hand or rod. If a 'good sound whipping' fails you are in a worse plight than before, and school is the only chance of breaking in the troublesome girl.[17]

Further correspondence trickled in, including desperate pleas for advice from 'AN ENGLISH MAMA' and 'PATER', whose inability to discipline their daughters elicited the letter which really acted as the igniting spark to the whole discussion. This was a dull, repetitious, badly written, but very decided epistle from a mother unequivocally signing herself 'PRO-ROD':

I see a subject discussed in your Magazine in the last two or three numbers on which, as a mother, I should like to say a few words. The subject I refer to is that of personal chastisement for children. I think that in the hands of a judicious mother the rod is a powerful aid in the proper bringing up of her children, both boys and girls. A whipping ought, though, to be effective, I believe, to be administered but seldom, and then, as I said before, only by a judicious mother. The operation ought, too, I think, to be strictly private, and ought to be really painful without being cruel. A child will, I think, often get into such a state that no kindness or reasoning with it will subdue its naughtiness, and when in such a condition I believe a good sound whipping from its mother's hands will generally have a wonderfully good effect. I have used the twigs with my two girls since they were quite little things, not often, it is true, sometimes only once in a month, and they are now—I believe in a great measure owing to these occasional whippings, which are always very private and tolerably severe—very good, well-behaved girls. I do not in the least think, with some of your correspondents, that any ignominy attaches to a private chastisement inflicted even on a girl of thirteen or fourteen by her mother, nor do I think that a kind, judicious mother will ever be hated by her children because she occasionally whips them. I do not, of course, know the circumstances of PATER's case, but I believe, if his wife is of the right kind, that she may find a good smart whipping from her own hand to have a good effect on her naughty daughters. I think that this is a subject which, from its general importance and the difference of opinion on it, might be very profitably discussed in your publication.[18]

This at once produced two more lengthy letters in favour of whipping. The first brought up the very relevant point, as did a great number of subsequent contributions, that the alternative 'moral' punishments were longer-lasting and often much crueller than a summary beating:

I dislike all prolonged punishments, such as sending to bed, shutting up in a room, and depriving a child of its usual food, as I think they are injurious to health and really do little good. Now a whipping is soon over and long remembered, and does not interfere with the daily occupation. I object to the rod as unfeminine, so, up to ten or twelve years old, I whip all my children, boys and girls alike, with my slipper; it punishes quite as much as a birch, and leaves no marks behind. . . .[19]

The second described the extremely severe punishment eventually resorted to by AN ENGLISH MAMA:

. . . that very morning, when my daughter was disobedient, I gave her a box on the ear. This seemed to have little or no effect. In the evening she was just as obstinate as ever, so I took her into my room and just raised her dress, and gave her three or four smart slaps, which, through her underclothing, she could hardly feel, but having the semblance of 'a good sound whipping,' I thought it might frighten her into obedience, and so it did for a day or two, but after that she became just as bad as ever. I told her to go to my room and wait till I came. I waited for about half-an-hour, as I had no wish to punish her in anger, but wished to think over the matter coolly. I made her take off her trousers in order that she might feel the chastisement sharply. I then put her across my knee 'in the good old-fashioned style,' and gave her about twenty sound strokes with the birch and then told her to dress herself, said the punishment was at an end, and there would be no further disgrace. But I also told her that whenever she disobeyed again the whipping would be repeated according to the fault, more or less severely. The effect, I must tell you, was magical; for three days afterwards I could not have had a better child. . . .[20]

From here, the correspondence was allowed to rip without editorial comment for the rest of the year, though care was taken to ensure that approximately the same number of letters appeared for and against (the latter were slower in coming, but no less vehement and numerous once they had begun). Schoolmistresses soon entered the arena, and it became evident that a great many girls' schools used the birch or its equivalent, with more pomposity and less frequency perhaps, but no more compunction, than boys'. The kind of weapon, where to buy it, and on what part of the body it was most expedient to use it were knowledgeably discussed, though the sexual implications of the subject were at this stage kept well in the background. The Scriptures were quoted as the ultimate authority for beating: a 'LOVER OF THE ROD' wrote:

I do believe in the Bible, and in the Proverbs, again and again, Solomon (inspired by God, if we believe the Bible) repeats the injunction in regard to the whipping of children. The rod is referred to not once only, but again and again, and although it is the custom in these days to say it only meant a rod figuratively, I am not one of those who hold that most absurd and dangerous opinion. . . .[21]

In January 1869 Sam endeavoured to put an end to the debate by giving a careful, judicious summary of the views put forward, from which it would seem that his own standpoint had shifted slightly from being absolutely anti to middling, though his condemnation of the thorough-going whipping faction was as firm as ever.

OUR READERS KNOW how fiercely was waged the controversy on the use of the Corset. . . . The discussion has been followed by one still more decided in tone, and upon a subject which has drawn very distinct enunciations of principle, and evidence of very positive practice, with regard to the chastisement of children. The positive party, in this instance, insist upon incalculable advantages to be derived from the use of the rod, slipper, or birch, or other instrument of punishment. They fortify their argument with reference to the sparing of the rod, which, on high authority, is asserted to spoil the child; they declare, absolutely, that corporal punishment is the safest, the kindest, the swiftest, the most effectual mode of correction. The more violent of the positive party, it is open to remark, do proceed, possibly, to further extremities than is, under usual or ordinary circumstances, desirable. There is much to be said, however, for this view, and we are unable to deny that a good deal has been said. As in the debate in our 'Conversazione' upon Tight-Lacing there was a moderate set of people, so there is in this matter of child-whipping; and with them probably lies the truth. The golden mean, which Mrs. Barton could never arrive at, is more likely to be reached by those who are wise enough to hear both sides, and determine for themselves what is best to do under their own particular set of circumstances. The third class of contributors to the discussion are numerous, and very decided in their views. They think there should be no whipping at all, that children—all children—may be made obedient without the use of the rod, and without the application of any personal chastisement whatever. They are ready with their experiences to support their view, and express themselves very strongly against those people who possess opposite opinions, and do not hesitate to brand them in very strong and opprobrious terms. . . . Here ends the discussion, however. Strong feelings have been aroused in the circle—an important and influential circle, listened to by thousands—which is called 'The Englishwoman's Conversazione.' Strong expressions have been used, and freedom has been given to all to express their opinions, for without such liberty nothing can be thoroughly sifted, and we have no desire to repress the candid thoughts of writers because they may differ from ourselves or from the majority. It has never been by any closing of the safety-valve of free discussion that any new truth has been spread, or any wrong set right. . . .[22]

So far, so good; what Sam said was fair enough, and the correspondence up to this point, as in the case of the previous one, served the important purpose of revealing a custom which stood in urgent need of examination and appraisal. There can be no question as to the truth of what was said; a similar correspondence had been carried on in *The Queen* several years before, some time after it had been sold, where complete freedom of expression had also been permitted, and the issue brought to a close in much the same manner as in the *EDM*: 'In the performance of what we regarded as a public duty which might lead to social benefit, we have persuaded ourselves to go to the utmost verge and limit . . . but . . . we must decline to insert any more communications regarding it.'[23] There were horrible reports of floggings and other fearful punishments imposed in schools in the newspapers; and even the *Pall Mall Gazette* was quoted by one Consersazione correspondent, on the subject of the Scottish taws. Nor can we comfortably assume that the violence with which some Victorians treated their children was peculiar to them, since although their obsession with discipline and punishment has faded with the advance of the permissive society, the issue of corporal punishment is with us as forcefully as ever— and not just in public schools, or for boys only, as every parent of school-age children must know; one has only to glance through the newspapers to see that caning is still a standard punishment. 'The hidden truth of school beatings' ran a heading in *The Guardian* of June 1976, where a London comprehensive teacher was quoted as saying: 'Much here isn't entered in the books but even so there were recorded 23 canings for "failure to complete homework" in the last term—five on one boy. A number of girls were included in this punishment.' And a Midland supply teacher wrote: 'At most of the schools I've just taught in I saw canings every day, some for the "crimes" you mention. I used to think girls were seldom or never caned. Now I know otherwise.

Young teachers seem even more ready to cane than older ones.'[24] 'Walloping backsides or licensed, sexually dangerous physical assault?' demanded another headline. 'Outwardly there is still in our society a conspiracy of silence on the sexual aspect of corporal punishment even more profound than that on the frequency of its occurrence. . . .'[25]

Unhappily for the reputation of the magazine, Sam followed up his editorial with a final selection of some twenty letters to illustrate the three points of view he had defined. Apparently he did not foresee the effect of publishing so many in the same issue—the others, it must be remembered, having been scattered in ones and twos amongst the constant queries about rouge and mascara, etiquette, etc. Extracts from two which summed up the anti and moderate arguments particularly concisely were as follows:

It has been with feelings of deep indignation and pain that we have perused the correspondence upon this subject. This correspondence reveals the fact that from grave faults of temper in the parents, or weakness and indecision of character, they have brought upon themselves the evils which they now seek to eradicate by measures as vain as they are reprehensible, and have plainly forgotten that they who would rule others must first learn to rule themselves![26]

I am a mother myself, and should be sorry if I could not manage my children myself without treating them like rough schoolboys or chastising them like dogs, but even these would have their coats on. There are many ways to be found for punishing children, but regular whippings would, in my opinion, render them callous. As the dispositions of children vary, so must your mode of treatment vary. There should be no rule, therefore, to govern them by.[27]

Finally, on behalf of the whippers, 'A HAPPY MOTHER' wrote:

H.M. has always found that the birch has answered capitally for disobedience, but has never put her children across the knee or across the chair, as it was never wide enough. H.M.

invariably takes hers to Birch's, in Cornhill, and lays them
across the counter, where they receive it hot and strong.
H.M. never leaves any underclothing on, but puts a layer or
two of cream, and naturally when she whips them it is a case
of I scream—Ice cream. . . .[28]

Page after page of such material of course cried out for sensational treatment in the press, and Sam ought to have been
grateful that in the first instance it was reported seriously and
fairly, in something like the same spirit in which it had been
published. It was picked up by *The Daily Telegraph*, which
reported it dramatically but condemned only the views expressed
and not the policy of the magazine for publicizing them, and had
the grace, after quoting a vivid selection of extracts from the pro-
whipping letters, to give an equal amount of space to the other
faction, observing drily, 'We owe it to the *Englishwoman's Journal*
[they had got the name wrong] and Englishwomen generally,
that we should set off against these abominable letters a few of the
indignant protests which happily appear on the other side.' It did
not, however, spare its language in its conclusion:

No wonder that girls go wrong, and throw their womanhood
away in sin and anguish, when their youth is passed with
fathers and mothers whose stupidity is such that they confound
brutality with discipline, and are not afraid to boast of the out-
rages which they commit on their own flesh and blood. If we
have appeared to cite the complacent suggestions of such
people with patience, it was because no words of condemnation could be so severe as their own descriptions of themselves and their ways. To those parents the great and sacred
gift of children has come as pearls to swine. . . . This correspondence is a serious thing; it reveals the existence of a whole
world of unnatural and indefensible private cruelty, of which
the law ought to have cognisance . . .[29]

The next to seize on the story, needless to say, was the ever-
vigilant *Saturday Review*, which produced a devastatingly witty
piece called 'The Birch in the Boudoir'. It began by remarking
that as women were trying to usurp all other male prerogatives,
it was only to be expected that they should wish to take over that

of flogging also, and went on to outline the rules for a Society for the Whipping of Young Women, among which were: that girls up to the age of twenty-one were eligible for flogging; that floggings should always be severe; that in order to produce shame as well as pain, the procedure should be witnessed; and that victims should be stripped, since it was proven that underclothes interfered with efficacy. In spite of his explicit statements to the contrary, Sam was accused of siding with the flagellants; finally, as her pay-off line—for the article was surely the work of the inimitable Miss Linton—the writer suggested that he had written all the letters himself:

The French Commissioners who recently reported to the Emperor on our Public Schools express their astonishment that our great Head-Masters, with their huge salaries, their extensive learning, their high reputation, their dignified social position, and their good prospects of seats in the House of Lords, should condescend to use the birch; and they declare their conviction that the custom will soon die out. It seems plain, from what has been written during the last six months in the *Englishwoman's Domestic Magazine*, that if the English Head-Masters do abandon the custom of flogging, it will be enthusiastically maintained by English mothers and their governesses. Is it possible that before long the only creatures in Europe, besides cattle, that are flogged will be English criminals and English girls? Or is the whole of this amazing correspondence fictitious? Is it nothing more than an elaborate and vulgar hoax? Have 'Materfamilias,' the 'Marchioness,' the 'Perplexed Mother,' and the other 'Lovers of the Rod' no existence out of the fertile brain of the conductor of the *Englishwoman's Domestic Magazine*? One of these two hypotheses must be true; and it is hard to say which of them is the more preposterous.[30]

Finally, a fortnight later *Punch* produced a rather feeble piece entitled 'The Englishwoman's Domestic Brownrigg', which took up the suggestion that the letters were fakes and, rather on the level of I scream—Ice cream, suggested that the flogging chain should be extended, and that mothers who beat their daughters should be beaten in turn by their husbands.

Naïvely, Sam was furious at all three articles, even the conscientious *Daily Telegraph*, and wrote an impassioned protest saying that rather than all the letters having been written by one person (which, as he pointed out, was physically impossible), all the articles had been—adding angrily of the *Saturday Review*, '... it is that Journal of Society which has done more to lower the tone and damage the purity of honest English girls and good women than a thousand whippings; it is the pen, and not the taws, that has done the bad work....'[31]

This outburst, which was not as effective as Myra's against the same publication, did not do much to clear his name; but the notoriety, however unwelcome, at least served to strengthen his resolve to maintain his ban, and for a year there were no more letters. Early in 1870, however, they began to trickle back; as before, the second wave was more prurient and sadistic than the first and the flavour of flagellation in the perverted sense was now noticeable, perhaps as a result of Miss Linton's efforts.

Several correspondents now suggested that the letters on whipping should be collected into a separate volume. At first Sam was indignant, but in April he gave in once again and announced that all future correspondence on the topic would be published in a 2d supplement instead of in the magazine proper, where the ban was to be firmly and finally re-imposed. These supplements continued to appear for the rest of that year. Their contents were of precisely the same nature as the later letters in the Conversazione, but, as with the editorial, the impression produced by a large number all at once was overwhelming, and, to the present writer at least, extremely distasteful—though they certainly did not deserve to be classified in the British Library as pornography, as for a period they were (the classification no longer exists).

The letters on the corset controversy, however, dragged on in the magazine for another couple of years; even to the end, interest never flagged. Two more books were frequently referred to, *The Art of Figure-Training*, and *Art the Handmaid of Beauty*. Men became increasingly frank about the attractions of tight-lacing:

> There is something to me extraordinarily fascinating in the
> thought that a young girl has for many years been subjected to

the strictest discipline of the corset. If she has suffered, as I have no doubt she has, great pain, or at any rate inconvenience, from their extreme pressure, it must be quite made up to her by the admiration her figure excites. . . .[32]

But the last word belonged to 'A MORALIST', who produced a theory of tight-lacing which undoubtedly struck very near the truth: it was not so much the appearance of the tiny waist that was attractive, he maintained, as the implication that its owner was schooled to submission; in other words, that the corset served to keep women in their place—which of course it did: 'If you want a girl to grow up gentle and womanly in her ways and feelings, lace her tight.'[33]

THE DEATH OF SAM

———————————◇———————————

THERE IS NO evidence that Ward, Lock, and Tyler interfered with Sam in any way during the five years over which the letters were published. What with the book, or books, the unsavoury monthly supplements, and the publicity, it is inconceivable that they did not know about them, as they claimed in the case of several of his subsequent publications, and the Conversazione was undoubtedly the chief reason for tensions which grew up between the partners and their editor. There are several possible reasons as to why they let him be, the chief one being simply the power of his personality: though Lock, at any rate, was also a forceful character, Sam could almost certainly have persuaded them that some discussion of the points the controversies raised was in the public interest; and his arguments were of course strengthened in their eyes by his past success and reputation. Their protests may also have been partly stifled by their very laudable resolve to be as accommodating towards him as possible. There was also the financial aspect of the question, for the letters raised the *EDM*'s circulation considerably, and the additional publications were also profitable; readers were still inquiring for the book years after its appearance, and the supplements would certainly not have been continued for so long without adequate justification. Finally, despite the attention the correspondences attracted, the publishers knew that they were unlikely to have any serious consequences, since they were of domestic relevance only and concerned no one of public importance.

But the latter was far from the case with Sam's next mode of social exposé, one of the chief features of which was that it attacked, under only nominal disguise, the highest persons in the land—beginning at the social apex with the Prince of Wales. In 1872, instead of the usual innocuous mixture of light entertainment in his Christmas annual, he turned over almost the whole of it to a take-off of Tennyson's poem about the Arthurian legend, *Idylls of the King*, in which he poked fun at Edward and his friends of the Marlborough House set (Tennyson's portrait was included on a page of caricatures of eminent men which followed the verses, one of the few miscellaneous items the volume contained). The next year, he produced a more politically orientated sequel, in which Gladstone, Disraeli, Cobden, and other political leaders were the chief characters; and two more, in 1874 and 1876, freely criticized not only the royal family but every aspect of the Establishment—however, by the time these appeared, Ward and Lock were no longer implicated (Tyler left the partnership in 1873).[1] Domestic revelations might not carry much risk, but radicalism was another matter, and having to be accountable for Sam's uncompromising views proved more than their nerves could stand. But they were still fairly long-suffering, for although they expressed disapproval of the earlier pair of books, and stopped a second edition of the first, it was not until they were involved in a silly wrangle over the publication of the third that they took positive action, and even then only under considerable provocation from Sam.

As his first and only political writings, the radical annuals come as something of a shock, the more for being found in such an unexpected and inappropriate place; to Edward Liveing, for instance, his conduct seemed incomprehensible: 'Beeton began to display traits of eccentricity. He was obviously suffering from the effects of shock.'[2] But when one recalls the slant of his early convictions, the really surprising thing is that he did not do something of the kind before—as he certainly would have done had it not been for Isabella and the fact that his energies had been entirely absorbed elsewhere. He was setting out the views of a life-time, encouraged perhaps by the publication of the letters, and spurred on (but only spurred on, not motivated) by the knowledge that he had nothing left to lose; his wife and business, the only two things he had ever cared for except his sons, had gone already, and by now he must have known that his own life too was nearly over. He was one of the few, one might say privileged few, who could afford to be disinterested and put humanity at large before themselves—and to enjoy doing it; for he obviously got more pleasure from penning these polemics than from anything else he ever wrote, except perhaps his replies as Cupid in the *EDM*'s first year or so.

The choice of his Christmas annual as a political vehicle was as fortuitous as the start of the Conversazione controversies, for the idea grew, as Mr Montgomery Hyde observes,[3] from a light-hearted item on the siege of Paris in 1871, and when he began the first in the series, *The Coming K*——, he almost certainly did not envisage that it would be anything more. In mood it was similar, its main aim being to amuse rather than arouse—and indeed, most of it was too puerile to do much else, the main action being the treachery of the Prince's best friend Loosealot (after Lancelot), who dosed the royal horse in the Derby with a bucket of Epsom salts. This had such a salutary effect upon the pleasure-loving 'Coming K——' that

> Henceforward did he lead a different life,
> His follies all forsook, and was a King—[4]

The effect was further softened by the setting in the Dark Ages, inaccurately carried through in the illustrations (by 'S.E.M.', and not up to Beeton's usual standard), which showed the characters in an improbable mixture of medieval-cum-Elizabethan dress.

The second, *The Siliad*, was in imitation of the *Iliad*, and correspondingly heavier in tone as well as import. The various ministers' names were approximately Latinized, as, for instance, 'Gladimemnon', 'Dudizzy', 'Cobdenus', 'Peelides'. The third, *Jon Duan*, was modelled on Byron's *Don Juan*; and the fourth, *Edward VII*, was a copy of Shakespeare. The latter was the most accomplished, probably because by this time Sam was inde-pendent and could give more time to it; but both the later pieces were not only wider-ranging in aim but sharper and more closely related to current events than the earlier ones, partly because of Sam's own increased impetus, and partly because of a change in his team of collaborators—for he did not write the verses unaided. He was helped by a writer called A. A. Dowty—a long-standing contributor of romantic verse to his magazines—and, to begin with, by an otherwise unknown journalist, S. R. Emerson. Emerson, however, was induced by Ward and Lock to abandon the others the summer after the publication of *The Siliad* in order to produce an independent Christmas annual. His replacement was Evelyn Jerrold, the son of the editor of *Lloyd's Newspaper*, a thoroughly radical gutter-press publication which habitually tore the royal family and other privileged persons to pieces; he can therefore be said to have been born to the job and his contribution was a great deal more full-blooded than Emerson's, whose own annual infuriated Sam because of its feebleness.

The political significance of the annuals has already been discussed by several authors, including Kinley Roby in his recent biography of Edward VII, and H. Montgomery Hyde, who gives a particularly thorough and informed account. Both are of the opinion that the annuals were among the cleverest and most spectacular radical writings of the period, despite the fact that they did not appear until the crest of the wave of Victorian republicanism was past its peak—a further indication that *The Coming K——* was undertaken spontaneously; if Sam had been meditating such a work for any length of time, he would surely have chosen a more apposite moment to bring it out, whereas, as it chanced, it appeared the year following the Prince's nearly fatal attack of typhoid, which produced an overwhelming resurgence of loyalty towards the monarchy.

It would be superfluous to say more about this aspect of Beeton's work than is necessary to show just what his views were. With regard to the royal family, he felt that the Queen should either spend the money allocated to her by Parliament for State purposes, or abdicate in Edward's favour. Towards Edward, he was on the whole sympathetic, especially over his financial problems, which, as he pointed out, were to a large extent caused by his mother's refusal to acknowledge his position or pay him for taking over some of her functions. One of the many passages designed to illustrate the Prince's predicament came in a comic scene in *Edward VII*, in which Edward went to ask his mother for money and found her asleep, her bank book lying unguarded beside her:

> The Prince (aside)—Oh, that I could
> Muster up resolution; tell her all,
> And claim full payment for the work I do.
> To tell all or not tell all, that is the question. . . .
> This then's my mother's bank book! I dare swear

Its pages bear a different tale from mine.
Mine's not a book I'd choose to foster slumber,
Or make a favourite bedfellow; . . .
Was it a shame to him [Albert] to leave so much?
And much it must have been, if what I see
Written in this book be right; much, do I say?
Much is no word for it; I see arrays
Of revenue, that capitalized, amount
To well-nigh what the navy costs each year.
I figures see which mean the Sovereign draws
An annual sum ten times as great as mine.
I must have courage, knowing what I do,
To strike for more.[5]

To Disraeli, Sam was surprisingly lenient, conceivably because of his friendship with Greenwood, whose affiliation to Disraeli was becoming increasingly important to him personally as well as professionally in his capacity as editor of the *Gazette*. But other ministers were depicted in a variety of disreputable situations: in dancers' dressing-rooms after the theatre; on a tour of brothels (this was in *The Siliad*, where, in the choicest establishment of all, they were made to encounter the Shah, whose much-publicized visit to London had taken place earlier that year); and (also in *The Siliad*) in a blood-curdling fight with the police, from which they emerged triumphant with the inevitable helmets and truncheons as trophies.

The institutions which came under fire included the press, the legal system, the army, upper-class sports, and to a lesser extent the police, but Sam's chief hatred was directed against the more generalized targets of Society, hypocrisy, and the Church. His feelings about the Church have already been spoken of; his disapproval of it in all its forms was reiterated constantly, perhaps most tellingly in his story of the priest who tried to seduce Jon Duan's sister in the confession-box, whereat the irate Duan dressed himself up in women's clothes, went to confession in her place, and assaulted him.

All suddenly the female form arose,
    And as the vicar stretched his arms to seize her,
A manly fist dash'd right into his nose,

A crushing blow, call'd vulgarly a 'sneezer';
And whilst he felt all nose and strange surprise,
    The fist work'd piston-like just twice or thrice,
And bunged up straightway were his sunken eyes,
    And then his throat was seized as in a vice.
Whilst, as his breath was being shaken out,
    And he felt he would very quickly smother—
Then, just before he fainted, came a shout,
    Of 'Alice could not come! but I'm her brother!'[6]

The whole story of Duan, like that of his prototype, was a protest
against the conventional values of Society and the Establishment,
and abounded with expostulations against their injustice and
malignity. One particularly vehement outburst occurred in the
course of a description of one of the all-too-rare 'Drawing-rooms'
given by the Queen:

Society! O what a hideous sham
    Is veiled and masked beneath that specious name!
Society! its mission is to damn,
    To curse, and blight; to burn with withering flame
All that is worthiest in us—to cram
    The world with polished hypocrites, who claim
To sin, of right—Society has said it—
And think their crimes are greatly to their credit![7]

There was a similar passage on hypocrisy in *The Siliad* :

O vile Hypocrisy, the Nation's bane,
With thee no mind is sound, no body sane;
Murder thou dost all honourable hopes;
And as the Borgia stands amongst the Popes,
So thou, amidst the curses of the world,
Dost stand pre-eminent, meet to be hurled
To Pandemonium; . . .[8]

The political and sociological content of the poems (if such
they can be called), although their *raison d'être* and certainly one of
their most noticeable features, was not, however, the main reason
for their success at the time. This was due primarily to their

tremendous liveliness and high-spirited, if crude, humour. The samples above give some idea of the style and quality of the verse, which in places was awful, but it is impossible in a few scattered quotations to give any idea of the zest and vigour of the narrative, which made them as gripping as a best-selling novel, if hardly as compulsive as the originals on which they were modelled. The description of the police fight and the tale of the serpentine priest were but two in a long procession of colourful incidents; sex, as opposed to romantic love or Byronic passion, was everywhere, and served as one of the writers' chief sources of comic situations. In *The Coming K——*, for instance, instead of Elaine of Astelot dying of love for the indifferent Lancelot, Delaine of Clapham Rise took her revenge on the fickle Loosealot by bluffing her way into the Prince's garden fête armed with the erring knight's letters and umbrella:

> . . . like Amazon
> Who flings with doomful aim the poisoned dart,
> Or as a schoolboy, fresh from tedious tasks,
> Propels the unboiled adamantine pea,
> She launched the green umbrella at him full,
> And met him with the ferrule in the chest;
> Then followed with the packet, which, well sent,
> Landed on 'chimney pot,' and knocked it off.
> And ever as this happened lords and dames
> Laughed, looking often from her face who read
> To his she read at, which was pale with rage;
> And ever Guelpho [the Prince] tittered at his plight;
> And not a knight but teased and rallied him;
> But worse the ladies, who all looked upon
> The fair Delaine as champion of their sex.[9]

It was characteristic of Sam that all the women in the poems, even the belligerent goddesses in *The Siliad*, were portrayed much more vigorously and convincingly than the male characters, and that the authors' sympathy was invariably with them. No opportunity was lost for ramming home their situation as the exploited half of the population: if they were not virtuous—and almost all of them were as scheming and amoral as imagination can conceive—it was entirely the fault of society, to which they were

martyrs all, prostitutes and heiresses alike. Anyone in a position
to know better might also have observed how far from the
tawdry reality were the incredibly luxurious places of pleasure
conjured up by the authors, who had obviously never set foot
inside any such establishment (in contrast, for instance, to
newspaper offices, which they described with the keenest
accuracy). This was their vision of a room in a high-class brothel:

> The ceiling glass, tall mirrors line the walls,
> Beneath, the footstep on pile velvet falls.
> Three satin-covered couches—one sky blue,
> And one coal-black, and one rich crimson's hue;
> Such charming couches, too so full of Spring,
> That you expect to hear the cuckoo sing;
> The pictures all one sentiment express—
> 'Tis female loveliness, unmarred by dress. . . .
> A fountain bubbles with a rich perfume,
> Soft waxen tapers soothe while they illume;
> Celestial music fills the sensuous air,
> And steeps the soul in rapturousness rare.[10]

The dispute which arose over the publication of *Jon Duan*
originated from the fact that Ward and Lock, having formally
protested against *The Siliad*, asked Sam the following summer
to produce a less controversial annual for the next season, and
when he appeared to be doing nothing about it they commissioned Emerson to compile one instead. According to their
subsequent statement, they had not read the manuscript of *The
Siliad* in time to prevent its being published; this would have been
a surprisingly careless omission on their part and is somewhat
difficult to believe, especially in view of the nature of Emerson's
annual, which was on the same radical plan as its predecessor but
rather less direct in its implications, its theme being the corrupt
influence of civilized society on a tribe of virtuous cannibals. One
cannot help suspecting that rather than disapproving of the
principle of the annuals, they were merely scared by the publicity
they attracted (*The Siliad* provoked at least one reply and was
commented on by Gladstone, who did not attempt to suppress it
for fear of adding to its already embarrassing notoriety).[11]
Probably, therefore, they would have been quite prepared to

tolerate a third in the series from Beeton if he had shown himself willing to co-operate, and compromise, as Emerson did, with something more moderate. However, when they read *Jon Duan* in October, the preparation of which it was implied was unknown to them, they were considerably dismayed—though even if its contents had been acceptable to them, they were not at this stage in a position to publish it because of their commitment to Emerson.

It was duly brought out, not by them, but by Sam's friend and erstwhile employee, Christopher Weldon, who had by this time set up as a publisher on his own. To publish anything without Ward and Lock's consent was of course a violation of Sam's contract; but, as he later said in court, his co-authors, Dowty and Jerrold, were bound by no such restriction, and he could not, as a friend, withhold his assistance from them or prevent them from profiting from their work—adding that he had made no arrangement for sharing the proceeds.[12] Yet even this infringement, which meant the simultaneous publication of two *Beeton's Christmas Annuals* for that year, might have been smoothed over if he had been content to leave it at that, and allow his own work to make its way quietly, unaccompanied by publicity. But that was not in his nature: indignant at his implied association with Emerson's composition, he publicly repudiated all connection with it, and inserted large announcements proclaiming *Jon Duan* as the true Beeton's Annual in the *Athenaeum*, the *Standard*, and other papers. The page before his announcement in the *Athenaeum* carried Ward and Lock's advertisement for *The Fijiad*, which ended with a discreet note saying:

Mr. S. O. Beeton, as his advertisements proclaim, has been (notwithstanding our protest and legal agreement to the contrary) concerned in the publication of another Annual, which, for well-founded reasons, we have objected to publish, or be in any way concerned with. We have, in consequence, made arrangements with an author of 'The Siliad' for the production of Beeton's Annual in such an attractive form as to commend itself to popular favour and support.[13]

The rivalry of the two annuals being thus publicly declared, it was impossible for the partners to allow the matter to stand, and

they promptly applied for a court injunction to restrain Sam
from issuing advertisements calculated to damage their interests
or imply that their use of his name was incorrect. Sam was in bed
with one of his ever-worsening coughs when the hearing came
up, and a temporary injunction pending his appearance was
granted, which the triumphant applicants duly published in the
next issue of the *Athenaeum*; thereafter, Weldon took over the
advertising of *Jon Duan*, which he did in style, for a whole page
the next week was devoted to an assurance that its publication
would be in no way affected by the court's ruling. The case was
heard on 10 December, and in spite of a vigorous defence, the
injunction was upheld.

The practical outcome of the case was that Sam's contract with
Ward and Lock was terminated. Myra also left, not only on his
account, though no doubt she would have resigned with him in
any case, but also because she too had had a part in *Jon Duan*: at
the conclusion of the poem (which, like *Don Juan*, was left without
an end) was a rhyming version of Spinnings in Town, spattered
with apologies for her ineptitude at writing in verse—which, on
this showing, was certainly not her forte. Fortunately, as was
almost inevitable after so much publicity, *Jon Duan* was easily the
most successful of the annuals so far, and netted its authors and
publisher a handsome profit. This enabled Sam and Weldon to
set Myra up with a magazine of her own, *Myra's Journal of Dress
and Fashion*. It was the first of an empire of similar journals to
come from the house of Weldon, the next being the famous
Weldon's Ladies' Journal—which, however, was not founded for
another five years, when Sam was dead, and the *EDM*, crippled
beyond recovery by the loss of its two leading spirits, had also
been terminated. Ward and Lock ended it in the same year as
Sam's death, and, unless they let it remain out of a gentlemanly
regard for the feelings of its founder, which once he had left
them they did not display over other matters, it is surprising that
they allowed it to limp on for as long as they did.

Once they had got over their initial anger, they had cause to
look on his departure with mixed feelings. In the short term
view, they had plenty on which to congratulate themselves, since
they were finally rid of the troublesome pair—for both Sam and
Myra had become an increasing embarrassment to them; and at
the same time they retained a noble legacy of profitable titles. Sam

had added over a dozen new books to his list in the past couple of years, including a remarkable volume called *Beeton's Complete Letter-Writing*, which contained sample letters for every situation, even parents with erring children at school (and children with angry parents); and as well as the doomed *EDM*, they had the *Young Englishwoman* and the *Boys' Own Magazine*, still the leading children's publications. On the other hand, they were faced with the problem of Sam's independence, which because of the commercial value of his name substantially threatened the acquisitions they inherited from him. The judge, in ruling in their favour, had pronounced that their purchase of his business entitled them to the continued use of his name with regard to the Christmas annual whether or not he himself had been directly connected with it, the annual being regarded as a regular publication in the same sense as a magazine. When, as he shortly did, he set himself up once again as a publisher, they were naturally apprehensive lest the value of their own Beeton list should be degraded by a rival stream of Beeton publications, and threatened legal sanction for a second time. Sam retorted with the equally justifiable complaint that they were appending his name to works in which he had had no part, and of which in certain instances he strongly disapproved. Another court case ensued, which ended rather less favourably for the partners, who were recommended either to come to some agreement with him or refrain from putting his name to new publications. They adopted the latter course, and thereafter only books originated before his departure were designated 'Beeton'.

To Sam, release from his employment, which by now had degenerated into a frustrating obligation, was a profound relief, despite his illness and the financial uncertainty entailed; and in other circumstances, he would undoubtedly have settled down to re-establish himself immediately. But over the last few years his health had deteriorated seriously. The bronchial attack which had prevented his appearance in court had been so severe that his doctor, Morell Mackenzie (the throat specialist who later treated the Emperor Frederick III) prevailed upon him to go abroad, and he spent the next six months in Italy, though his tubercular condition was by this time past the stage where any more favourable climate or other known remedy could do much for him. On his return, he took offices at 39 and 40 Bedford Street, and with

Goubaud's backing and the advantages of nearly twenty-five years of experience plus a ready-made reputation, started out from the beginning once again.

He was by this time an alarming figure, emaciated and ghoulishly white, his eyes sunken and unnaturally brilliant, living off little more than cups of soup, frequent doses of medicine, and the conversation of his friends, who were as numerous and attentive as ever and ranged from the allies of his youth such as Frederick Warne and Tom Hood (then the editor of *Fun*, a bitterer rival to *Punch*), to hopeful young men such as T. P. O'Connor, whose biography of Disraeli was originally commissioned by him; sadly, the first volume was reviewed under his imprint in the same month as his death. But if he had had more time, he would certainly soon have reached the point where he left off in terms of turnover and prosperity—though the nature of his output would have been different, radicalism rather than education being now the ruling passion of his precarious existence; besides this, literature for children had now advanced so far, and magazines proliferated to such an extent, that the corners of the market that had formerly been his were now becoming common property. As far back as 1869 he had commented upon the 'piles upon piles of magazines, in every variety of type and wrapper!'[14] Not that he was pessimistic about the future of periodicals, for he regarded the demand as being virtually insatiable; but, if he had founded more magazines, they would have been for the discontented segment of the population who fed their minds on *Lloyds*, and those who were really poor and underprivileged.

But this was not to be. His last achievement, apart from the publication of the Disraeli biography, was *Edward VII*, described by Kinley Roby as the most unflattering of all the criticisms of the Queen that had yet been published.[15] It produced a reply called *The Key to Edward the Seventh*, which it is tempting to suppose from the title was written by Frederick Greenwood.

He died on 6 June 1877 at the age of forty-six in a sanatorium in Richmond, where Mackenzie had placed him a few weeks before. His sons and the Brownes had long been prepared, and had already in some degree grown used to his absence, for, too weak to commute regularly, he had already for some time past been in the habit of sleeping over his offices, constantly watched over by the conscientious doctor, who had become one of his most

10

valued friends.[16] He was buried next to Isabella and their second son in Norwood cemetery.

It is impossible to measure the extent of his achievement. Lord Northcliffe was indebted to him in the matter of his children's magazines; Christopher Weldon was the chief inheritor of his innovations for women, in particular the popularization of paper patterns, which were the foundation of his fortune—which, in view of his consistent aid and loyalty, was doubtless no less than Sam would have wished. Ward, Lock retained the copyright of his books, and in promoting *Management* into a household byword must take the credit for the survival of his name. Overall, his work has been disseminated over so many facets of journalism that all one can say is that publishers, editors, writers, and women and children everywhere have benefited directly and indirectly from the fecundity of his mind.

His obituaries were generous, though far from adequate in view of the ultimate contribution he made; the *Athenaeum* said, regretfully but matter-of-factly, 'We are sorry to hear of the death of Mr. S. O. Beeton, the publisher of many cheap and popular works. Although from an early age a sufferer from the disease from which he died, he displayed throughout his life immense energy and perseverance. . . . In his literary labours he was much assisted by his wife, who died some years ago.'[17]

Far more moving were the verses to him written by Dowty and Jerrold in their Christmas annual for that year, *Finis, or, Coelebs and the Modern Sphinx*, the last of the series, and devoted not to radicalism but, as the title indicated, to women—the subject to which Sam had addressed himself longer and more consistently than any other in his life.

In Memoriam

S.O.B.

We lack fit words to tell our grief,
For his great soul from earth removed;
A staunch companion, often proved,
His noble life was all too brief.

High-spirited, yet like a child
Though modest, yet as lion bold;
A man whom years could not make old,
Who through a life of torture smiled.

Who through a life of torture worked;
With busy brain and facile pen,
He wrought good for his fellow-men
No labour shunned, nor duty shirked. . . .

All he thought right he dared to do,
Nor pause a moment to ask why;
Right must be done, though he may die,
And so he bore his purpose through. . . .[18]

Even more than serving as a tribute to the purity of his motives
and his genuine concern for the lot of his fellow-men, this, in
showing the unbounded admiration he inspired in his friends,
managed to convey something of the quality of the man: always
hopeful, always generous, always kind—though it did not, as in
this context it could not have been expected to, express the
complexities and contrarieties of his character: the mixture of
ambition with his altruism; of vanity, sometimes silliness, with
brilliant far-sightedness; and of frivolity with an earnestness and
determination of purpose exceptional even among his generation.
But it did, above all, commemorate his lasting grief over the death
of his wife—not a grief that constantly asserted itself, for he was
always too cheerful and ebullient to be sad or morose for long
periods, but a grief that he tried to turn to other men's advantage. As a final gesture, although they had never known
Isabella except from his oft-repeated, idealized description, his
friends left a memory to her also:

Never have I known a girl so nice,
Her character unspoiled by any vice,
So sweet, so pure, so gentle, and so kind,
And yet with such a great and earnest mind,
Nothing's too deep for her to understand,
No task too simple for her loving hand;
Her home's the pink of comfort and of neatness;
Her management the acme of discreetness. . . .[19]

Myra and Charlie continued to look after the orphaned brothers until they grew up, and Myra's magazine flourished until well after the turn of the century, continuing until 1912. The *Young Englishwoman* became *Sylvia's Home Journal*, while the *Boys' Own Magazine* survived its founder by thirteen years. Two years before its demise, the first enlarged edition of *Household Management* appeared, and four years later, in 1892, another, still further enlarged; thus the Beetons' publications were never eclipsed, though their originators were obliterated almost at once by a blanket of obscurity and misunderstanding.

APPENDICES

NOTES

BIBLIOGRAPHY

INDEX

APPENDIX I

EDITIONS AND DERIVATIONS OF
HOUSEHOLD MANAGEMENT

Beeton's Book of Household Management, 1859 (in volume form, 1861),
1863, 1868, 1879–80, 1888 (enlarged), 1892 (greatly enlarged),
1906 (enlarged), 1915 (enlarged), 1923, 1936, 1950, 1960, 1968
(Facsimile of first edition published by Cape)
The Englishwoman's Cookery Book, 1863, 1867?, 1870?, 1879, 1882
Dictionary of Everyday Cookery, 1865
Mrs. Beeton's House and Home Books, 1866–7
Mrs. Beeton's All About Cookery, 1871, 1890, 1907, 1923, 1951,
1961, 1963; also as a paperback (Pan Books) 1963
Mrs. Beeton's How to Manage House, Servants, and Children, 1871
Beeton's Every-Day Cookery and Housekeeping Book, 1872, 1877?, 1890,
1907, 1923, 1950
Mrs. Beeton's Cookery Book and Household Guide, 1890, 1901, 1902,
1909, 1912, 1915, 1923, 1950
Mrs. Beeton's Family Cookery, 1893, 1907, 1923, 1951, 1962
Mrs. Beeton's Penny Cookery, 1908
Mrs. Beeton's Sixpenny Cookery, 1910, 1923
Mrs. Beeton's Jam Making, 1924
Mrs. Beeton's Cake Making, 1924, 1952
Mrs. Beeton's Puddings and Pies, 1925
Mrs. Beeton's Sauces and Soups, 1925
Mrs. Beeton's Hors d'Oeuvres and Savouries, 1925
Mrs. Beeton's Cold Sweets, 1925
Mrs. Beeton's Fish Cookery, 1926, 1964
Mrs. Beeton's Poultry and Game, 1926, 1963
Mrs. Beeton's Hints to Housewives, 1928
Mrs. Beeton's Hot and Cold Sweets, 1963
Mrs. Beeton's Preserves, 1963
Mrs. Beeton's Cakes and Pastries, 1963
Mrs. Beeton's Continental Cookery, 1964
Mrs. Beeton's Hors d'Oeuvres and Salads, 1964
Mrs. Beeton's Meat Dishes, 1965

APPENDIX II

LIST OF BEETON BOOKS

1852 *Uncle Tom's Cabin*, by Harriet Beecher Stowe
1853 *The Key to Uncle Tom's Cabin*, by Harriet Beecher Stowe

From 1852: READABLE BOOKS commissioned by Vizetelly:
  Tales of Mystery, Imagination, and Humour, by Edgar Allan Poe
  Philosophers and Actresses, or, Scenes Vivid and Picturesque, from the Hundred and One Dramas of Art and Passion, by Arsène Houssaye (in translation)
  The Letters of Peter Phymley, Essays, and Speeches, by Sydney Smith
  Nile Notes of a "Howadje"; or, The American in Egypt, by G. W. Curtis
  The Old Guard, by J. T. Headley
  Wellington: The Story of His Life, His Battles, and Political Career, by Alfred Cooke

  READABLE BOOKS commissioned by Sam:
  Reveries of a Bachelor, by Ik Marvel
  The Life of Nelson, by Robert Southey
  Three Tales, by the Countess D'Abouville
  Pictures of European Capitals, by William Ware
  The Cavaliers of England, by H. W. Herbert
  The Adirondack; or, Life in the Woods, by J. T. Headley
  The Guards, or, The Household Troops of England, by Captain Rafter

1858–62 *Beeton's Dictionary of Universal Information*, Vol. I
1861–5 *Beeton's Dictionary of Universal Information*, Vol. II
  Both compiled and edited by S. O. Beeton and John Sherer

1858–60 *Beeton's Historian*
1859–61 *Beeton's Book of Household Management*, by Isabella Beeton
1861 *Beeton's Book of Garden Management*

1861–73 *Beeton's Christmas Annual*
1863 *Beeton's Illuminated Family Bible*
  Beeton's Dictionary of Universal Biography
  Boys' Own Library
  Beeton's Guide to Journalism
1864? *Beeton's Book of Birds*
1865 *Beeton's Riddle Book*
  Beeton's Book of Songs
  Beeton's Book of Chemistry (also published by F. Warne)
  Beeton's Book of Anecdote, Wit, and Humour (3rd ed.)
  Cressy and Poitiers, by John G. Edgar, ed. S. O. Beeton
  The Nasby Papers, by "P. V. Nasby" (pseud.). Preface
  signed S. O. B.
1866 *Beeton's Book of Anecdote, Jokes, and Jests; or, Good Things*
  Said and Sung (also published by Frederick Warne)
  Beeton's Book of Games (2 vols.)
  Beeton's Book of Acting Charades
  Beeton's Sixpenny Book of Songs
1865–79 Beeton's "All about it" Books (*Cookery, Everything, Gardening, Country Life, Mothers' Homebook*)

PUBLISHED BY WARD, LOCK, AND TYLER, OR WARD AND LOCK:
1867 *Our Soldiers and the Victoria Cross*
1868 *The Corset and the Crinoline*, by W. B. L.
  Beeton's Dictionary of Geography
  History of France, by Boisnormand de Bonnechose (F. P. E.),
  ed. S. O. Beeton
  London's Great Outing: the Derby Carnival, by "Phiz", ed.
  S. O. Beeton
1868–70 *Beeton's Great Book of Poetry*
1870 *Beeton's Guide to Investing Money with Safety and Profit*
  Beeton's Guide Book to the Stock Exchange and Money Market
  Beeton's British Biography—From earliest times to the accession of
  George III
  Beeton's Bible Dictionary
  Beeton's Boys' Annual
  Beeton's Book of Needlework
  Beeton's Book of Poultry and Domestic Animals
  Beeton's British Gazeteer
  Beeton's Fact, Fiction, History, and Adventure
10*

Beeton's Modern Men and Women; *or, British biography from the accession of George III to the present time*

(or '71) *Beeton's Dictionary of the British Navy*

Beeton's Penny Cookery

1871 *Beeton's British Biography* (to the present day)

Beeton's Book of the Laundry

Beeton's Book of the War

Beeton's Classical Dictionary

Beeton's Dictionary of Natural History

Beeton's Dictionary of Practical Recipes and Everyday Information

Beeton's Ready Reckoner

Beeton's Medical Dictionary

Beeton's Historical Romances, Daring Deeds, and Animal Stories

Beeton's Law Books: *Property*; *Women and Children*; *Divorce and Matrimonial Causes*; *Wills, Executors, and Trustees*

1872 *Beeton's Brave Tales, Bold Ballads, and Travels and Perils by Land and Sea*

Beeton's Date Book

Beeton's Nine Hours Wages Book

Livingstone and Stanley, by S. O. Beeton and Ronald Smith

The Coming K—

1872–4 Beeton's Penny Books

1872–8 Beeton's Humorous Books

1873 *Beeton's Book of Cottage Management*

Beeton's Family Register

Beeton's Complete Letter-Writer for Ladies and Gentlemen

Beeton's Famous Voyages, Brigand Adventures, Tales of the Battlefield, Life and Nature

Beeton's Penny Children's Books

Beeton's Pictorial Speller

The Siliad

1873–6 Beeton's Good Aim Series

1874 *Arthur Bonnicastle*, by Josiah G. Holland. Preface signed S. O. B.

Beeton's Dictionary of Everyday Gardening

Beeton's Gardening Book

Beeton's Men of the Age and Annals of the Time

Beeton's Modern European Celebrities

Jon Duan (published by C. Weldon)

1874–9 Beeton's Books for All Time

PUBLISHED BY BEETON
1876 *Edward VII*
1877 *Benjamin Disraeli, Earl of Beaconsfield,* by T. P. O'Connor

EDITED BY S. O. BEETON, PUBLISHED BY WARD AND LOCK AFTER
HIS DEPARTURE, based on previous publications:
1875 *Beeton's Counting House Book*
  Beeton's Public Speaker
1876 *Family Etiquette*
  Beeton's Complete Etiquette for Ladies
  Beeton's Complete Etiquette for Gentlemen
  *Beeton's Manners of Polite Society: or, Etiquette for Ladies,
  Gentlemen, and Families* (containing memoir signed S. O. B.)
1877 *The Works of Lord Bacon*
  Essays Social and Political, by the Canon of St Paul's

APPENDIX III

ORIGINAL RECIPES

Here is a practical selection of recipes from the original edition of *Household Management*. It does not include any soups, because most of these were based on home-made meat stock which as well as being time-consuming would be disproportionately expensive to make now, and in most cases stock cubes are not a satisfactory substitute. Nor are there any of the impossibly extravagant Victorian roasts or other meat dishes calling for garnishes of oysters, truffles, etc.; nor, for technical reasons, such as that gelatine had to be treated differently from its modern equivalent, are there any of the delicious cream desserts in the pudding section. There are, however, traditional English recipes for mutton stew, Bakewell tart, treacle pudding, custard, gingerbread, seed cake, and toffee. There are also several excellent basic fish recipes, for the fish chapter was one of the best and most practical in the book. If none of these dishes seems very exotic, it is because of the above limitations and because Isabella's recipes have long since come to be regarded as standard, which was far from the case in her own day.

Apart from a few comments and additions and up-to-date costs (all in square brackets or marked by asterisks), they are presented exactly as she wrote them.

BAKED MACKEREL

INGREDIENTS.—4 middling-sized mackerel, a nice delicate forcemeat (see Forcemeats), 3 oz. of butter; pepper and salt to taste.

Mode.—Clean the fish, take out the roes, and fill up with forcemeat, and sew up the slit [or pin with toothpicks or cocktail sticks]. Flour, and put them in a dish, heads and tails alternately, with the roes; and, between each layer, put some little pieces of butter, and pepper and salt. Bake for ½ an hour [1 hour in a low oven], and either serve with plain melted butter or a *maître d'hotel* sauce.

Time.—½ [or 1] hour.

Average cost for this quantity, 1s 10d. [March 1977, mackerel 36p per lb.]

Seasonable from April to July [and throughout the winter].

Sufficient for 6 persons. [This was for a first course, as an alternative to soup; as a main course, 1 fish each is required.]

FORCEMEAT FOR PIKE, CARP, HADDOCK, AND VARIOUS KINDS OF FISH

INGREDIENTS.—1 oz. of fresh butter, 1 oz. of suet, 1 oz. of fat bacon, 1 small teaspoonful of minced savoury herbs, including parsley; a little onion, when liked, shredded very fine; salt, nutmeg, and cayenne to taste; 4 oz. of bread crumbs, 1 egg.

Mode.—Mix all the ingredients well together, carefully mincing them very finely; beat up the egg, moisten with it, and work the whole very smoothly together. Oysters or anchovies may be added to this forcemeat, and will be found a great improvement.

Average cost, 6d.

Sufficient for a moderate-sized haddock or pike.

*A SIMPLER FORCEMEAT

For each mackerel: 1 pounded anchovy, 1 egg yolk, 1 tablespoon chopped parsley, 1 oz. butter, ¼ cup fresh bread crumbs, squeeze of lemon juice, tiny pinch cayenne.

Melt the butter and mix all together.

FISH SCALLOP

INGREDIENTS.—Remains of cold fish of any sort, ½ pint of cream, ½ tablespoonful of anchovy sauce [or use 4 tinned anchovies pounded in ½ tablespoon of their own oil], ½ teaspoonful of made mustard [1 teaspoonful of French mustard], ditto of walnut ketchup [or Worcester sauce], pepper and salt to taste (the above quantities are for ½ lb. of fish when picked); bread crumbs [fresh].

Mode.—Put all the ingredients into a stewpan, carefully picking the fish from the bones; set it on the fire, let it remain till nearly hot, occasionally stir the contents, but do not allow it to boil. When done, put the fish into a deep dish or scallop shell, with a good quantity of bread crumbs; place small pieces of butter on the

top, set in a Dutch oven before the fire to brown, or use a sala-
mander [place under the grill or at the top of a hot oven 15–20
minutes].

Time.—¼ hour.

Average cost, exclusive of the cold fish, 10d. [March 1977, about
56p.]

[For 2 as a main course, 4 as a first course.]

SOLE WITH CREAM SAUCE

INGREDIENTS.—2 [large] soles [or 4 or 5 small ones]; salt, cayenne,
and pounded [ground] mace to taste; the juice of ½ lemon, salt and
water, ½ pint of cream [preferably double].

Mode.—Skin, wash, and fillet the soles, and divide each fillet in
2 pieces [if large soles are used]; lay them in cold salt and water,
which bring gradually to a boil. When the water boils, take out the
fish, lay it in a delicately clean stewpan, and cover with the cream.
Add the seasoning, simmer very gently for ten minutes, and, just
before serving, put in the lemon-juice. The fillets may be rolled,
and secured by means of a skewer; but this is not so economical a
way of serving them, as double the quantity of cream is required.

Time.—10 minutes in the cream.

Average cost, from 1s. to 2s. per pair. [March 1977, 4 servings,
£2.50.]

Sufficient for 4 or 5 persons.

Seasonable at any time.

This will be found a most delicate and delicious dish.

WHITING AU GRATIN, or BAKED WHITING

INGREDIENTS.—4 whiting, butter, 1 tablespoonful of minced
parsley, a few chopped mushrooms when obtainable; pepper,
salt, and grated nutmeg to taste; butter, 2 glasses of sherry or
Madeira [or white wine], bread crumbs.

Mode.—Grease the bottom of a baking-dish with butter, and
over it strew some minced parsley and mushrooms. Scale,
empty, and wash the whitings, and wipe them thoroughly
dry. . . . Lay them in the dish, sprinkle them with bread crumbs
and seasoning, adding a little grated nutmeg, and also a little more

minced parsley and mushrooms. Place small pieces of butter over the whiting, moisten with the wine, and bake for 20 minutes in a hot oven. If there should be too much sauce, reduce it by boiling over a sharp fire for a few minutes, and pour under the fish. Serve with a cut lemon, and no other sauce.

Time.—20 minutes.

Average cost, 4d each. [March 1977, whiting 45p per lb.]

Seasonable all the year, but best from October to March.

Sufficient.—This quantity for 4 or 5 persons [4 persons as a main course].

* This recipe is equally good with sole.

HARICOT MUTTON II

INGREDIENTS.—Breast or scrag of mutton, flour, pepper and salt to taste, 1 large onion, 3 cloves, a bunch of savoury herbs, 1 blade of mace [pinch ground mace], carrots and turnips, sugar.

Mode.—Cut the mutton into square pieces, and fry them a nice colour; then dredge over them a little flour and a seasoning of pepper and salt. Put all into a stewpan, and moisten with boiling water, adding the onion, stuck with 3 cloves, the mace, and herbs. Simmer gently till the meat is nearly done, skim off all the fat, and then add the carrots and turnips, which should previously be cut in dice and fried in a little sugar to colour them. Let the whole simmer again for 10 minutes; take out the onion and bunch of herbs, and serve.

Time.—About 3 hours to simmer.

Average cost, 6d per lb. [March 1977, lamb 35p per lb.]

Sufficient for 4 or 5 persons.

Seasonable at any time.

VEAL AND HAM PIE

INGREDIENTS.—2 lbs. of veal cutlets [pie veal], ½ lb. of boiled ham, 2 tablespoonfuls of minced savoury herbs, ¼ teaspoonful of grated nutmeg, 2 blades of pounded [ground] mace, pepper and salt to taste, a strip of lemon-peel finely minced, the yolks of 2 hard-boiled eggs, ½ pint of water, nearly ½ pint of good strong gravy, puff-crust.

Mode.—Cut the veal into nice square pieces, and put a layer of them at the bottom of a pie-dish; sprinkle over these a portion of the herbs, spices, seasoning, lemon-peel, and the yolks of the eggs cut in slices; cut the ham very thin, and put a layer of this in. Proceed in this manner until the dish is full, so arranging it that the ham comes at the top. Lay a puff-paste on the edge of the dish, and pour in about ½ pint of water; cover with crust, ornament it with leaves, brush it over with the yolk of an egg, and bake in a well-heated oven for 1 to 1½ hour, or longer, should the pie be very large. When it is taken out of the oven, pour in at the top, through a funnel, nearly ½ pint of strong gravy: this should be made sufficiently good that, when cold, it may cut in a firm jelly. This pie may be very much enriched by adding a few mushrooms, oysters, or sweetbreads; but it will be found very good without any of the last-named additions.

Time.—1½ hour, or longer, should the pie be very large.

Average cost, 3s. [March 1977, £2.05, exclusive of pastry.]

Sufficient for 5 or 6 persons [6 to 8].

Seasonable from March to October [virtually any time].

Stewed Red Cabbage*

INGREDIENTS.—1 red cabbage, a small slice of ham, ½ oz. of fresh butter, 1 pint of weak stock or broth, 1 gill [¼ pint] of vinegar, salt and pepper to taste, 1 tablespoonful of pounded [lumpless] sugar.

Mode.—Cut the cabbage into very thin slices, put it into a stewpan, with the ham cut in dice, the butter, ½ pint of stock, and the vinegar; cover the pan closely, and let it stew for 1 hour. When it is very tender, add the remainder of the stock, a seasoning of salt and pepper, and the pounded sugar; mix all well together, stir over the fire until nearly all the liquor is dried away, and serve. Fried sausages are usually sent to table with this dish: they should be laid round and on the cabbage, as a garnish.

Time.—Rather more than 1 hour.

Average cost, 4d. each. [March 1977, 1 medium-sized cabbage, 56p.]

Sufficient for 4 persons.

Seasonable from September to January.

* This recipe appears unchanged in the 1960 edition.

Baked Tomatoes
(Excellent)

INGREDIENTS.—8 or 10 tomatoes, pepper and salt to taste, 2 oz. of butter, bread crumbs.

Mode.—Take off the stalks from the tomatoes; cut them into [halves or] thick slices, and put them into a deep baking-dish; add a plentiful seasoning of pepper and salt,* and butter in the above proportion; cover the whole with bread crumbs; drop over these a little clarified butter; bake in a moderate oven from 20 minutes to ½ hour, and serve very hot. This vegetable, dressed as above, is an exceedingly nice accompaniment to all kinds of roast meat. The tomatoes, instead of being cut in slices, may be baked whole; but they will take rather longer time to cook.

Time.—20 minutes to ½ hour.

Average cost, in full season, 9d. per basket. [March 1977, tomatoes 40p per lb. This would be a far cheaper dish in the autumn.]

Sufficient for 5 or 6 persons.

* This is greatly improved by the addition of a little chopped garlic with the seasoning.

Very Good Puff Paste

INGREDIENTS.—To every lb. of [plain] flour allow 1 lb. of butter, and not quite ½ pint of [very cold] water.

Mode.—Carefully weigh the flour and butter, and have the exact proportion. . . . Sift the flour; see that it is perfectly dry, and proceed in the following manner to make the paste, using a very *clean* paste-board and rolling pin:—Supposing the quantity to be 1 lb. of flour, work the whole into a smooth paste, with not quite ½ pint of water, using a knife to mix it with: the proportion of this latter ingredient must be regulated by the discretion of the cook; if too much be added, the paste, when baked, will be tough. Roll it out until it is of an equal thickness of about an inch; break 4 oz. of the butter into small pieces; place over the paste, sift over it a little flour, fold it over, roll out again, and put another 4 oz. of butter. Repeat the rolling and buttering until the paste has been rolled out 4 times, or equal quantities of flour and butter have been used. Do not omit, every time the paste is rolled out, to dredge a little flour over that and the rolling pin, to prevent both from sticking. Handle the paste as lightly as possible, and do not press heavily upon it with the rolling pin. The next thing to be considered is the oven, as the baking of pastry requires particular attention. Do not put it into the oven until it is sufficiently hot to raise the paste [Gas Mark 8, 450 F, or 240 C]; for the best-prepared paste, if not properly baked, will be good for nothing. Brushing the paste as often as rolled out, and the pieces of butter placed thereon, with the white of an egg, assists it to rise in *leaves* or *flakes*. As this is the great beauty of puff-paste, it is as well to try this method.

Average cost, 1s. 4d. per lb. [March 1977, 70p for the above quantity.]

BAKEWELL PUDDING
(*Very Rich*)

INGREDIENTS.—¼ lb. of puff-paste, 5 eggs, 6 oz. of sugar, ¼ lb. of butter, 1 oz. of [ground] almonds, jam.

Mode.—Cover a dish with thin paste, and put over this a layer of any kind of jam, ½ inch thick; put the yolks of 5 eggs into a basin with the white of 1, and beat these well; add the sifted sugar, the butter, which should be melted, and the almonds . . .; beat all together until well mixed, then pour it into the dish over the jam, and bake for an hour in a moderate oven.

Time.—1 hour.

Average cost, 1s. 6d. [March 1977, 60p exclusive of pastry.]

Sufficient for 4 or 5 persons.

Seasonable at any time.

BOILED CUSTARDS

INGREDIENTS.—1 pint of milk, 5 eggs, 3 oz. of loaf sugar, 3 laurel-leaves, or the rind of ½ lemon [or juice, added at the end with the brandy], or a few drops of essence of vanilla, 1 table-spoonful of brandy.

Mode.—Put the milk into a *lined* saucepan, with the sugar, and whichever of the above flavourings may be preferred (the lemon-rind flavours custards most deliciously), and let the milk steep by the side of the fire until it is well flavoured. Bring it to the point of boiling, then strain it into a basin; whisk the eggs well [using yolks only gives a smoother custard], and, when the milk has cooled a little, stir in the eggs, and *strain* this mixture into a jug [a bain-marie or another saucepan is more practical]. Place this jug in a saucepan of boiling water over the fire [provided the mixture is stirred continuously, a saucepan can be used directly over low heat]; keep stirring the custard *one way* until it thickens; but on no account allow it to reach boiling-point, as it will instantly curdle and be full of lumps. Take it off the fire, stir in the brandy, and, when this is well mixed with the custard, pour it into glasses, which should be rather more than three-parts full; grate a little nutmeg over the top, and the dish is ready for table. To make custards look and eat better, ducks' eggs should be used, when obtainable; they add very much to the flavour and richness, and so many are not required as of the ordinary eggs, 4 ducks' eggs to the pint of milk making a delicious custard. When desired extremely rich and good, cream should be substituted for the milk, and double the quantity of eggs used, to those mentioned, omitting the whites.

Time.—½ hour to infuse the lemon-rind, about 10 minutes to stir the custard.

Average cost, 8d. [March 1977, 35–40p, exclusive of brandy.]

Sufficient to fill 8 custard-glasses.

Seasonable at any time.

Aunt Nelly's Pudding

INGREDIENTS.—½ lb. of [plain] flour, ½ lb. of treacle, ½ lb. of suet, the rind and juice of 1 lemon, a few strips of candied lemon-peel, 3 tablespoonfuls of cream, 2 eggs.

Mode.—Chop the suet finely; mix it with the flour, treacle, lemon-peel minced, and candied lemon-peel; add the cream, lemon-juice, and 2 well-beaten eggs; beat the pudding well, put it into a buttered basin, tie it down with a cloth, and boil from 3½ to 4 hours.*

Time.—3½ to 4 hours.

Average cost, 1s. 2d. [March 1977, 55p.]

Sufficient for 5 or 6 persons.

Seasonable at any time, but more suitable for a winter pudding.

* Serve with heated treacle and/or lemon-flavoured Boiled Custard.

APPLE TRIFLE
(A Supper Dish)

INGREDIENTS.—10 good-sized apples [2 lb. Bramleys or other cooking apples is ample], the rind of ½ lemon, 6 oz. of pounded [caster] sugar, ½ pint of milk, ½ pint of cream, 2 eggs, whipped cream.

Mode.—Peel, core, and cut the apples into thin slices, and put them into a saucepan with 2 tablespoonfuls of water, the sugar, and minced lemon-rind. Boil all together until quite tender, and pulp the apples through a sieve; if they should not be quite sweet enough, add a little more sugar, and put them at the bottom of the dish to form a thick layer. Stir together the milk, cream, and eggs, with a little sugar, over the fire, and let the mixture thicken, but do not allow it to reach the boiling-point. When thick, take it off the fire; let it cool a little, then pour it over the apples. Whip some cream with sugar, lemon-peel, &c. . . .; heap it high over the custard, and the dish is ready for table. It may be garnished as fancy dictates, with strips of bright apple jelly, slices of citron, &c. [Serve chilled.]

Time.—From 30 to 40 minutes to stew the apples; 10 minutes to stir the custard over the fire.

Average cost, 1s. 6d. [March 1977, about £1.40.]

Sufficient for a moderate-sized trifle.

Seasonable from July to March.

DESSERT BISCUITS,

which may be flavoured with Ground Ginger, Cinnamon, &c. &c.

INGREDIENTS.—1 lb. of plain flour, ½ lb. of butter, ½ lb. of sifted sugar, the yolks of 6 eggs, flavouring to taste.

Mode.—Put the butter into a basin; warm it, but do not allow it to boil; then with the hand beat it to a cream. Add the flour by degrees, then the sugar and flavouring, and moisten the whole with the yolks of the eggs, which should previously be well beaten. When all the ingredients are thoroughly incorporated, drop the mixture from a spoon to a buttered paper [baking tray], leaving a distance between each cake, as they spread as soon as they begin to get warm. Bake in a rather slow oven from 12 to 18 minutes, and do not let the biscuits acquire too much colour. In making the above quantity, half may be flavoured with ground ginger and the other half with essence of lemon or currants, to make a variety. With whatever the preparation is flavoured, so are the biscuits called; and an endless variety may be made in this manner.

Time.—12 to 18 minutes, or rather longer, in a very slow oven.
Average cost, 1s 6d. [March 1977, 80p.]
Sufficient to make from 3 to 4 dozen cakes.
Seasonable at any time.

* This is one of the best biscuit recipes I have ever come across; particularly recommended flavoured with grated orange peel. For most purposes, half the amount given is enough.

THICK GINGERBREAD
[A large, rich gingerbread cake]

INGREDIENTS.—1 lb. of treacle, ¼ lb. of butter, ¼lb. of coarse brown sugar, 1½ lb. of [plain] flour, 1 oz. of ginger, ½ oz. of ground allspice [or mixed spice], 1 teaspoonful of carbonate of soda, ¼ pint of warm milk, 3 eggs.

Mode.—Put the flour into a basin, with the sugar, ginger, and allspice; mix these together; warm the butter, and add it, with the treacle, to the other ingredients. Stir well; make the milk just warm, dissolve the carbonate of soda in it, and mix the whole into a nice smooth dough with the eggs, which should be previously well whisked; pour the mixture into a buttered tin, and bake it from ¾ to 1 hour, or longer, should the gingerbread be very thick [Gas Mark 6, 400 F, or 200 C]. Just before it is done, brush the top over with the yolk of an egg beaten up with a little milk, and put it back in the oven to finish baking.

Time.—¾ to 1 hour.
Average cost, 1s. per square [March 1977, 70p.]
Seasonable at any time.

A VERY GOOD SEED-CAKE*

INGREDIENTS.—1 lb. of butter, 6 eggs, ¾ lb. of sifted sugar, pounded [ground] mace and grated nutmeg to taste, 1 lb. of flour [the cake rises adequately with plain flour, but is lighter if made with self-raising], ¾ oz. of caraway seeds, 1 wineglassful of brandy.

Mode.—Beat the butter to a cream; dredge in the flour; add the sugar, mace, nutmeg, and caraway seeds, and mix these ingredients well together. Whisk the eggs, stir to them the brandy, and beat the cake again for 10 minutes. Put it into a tin lined with buttered paper [unnecessary if the tin has a moveable bottom], and bake it [at Gas Mark 3, 325 F, or 160 C] 1½ to 2 hours. This cake would be equally nice made with currants [or chopped walnuts], and omitting the caraway seeds.

Time.—1½ to 2 hours [1½ hours in middle of oven].

Average cost, 2s. 6d. [March 1977, £1.05, exclusive of brandy.]

Seasonable at any time.

* This is one of the few cakes which goes very agreeably with red wine or sherry.

RHUBARB JAM

INGREDIENTS.—To every lb. of rhubarb allow 1 lb. of loaf [granulated] sugar, the rind of ½ lemon.

Mode.—Wipe the rhubarb perfectly dry, take off the string or peel, and weigh it; put it into a preserving-pan, with sugar in the above proportion; mince [grate] the lemon-peel very finely, add it to the other ingredients, and place the preserving-pan by the side of the fire; keep stirring to prevent the rhubarb from burning, and when the sugar is well dissolved, put the pan over the fire, and let the jam boil until it is done, taking care to keep it well skimmed and stirred with a wooden or silver spoon. Pour it into pots, and cover down with oiled and egged papers.

Time.—If the rhubarb is young and tender, ¾ hour, reckoning from the time it simmers equally; old rhubarb, 1¼ to 1½ hour [if only a small quantity of jam is made, using 2–4 lb. rhubarb, simmering takes only ½–¾ hour].

Average cost, 5d. to 7d. per lb. pot. [March 1977, 36p per lb. of prepared fruit.]

Sufficient.—About 1 pint [1½ lb.] sliced rhubarb to fill a lb. pot.

Seasonable from February to April.

To Make Everton Toffee

INGREDIENTS.—1 lb. of powdered loaf [granulated] sugar, 1 teacupful of water, ¼ lb. of butter, 6 drops of essence of lemon [or juice of ½ lemon].

Mode.—Put the water and sugar into a brass pan, and beat the butter to a cream. When the sugar is dissolved, add the butter, and keep stirring the mixture over the fire until it sets, when a little is poured on to a buttered dish; and just before the toffee is done, add the essence of lemon [or lemon juice]. Butter a dish or tin, pour on it the mixture, and when cool, it will easily separate from the dish. [Cut as soon as it is sufficiently set.] Butter-Scotch, an excellent thing for coughs, is made with brown, instead of white sugar, omitting the water, and flavoured with ½ oz. of powdered ginger. It is made in the same manner as toffee.

Time.—18 to 35 minutes [about twenty minutes].

Average cost, 10d. [March 1977, 30p.]

Sufficient to make a lb. of toffee.

NOTES

Abbreviations used in Notes: *BOM:* The *Boys' Own Magazine;*
EDM: The *Englishwoman's Domestic Magazine; EDM* . . . NS:
The *Englishwoman's Domestic Magazine* . . . New Series.

CHAPTER I

1. *Household Words,* 7 June 1851, pp. 241–6.
2. E. E. Dorling, *Epsom and the Dorlings,* p. 13.
3. According to David Hunn, *Epsom Racecourse,* p. 66, when the Association was founded shares were bought for himself, Henry, and his eldest grandson Henry Mayson. H. Montgomery Hyde, in *Mr. and Mrs. Beeton,* says the shares were purchased at a later date (p. 23).
4. This was the figure given by the *Mirror of Literature, Amusement, and Instruction,* 30 May 1829, Vol. XIII, p. 372.
5. See E. E. Dorling, *op. cit.,* p. 21.
6. *The Times* reported Mr Farrall as clerk of the course in June 1840, at the time of Queen Victoria's visit to the Derby.
7. H. Montgomery Hyde, *op. cit.,* p. 24.

CHAPTER II

1. The entries in the parish rent book ceased in 1839.
2. *Carlisle Journal,* 1 August 1840.
3. E. E. Dorling, *Epsom and the Dorlings, op. cit.,* p. 93.

CHAPTER III

1. E. E. Dorling, *Epsom and the Dorlings, op. cit.,* p. 26.
2. *Ibid,* p. 22.
3. Nancy Spain, *The Beeton Story,* p. 34.
4. *Mirror of Literature, Amusement, and Instruction.*
5. *Household Words.*
6. *The Times,* 1 June 1840, p. 6.
7. David Hunn, *op. cit.,* p. 78.
8. E. E. Dorling, *op. cit.,* p. 22.
9. Nancy Spain, *op. cit.,* p. 78.

CHAPTER IV

1. *EDM*, Vol. 1, p. 58.
2. Nancy Spain, *The Beeton Story*, *op. cit.*, p. 39.
3. H. Montgomery Hyde, *Mr. and Mrs. Beeton*, *op. cit.*, p. 59.

CHAPTER V

1. Nancy Spain, *The Beeton Story*, *op. cit.*, p. 170.
2. *The Derby Carnival* (Ward, Lock, and Tyler, 1869), p. 6.
3. The curtains went for £27 6s, a carved couch for 10 gns., an easy chair for £3 10s, and a pair of Victoria-back chairs for 10 gns.
4. *Household Management*, para. 48.
5. Letter from Rosemary Fellowes; see below.
6. G. D. Roberts, author of many sea stories.
7. Nancy Spain, *op. cit.*, p. 33.
8. Aileen Smiles, *Samuel Smiles and his Surroundings*, p. 129.

CHAPTER VI

1. *Beeton's Dictionary of Universal Information*, 1859, Vol. 1, p. 188.
2. *Illustrated London News*, 1843, p. 431.
3. The house is now run as a Christian Training Centre.
4. Letter in Chelmsford Public Library.
5. *EDM*, Vol. III NS (1867), p. 277.
6. *EDM*, Vol. VI NS (1869), p. 52.

CHAPTER VII

1. Oxford University Press, 1950.
2. *The Path of Roses*, serialized in the *EDM* in 1856, published as a volume 1860; *The Lover's Lexicon*; and *Imagination in Dreams*. See J. W. Robertson Scott, *The Story of the Pall Mall Gazette*, pp. 120–1.
3. J. W. Robertson Scott, *op. cit.*; H. Montgomery Hyde, *Mr. and Mrs. Beeton*, *op. cit.*, p. 121; Robert Blake, *Disraeli*, p. 582.
4. J. W. Robertson Scott, *op. cit.*, pp. 166–7.
5. *Jon Duan* (Ward, Lock, and Tyler, 1874) Canto the Fourth, XI–XII.
6. Nancy Spain, *The Beeton Story*, *op. cit.*, p. 42.
7. *Ibid*, p. 42.
8. Pelican, 1971, p. 285.

CHAPTER VIII

1. The advertisement tax was abolished in 1853, stamp duty in 1855, and paper duty in 1861.

2. Clarke and Beeton's account of the publication of *Uncle Tom's Cabin*, together with another by the rival publisher Sampson Low (who later published many more of Mrs Stowe's works) appears in Charles Edward Stowe, *The Life of Harriet Beecher Stowe*, pp. 189–92. Vizetelly left a third version in his autobiography *Glances Back Through Seventy Years*, pp. 359–61.

3. *The Tatler*, No. 23, 4 December 1901, p. 448.

4. Sampson Low's estimate. See Charles Edward Stowe, *op. cit.*

5. *The Times*, 3 September and 11 November 1852.

6. Charles Edward Stowe, *op. cit.*, p. 188.

7. H. Montgomery Hyde, *Mr. and Mrs. Beeton*, *op. cit.*, p. 57; Henry Vizetelly, *op. cit.*, p. 361.

8. Frederick Greenwood once said: 'The sharpest pang the editor's mind can know, a mental pain that smites the Herr Pretender to Critical Acumen through midriff to backbone' is the knowledge that 'some good thing which all the world applauds and buys was by him declined'. J. W. Robertson Scott, *The Story of the Pall Mall Gazette*, *op. cit.*, p. 194.

9. See Appendix II for a complete list of Readable Books.

10. Copyright laws were not established until 1891.

11. Charles Edward Stowe, *op. cit.*, p. 198.

12. *EDM*, Vol. I, pp. 289–92.

CHAPTER IX

1. This presumably referred to the total number of copies sold since it began.

2. Poetry was almost as popular as prose; Tennyson was a best-seller.

3. *Family Friend*, Preface, Vol. I (1849).

4. *Ibid*, 'The Editor to his Friends', Appendix (Letters), June 1850.

5. A key passage in *The Scarlet Letter* was: 'Indeed, the same dark question often arose in her mind, with reference to the whole race of womanhood. Was existence worth accepting, even to the happiest among them? As concerned her own individual existence, she had long ago decided in the negative, and dismissed the point as settled. A tendency to speculation, though it may keep woman quiet, as it does man, yet makes her sad. She discerns, it may be, such a hopeless task before her. As a first step, the whole system of society is to be torn down, and built up anew. Then, the very nature of the opposite sex, or its long hereditary habit, which has become like nature, is to be essentially modified, before woman can be allowed to assume what seems a fair and suitable position. Finally, all other difficulties being obviated, woman cannot take advantage of these preliminary reforms, until she herself shall have undergone a still mightier change; in which,

perhaps, the ethereal essence, wherein she has her finest life, will be found to have evaporated.' Holt, Rinehart, and Winston, New York, paperback ed., 1900, p. 157.

6. *EDM*, Vol. I, p. 227.

7. *Ibid*, Vol. III, p. 74.

8. *Ibid*, Vol. III, p. 32.

9. *Ibid*, Vol. I, p. 63.

10. *Ibid*, Vol. II, p. 224.

11. *Ibid*, Vols. III and IV, March-July 1855.

12. From a series of advertisements in the *EDM*.

13. Advertisement in the *EDM* and *BOM*, 1855.

14. *BOM*, Vol. IX NS, p. 115.

15. *Ibid*, Address, Vol. I.

16. *Ibid*, Preface, Vol. I.

17. *Ibid*, Address, Vol. VIII.

18. See E. S. Turner, *Boys Will Be Boys* (Penguin 1976) p. 75.

CHAPTER X

1. Her admiration was returned. Miss Lind wrote to Mrs Stowe: 'You must feel and know what a deep impression "Uncle Tom's Cabin" has made upon every heart that can feel for the dignity of human existence: so I with my miserable English would not even try to say a word about the great excellency of that most beautiful book, but I must thank you for the great joy I have felt over that book.' Charles Edward Stowe, *The Life of Harriet Beecher Stowe, op. cit.*, p. 183.

2. The last verse of 'A Table of Errata' by Tom Hood senior (his son was a contributor to the *BOM*).

CHAPTER XI

1. A practice often resorted to as a means of saving paper, which because of the tax was disproportionately expensive.

CHAPTER XII

1. *The Times*, 28 July 1856; *Surrey Gazette, Sussex Advertiser, West Kent Courier*, 23 July 1856.

2. *Daily Mail*, 14 March 1936.

3. *Household Management*, para 2143.

4. *The Queen*, 14 September 1861, p. 18.

CHAPTER XIII

1. *Household Management*, para. 65.

2. According to her family and Nancy Spain, *The Beeton Story, op. cit.*,

p. 98; but as translators were not credited, it is impossible to verify by reference to the magazine.
3. *EDM*, Vol. V, p. 373.
4. *Household Management*, para. 265.
5. *Ibid*, para. 1810.
6. *Ibid*, para. 1814.
7. *EDM*, Vol. V, trailer for next issue.
8. *A Complete System of Cookery* by John Simpson. A fourth edition appeared in 1822.
9. *Household Management*, para. 180.
10. Alexis Soyer, *Modern Housewife* (1851 ed.), p. 88.
11. *EDM*, Vol. VI, p. 63.
12. *Household Management*, para. 2568.

CHAPTER XIV

1. The exact number of pages was 1,112, but the last three chapters were not written by Isabella.
2. Preface. The original Preface is reprinted in the 1960 edition.
3. It was priced at 1½d per quart (twice as much as Soyer's, which he claimed cost the almost incredibly small sum of ¾d. See Helen Morris, *Portrait of a Chef: (Alexis Soyer*, p. 76).
4. *Household Management*, para. 148.
5. *Ibid*, para. 154.
6. *Ibid*, para. 1244.
7. *Ibid*, para. 605.
8. According to André Simon, *Bibliotheca Gastronomica*, which lists about 100 published in England 1800–1860.
9. Mrs Rundell, *A New System of Domestic Cookery* (1819 ed.), p. 6.
10. Eg Giblet Soup, *Household Management*, para. 168, Rundell p. 99; Gooseberry Fool, *Household Management*, para. 1433, Rundell p. 190.
11. William Kitchener, *The Cook's Oracle*, 1840 ed., pp. 20–21.
12. *Ibid*, p. 20.
13. *Ibid*, p. 30.
14. First published 1829. Kitchener also wrote *The Traveller's Oracle*, 1817, and *The Art of Invigorating and Prolonging Life*, 1822.
15. Eg Chili Vinegar, *Household Management*, para. 393, Kitchener 347; and Carrot Soup, *Household Management*, para. 120, Kitchener 198.
16. *Household Management*, para. 189.
17. See Elizabeth Ray (ed.), *The Best of Eliza Acton*, p. vi.
18. *Household Management*, preface.
19. Examples of Isabella's adaptations are: Crab Sauce, *Household Management*, para. 396, Acton (1855 ed.) p. 114, where Isabella specified the amount of butter; Soup à la Cantatrice, *Household Management*, para.

119, Acton (who called it Mademoiselle Jenny Lind's Soup) p. 16, where Isabella decreased the amount of cream; Christopher North's Sauce for Game or Meat, *Household Management*, para. 394, Acton p. 119. This was Miss Acton's version of Christopher North's Sauce:

CHRISTOPHER NORTH'S OWN SAUCE FOR MANY MEATS

Throw into a small basin a heaped saltspoonful of *good* cayenne pepper, in a very fine powder, and half the quantity of salt; add a small dessertspoonful of well-refined, pounded, and sifted sugar; mix these thoroughly; then pour in a tablespoonful of the strained juice of a fresh lemon, two of Harvey's sauce, a teaspoonful of the very best mushroom catsup (or of cavice), and a small wineglassful of port wine. Heat the sauce by placing the basin in a saucepan of boiling water, or turn it into a jar, and place this in the water. Serve it directly it is ready with geese or ducks, tame or wild; roast pork, venison, fawn, a grilled blade-bone, or any other broil. A slight flavour of garlic or eschalot vinegar may be given to it at pleasure. Some persons eat it with fish. It is good cold; and, if bottled directly it is made, may be stored for several days. It is the better for being mixed some hours before it is served. *The proportion of cayenne may be doubled when a very pungent sauce is desired.*

* Characteristically, the salt of this sauce ought, perhaps, to prevail more strongly over the *sugar*, but it will be found for most tastes sufficiently *piquant* as it is.

In *Household Management* it appeared as follows:

CHRISTOPHER NORTH'S SAUCE FOR MEAT OR GAME

394. INGREDIENTS—1 glass of port wine, 2 tablespoonfuls of Harvey's sauce, 1 dessertspoonful of mushroom ketchup, ditto of pounded white sugar, 1 tablespoonful of lemon-juice, $\frac{1}{2}$ teaspoonful of cayenne pepper, ditto of salt. *Mode*—mix all the ingredients thoroughly together, and heat the sauce gradually, by placing the vessel in which it is made in a saucepan of boiling water. Do not allow it to boil, and serve directly it is ready. This sauce, if bottled immediately, will keep good for a fortnight, and will be found excellent.

20. Elizabeth David, Introduction, *The Best of Eliza Acton* (ed. Elizabeth Ray), p. xxiii.

21. *Ibid*, p. xxv.

22. Eliza Acton, (1855 edition), Preface.

23. *Chronicle; Weekly Chronicle; Literary Gazette; Morning Herald;* quoted from the end pages of the 1851 edition.

24. *The Times*, 23 November 1849, p. 8.

25. Eg Puff Paste, *Household Management*, para. 1209; Beef Tea, *Household Management*, para. 1859.
26. *Alexis Soyer, The Pantropheon*, p. 110.
27. *Household Management*, para. 455.
28. Jean-Anthelme Brillat-Savarin, trs. Anne Drayton, *The Philosopher in the Kitchen*, p. 21.
29. *Household Management*, para. 1885; Brillat-Savarin, 'Aphorisms', p. 13.
30. *Household Management*, para. 354; Brillat-Savarin, pp. 54–5.
31. Liebig's books included *Chemistry in its Applications to Agriculture and Physiology* (Taylor & Walton, 4th ed. 1847); *Principles of Agricultural Chemistry* (Walton & Maberley, 1855); *Letters on Modern Agriculture* (Walton & Maberley, 1859).
32. The full title was *A Cyclopedia of Agriculture, Practical and Scientific: in which The Theory, the Art, and the Business of Farming, In all Their Departments, are Thoroughly and Practically Treated by Upwards of Fifty of the most Eminent Farmers, Land Agents, and Scientific Men of the Day.*
33. *Household Management*, para. 95; Morton, Vol. II, p. 399.
34. *Household Management*, para. 822.
35. It is not mentioned in the *Dictionary of National Biography*, nor catalogued in the British Library.
36. Archibald Constable & Co., Edinburgh, 1825.
37. Wilkie & Robinson, 1812.
38. 1836; 4th revised ed., 1859.
39. *EDM*, Vol. VII, pp. 200–203.
40. *New Monthly Belle Assemblée*, Vol. XXXIII, p. 244.

CHAPTER XV

1. Nancy Spain, *The Beeton Story, op. cit.*, p. 94.
2. *Ibid*, p. 95.
3. H. Montgomery Hyde, *Mr. and Mrs. Beeton, op. cit.*, p. 83.
4. *EDM*, Vol. I NS, p. 47.
5. *Ibid*, Vol. III NS, p. 168.
6. *Ibid*, Vol. I NS, p. 139.
7. *Ibid*, Vol. I NS, p. 144.

CHAPTER XVI

1. Nancy Spain, *The Beeton Story, op. cit.*, p. 110.
2. *Ibid*, p. 97.
3. *The Queen*, 14 September 1861, p. 21.
4. *EDM*, Vol. I NS, p. 189.
5. From an advertisement in *The Queen*, 14 September 1861, p. 31.

There is no record in the Royal Archives that Queen Victoria either gave permission for or knew of the distribution of the photograph.
6. *The Queen*, 14 September 1861, p. 18.
7. *Ibid*, 7 September 1861, p. 11.
8. *Ibid*, 14 September 1861, p. 27.
9. *Ibid*, 7 September 1861, p. 11.
10. *Ibid*, 7 September 1861, p. 12.

CHAPTER XVII

1. *Household Management* 1861, para. 3.
2. *Ibid*, para. 4.
3. *Ibid*, para. 1.
4. *Ibid*, para. 7.
5. *Ibid*, para. 27.
6. *Ibid*, para. 33.
7. *Ibid*, para. 34.
8. *Ibid*, para. 36.
9. *Ibid*, para. 54.
10. *Ibid*, para. 2305.
11. *Ibid*, para. 2263.
12. *Ibid*, para. 2234.
13. *Ibid*, para. 2202.
14. *Ibid*, para. 2190.
15. *Ibid*, para. 2195.
16. *Ibid*, para. 2416.
17. *Ibid*, para. 2441.
18. *Ibid*, para. 2443.
19. Blood-letting was commonly prescribed in various emergencies, such as fever, apoplexy, and drowning.
20. *Household Management*, para. 2606.
21. *Ibid*, para. 5.
22. *Ibid*, para. 117.
23. *Ibid*, para. 1244.
24. *Ibid*, para. 726.
25. Alexis Soyer, *Modern Housewife, op. cit.*, 1851, p. 64.
26. *Household Management*, para. 5.
27. *Ibid*, para. 1326.
28. *Ibid*, para. 103.
29. *Ibid*, para. 658.
30. Alexis Soyer, *Gastronomic Regenerator*, p. xxii.
31. *The Times*, 12 September 1862, p. 4.
32. *Household Management*, paras. 1842–4.
33. *Ibid*, para. 1885.

34. Helen Morris, *Portrait of a Chef*, *op. cit.*, p. 70.
35. *Household Management*, para. 1908.
36. *Ibid*, para. 1963.
37. *Ibid*, paras 2144–6.
38. *Ibid*, para. 91.
39. *Ibid*, para. 76.
40. *Ibid*, paras 1879–80.
41. *Ibid*, para. 1881.
42. *Ibid*, para. 250.
43. *Ibid*, para. 309.
44. *Ibid*, para. 897.
45. *Ibid*, para. 1638.
46. *Ibid*, para. 1641.
47. *Ibid*, para. 976.
48. *Athenaeum* No. 1812, 19 July 1862, pp. 78–9.

CHAPTER XVIII

1. *Athenaeum*, No. 1881, 14 November 1863, p. 640.
2. *The Morning Herald*, 26 January 1863.
3. *EDM*, Vol. VI NS, p. 74.
4. Nancy Spain, *The Beeton Story*, *op. cit.*, p. 132.
5. *Penny Illustrated Paper*, 14 February 1863.
6. *Athenaeum*, No. 1882, 21 November 1863, p. 665.

CHAPTER XIX

1. *EDM*, Vol. X NS (1871), p. 344.
2. J. W. Robertson Scott, *The Story of the Pall Mall Gazette*, *op. cit.*, p. 115.
3. *EDM*, Vol. I NS (1865), p. 32.

CHAPTER XX

1. Nancy Spain, *The Beeton Story*, *op. cit.*, p. 175.
2. *Ibid*, pp. 173–4.
3. *EDM*, Vol. I NS (1865), p. 96.
4. *Ibid*, Vol. X NS (1871), p. 351.
5. Nancy Spain, *op. cit.*, p. 173.

CHAPTER XXI

1. *EDM*, Vol. I NS (1865), p. 94.
2. *The Times*, 11 May 1866, p. 11.

3. *Banker's Magazine*, 1865, p. 905; from W. T. C. King, *History of the London Discount Market* (Routledge, 1936).

4. Nancy Spain, *The Beeton Story, op. cit.*, p. 153.

5. *The Times*, 11 May 1866, p. 11.

6. *Punch*, 6 February 1869, p. 48.

7. Nancy Spain, *op. cit.*, p. 175; H. Montgomery Hyde, *Mr. and Mrs. Beeton, op. cit.*, p. 135.

8. H. Montgomery Hyde, *op. cit.*, p. 134.

9. S. O. Beeton (pseud. "Phiz"), *London's Great Outing: The Derby Carnival* (Ward, Lock, and Tyler, 1868) p. 6.

10. H. Montgomery Hyde, *op. cit.*, p. 135.

11. Edward Liveing, *Adventure in Publishing: The House of Ward, Lock, 1854–1954*, p. 37.

12. *Ibid*, p. 46.

13. Announcement in the *BOM*, Vol. VIII NS (1866).

14. *EDM*, Vol. XI NS (1871), p. 299.

15. *Ibid*, Vol. XIII NS (1872), p. 334.

16. *Ibid*, Vol. XII NS (1872), p. 106.

17. *Ibid*, Vol. XIV NS (1873), p. 314.

CHAPTER XXII

1. *EDM*, Vol. X NS (1871), p. 106.

2. From a letter from a 'Contessa', *EDM*, Vol. VII NS (1869), p. 110.

3. *EDM*, Vol. V NS (1868), p. 317.

4. *Ibid*, Vol. XIV NS (1873), p. 21.

5. *Ibid*, Vol. III NS (1867), p. 165.

6. *Ibid*, Vol. III NS (1867), pp. 223–4.

7. *Ibid*, Vol. III NS (1867), p. 279.

8. *Ibid*, Vol. III NS (1867), p. 335.

9. *Ibid*, Vol. III NS (1867), p. 334.

10. *Ibid*, Vol. IV NS (1868), p. 280.

11. *The Ladies' Treasury*, Vol. VII (1863), p. 11.

12. Doris Langley Moore, *Woman in Fashion*, Batsford, 1949, p. 17.

13. *EDM*, Vol. IV NS (1868), p. 109.

14. *Ibid*, Vol. IV NS (1868), p. 109.

15. *Ibid*, Vol. IV NS (1868), p. 109.

16. *Ibid*, Vol. III NS (1867), p. 277.

17. *Ibid*, Vol. III NS (1867), p. 503.

18. *Ibid*, Vol. V NS (1868), p. 168.

19. *Ibid*, Vol. V NS (1868), p. 221.

20. *Ibid*, Vol. V NS (1868), p. 221.

21. *Ibid*, Vol. VI NS (1869), p. 55.

22. *Ibid*, Vol. VI NS (1869), pp. 52–3.

23. *The Queen, The Ladies' Newspaper*, 3 February 1866, p. 88.
24. *The Guardian*, 15 June 1976, p. 8.
25. *The Guardian* 29 June 1976, p. 8.
26. *EDM*, Vol. VI NS (1869), p. 53.
27. *Ibid*, Vol. VI NS (1869), p. 54.
28. *Ibid*, Vol. VI NS (1869), p. 55.
29. *The Daily Telegraph*, 18 January 1869, p. 5.
30. *Saturday Review*, 30 January 1869, p. 144.
31. *EDM*, Vol. VI NS (1869), p. 165.
32. *Ibid*, Vol. X NS (1871), p. 62.
33. *Ibid*, Vol. X NS (1871), p. 127.

CHAPTER XXIII

1. According to Edward Liveing, *Adventure in Publishing: the House of Ward, Lock, 1854–1954, op. cit.*, p. 37. His name was retained in the firm's advertisements, however, throughout 1874.
2. Edward Liveing, *op. cit.*, p. 43.
3. H. Montgomery Hyde, *Mr. and Mrs. Beeton, op. cit.*, p. 146.
4. *The Coming K—* (Ward, Lock, and Tyler, 1872) 'Goanveer', 8th Lay.
5. *Edward VII*, Act II, Scene I.
6. *Jon Duan* (Weldon & Co., 1874) Canto the Fourth, XXXI, 'A Story of the Confessional', 10.
7. *Ibid*, Canto the Second, LXVI.
8. *The Siliad* (Ward, Lock and Tyler, 1873), Book VI.
9. *The Coming K—*, 'Loosealot and Delaine', 4th Lay.
10. *The Siliad*, Book IV.
11. Sir Philip Magnus, *King Edward VII* (Penguin, 1967), p. 166.
12. From a report in *The Times*, 26 November 1874, quoted in an advertisement in the *Athenaeum*, No. 2459, 12 December 1874, p. 778. The court records have been destroyed as of no historical interest.
13. *Athenaeum*, No. 2456, 21 November 1874, p. 690.
14. *EDM*, Vol. VI NS (1869), p. 153.
15. Kinley Roby, *The King, the Press and the People*, p. 199.
16. H. Montgomery Hyde, *op. cit.*, p. 175.
17. *Athenaeum*, No. 2589, 9 June 1877, p. 739.
18. *Finis, or, Coelebs and the Modern Sphinx* (Goubaud & Sons, 1877), Preface.
19. *Ibid*, 'Alice the Good'.

SELECT BIBLIOGRAPHY

Adburgham, Alison, *Women in Print: Writing Women and Women's Magazines from the Restoration to the Accession of Victoria* (George Allen & Unwin: 1972).

Avery, Gillian, *Childhood's Pattern* (Hodder & Stoughton: 1975).

Andrews, James, *Reminiscences of Epsom* (L. W. Andrews & Son: 1904).

Beeton, S. O., and Sherer, John, *Beeton's Dictionary of Universal Information* (S. O. Beeton: 1859).

Blake, Robert, *Disraeli* (Eyre & Spottiswoode: 1966).

Butler, David, *Edward the Seventh* (Futura Publications: 1974).

Cadogan, Mary, and Craig, Patricia, *You're a brick, Angela! A new look at Girls' Fiction from 1839–1975* (Gollancz: 1976).

Cundall, H. M., *Birket Foster* (A. & C. Black: 1906).

Dorling, Edward E., *Epsom and the Dorlings* (Stanley Paul: 1939).

Edgeworth, Maria, *Moral Tales* (J. Johnson: 1813).

Ellis, Sarah, *The Daughters of England, their Position in Society, Character, and Responsibilities* (Fisher, Son & Co.: 1842).

Harvey Barton, F. J., *Children's Books in England: Five Centuries of Social Life* (Cambridge University Press: 1958).

Hunn, David, *Epsom Racecourse* (Davis-Poynter: 1973).

Langley Moore, Doris, *Fashion through Fashion Plates, 1771–1970*. (Ward, Lock: 1971).

——, *Woman in Fashion* (Batsford: 1949).

Liveing, Edward, *Adventure in Publishing: The House of Ward, Lock, 1854–1954* (Ward, Lock: 1954).

Magnus, Philip, *King Edward VII* (Murray: 1964, Penguin: 1967).

Montgomery Hyde, H., *Mr. and Mrs. Beeton* (Harrap: 1951).

Morris, Helen, *Portrait of a Chef: Alexis Soyer* (Cambridge: 1938).

Mumby, F. A., *The House of Routledge* (Routledge: 1934).

O'Connor, T. P., *Memoirs of an Old Parliamentarian* (Ernest Benn: 1929).

Pearsall, Ronald, *The Worm in the Bud* (Weidenfeld & Nicolson: 1969, Pelican: 1971).

Quennell, Peter, *Mayhew's London* (William Kimber: 1951).

Reid, Captain Mayne, *The Chase of Leviathan* (Routledge: 1885).

Roby, Kinley, *The King, the Press, and the People: A Study of Edward VII* (Barrie & Jenkins: 1975).

Scott, J. W. Robertson, *The Story of the Pall Mall Gazette* (Oxford University Press: 1950).

Seth-Smith, Michael, *Lord Paramount of the Turf* (Faber: 1971).

Smiles, Aileen, *Samuel Smiles and His Surroundings* (Robert Hale: 1956).

Spain, Nancy, *The Beeton Story* (Ward, Lock: 1956).

Stowe, Charles Edward, *The Life of Harriet Beecher Stowe* (Sampson Lowe & Co.: 1889).

Trimble, William Tennant, *The Trimbles and Cowans of Dalston, Cumberland* (Charles Thurnam & Sons: 1935).

Turner, E. S., *Boys Will Be Boys* (Michael Joseph: 1948, Penguin: 1976).

Wheatley, Vera, *The Life and Work of Harriet Martineau* (Secker & Warburg: 1957).

White, Cynthia L., *Women's Magazines 1693–1968* (Michael Joseph: 1970).

Vizetelly, Henry, *Glances Back Through Seventy Years* (Kegan Paul & Co.: 1893).

COOKERY BOOKS

Acton, Eliza, *Modern Cookery for Private Families* (Longman: 1855 and 1868 editions).

——, *The English Breadbook* (Longman: 1857).

Brillat-Savarin, Jean-Anthelme, *The Philosopher in the Kitchen*. Translated by Anne Drayton (Penguin: 1970).

Francatelli, Charles Elmé, *Cook's Guide and Butler's and Housekeeper's Assistant* (Richard Bentley: 1880 edition).

——, *Plain Cookery for the Working Classes* (Richard Bentley: 1861).

——, *Modern Cook* (Richard Bentley: 1886 edition).

Glasse, Hannah, *The Art of Cookery Made Plain and Easy* (Wangford: c 1774).

Kitchener, Dr William, *The Cook's Oracle* (Robert Cadell, Edinburgh; Whittaker & Co., London: 1840).

——, *The Housekeeper's Oracle* (London: 1829).

Ray, Elizabeth, (editor) *The Best of Eliza Acton* (Longman: 1968).

Rundell, Mrs, *A New System of Domestic Cookery* (John Murray: 1819).

Soyer, Alexis, *Gastronomic Regenerator* (Simpkin, Marshall: 1846).

——, *Modern Housewife* (Simpkin, Marshall: 1851).

——, *The Pantropheon* (Simpkin, Marshall: 1853).

——, *A Shilling Cookery* (Routledge: 1855 edition).

Simon, André, (editor) *Bibliotheca Gastronomica: A Catalogue of Books and Documents on Gastronomy* (Wine and Food Society: 1953).

Ude, Louis Eustace, *The French Cook* (Ainsworth: 1827).

NEWSPAPERS AND PERIODICALS

Athenaeum
Boys' Own Magazine
Daily Telegraph
Family Friend
Family Tutor
The Guardian
Household Words
Illustrated London News
The Ladies' Cabinet
The Ladies' Magazine and Museum
The Ladies' Treasury
Mirror of Literature, Amusement, and Instruction
Le Moniteur de la Mode
The Monthly Packet
The Morning Herald
The New Monthly Belle Assemblée
The Queen
The Saturday Review
The Standard
The Times
Townsend's Monthly Selection of Parisian Costumes
The What-not or Ladies' Handy-book
The Young Englishwoman

INDEX

Compiled by H. E. Crowe